Named in remembrance of

the onetime *Antioch Review* editor

and longtime Bay Area resident,

the Lawrence Grauman, Jr. Fund

supports books that address

a wide range of human rights,

free speech, and social justice issues.

The publisher and the University of California Press Foundation gratefully acknowledge the generous support of the Lawrence Grauman, Jr. Fund.

Smoke but No Fire

Smoke but No Fire

CONVICTING THE INNOCENT OF
CRIMES THAT NEVER HAPPENED

Jessica S. Henry

UNIVERSITY OF CALIFORNIA PRESS

University of California Press
Oakland, California

© 2020 by Jessica S. Henry

Library of Congress Cataloging-in-Publication Data

Names: Henry, Jessica S., author.
Title: Smoke but no fire : convicting the innocent of crimes that never
    happened / Jessica S. Henry.
Description: Oakland, California : University of California Press, [2020] |
    Includes bibliographical references and index.
LCCN 2019053434 (print) | LCCN 2019053435 (ebook) | ISBN 9780520300644
    (cloth) | ISBN 9780520971943 (ebook)
Subjects: LCSH: Judicial error—United States. | False imprisonment—
    United States.
Classification: LCC KF9756 .H46 2020 (print) | LCC KF9756 (ebook) |
    DDC 345.73/0122—dc23
LC record available at https://lccn.loc.gov/2019053434
LC ebook record available at https://lccn.loc.gov/2019053435

Manufactured in the United States of America

27   26   25   24   23   22   21   20
10   9   8   7   6   5   4   3   2   1

To those wrongly convicted of crimes that never happened
And to Ken, Jack, and Max, with all my love

CONTENTS

PREFACE

For the past ten years or so, I have taught an undergraduate course on wrongful convictions. I teach about the factors that contribute to wrongful convictions, the legal standards that apply to wrongful convictions, and the stories of innocent people whose lives are destroyed after being convicted of crimes they did not commit. I write about wrongful convictions both in academic journals and in the popular press, and present my findings at academic conferences.

Yet, despite all that I know about wrongful convictions, I was shocked to learn that nearly one-third of all known exonerations involve people wrongfully convicted of crimes that never happened. Unlike the popular understanding of a wrongful conviction, where the wrong person was convicted of a crime committed by someone else, no-crime wrongful convictions involve innocent people convicted of crimes that did not happen in the first place. At the time of this writing, more than nine hundred entirely innocent people have been arrested, prosecuted, convicted, often incarcerated, and eventually exonerated for crimes that were never committed. They simply did not occur.

And those nine hundred cases are just the ones we know about, where the person was fortunate enough to be able to clear his or her name. Most people wrongly convicted in no-crime cases are not so lucky

When I stumbled across the data about no-crime wrongful convictions, I knew I had to learn more. I started researching. I started writing. *Smoke but No Fire* was born.

Smoke but No Fire has been a fascinating undertaking for me, particularly because of my own background. Before I was an academic, I was a public defender in New York City for nearly a decade. As a result, I bring to my research not just an academic's perspective but also rich experience as a criminal justice practitioner. *Smoke but No Fire* reflects the intersection of these two worlds. It relies heavily on the legal and social science literature to explore how and why no-crime convictions happen. It also draws heavily on the nonacademic world, from newspaper articles, judicial decisions, and exoneree accounts. In connecting the two realms, this book tells the stories of innocent people wrongly caught up in the criminal justice system's net, many of whom are marginalized, poor, and people of color.

I hope you will find the chapters that follow to be eye-opening, informative, and motivating. I know writing them was for me.

ACKNOWLEDGMENTS

I have read many times that "no book is written alone." This book is no exception. I could not have reached the finish line without the support of a whole host of incredibly generous people.

One of the most important decisions that a person can make is choosing a life partner. When I had the opportunity to marry Ken Waitz all those years ago, I grabbed it. Thank you, Ken. For this book alone, you edited my words, helped me with Excel spreadsheets, cheered me on, gave me space to write, and encouraged me throughout the process. You also made—and make—me laugh more than anyone I know. I am grateful for the life we have built together, and for the joy of having you by my side. Thank you. I am truly blessed.

Jack and Max, you are my reasons for being. The future is brighter with you in it. Thank you for your patience and encouragement throughout this year of writing. At least you know that I make *myself* write more than one draft, too.

Back in the early 1990s, I went to New York University School of Law to earn my law degree. I walked out with a pack of chosen sisters. Raman Gill, Ragini Gupta, and Miriam Spiro, you read my entire first draft (the *entire* draft!) with great insight, humor, and compassion. Thank you for having my back on this project, and always. Our never-ending chat is a lifeline that has saved me on more than one occasion. I love you, ladies, for everything.

A special shout-out to Raman Gill for agreeing to be interviewed for this book. In my humble opinion, she is the best criminal defense lawyer that Austin, Texas, has to offer.

James B. Jacobs was my law school mentor and has remained my dear friend for the past thirty years. He encourages me to write, and to keep on writing, even when it gets hard. My professional life would not be where it is without his support and guidance, and I am eternally thankful for his friendship.

Many dear friends from my beautiful town of Montclair and beyond encircled me with encouragement and friendship. You know who you are. Thank you.

Special mention must be made of Leslie Kaufman—a brilliant professional writer and friend; thank you for your wisdom and support. Pritha Gopalan, your suggestion for a preface was brilliant. Thank you to Sarah Damaskos, for her insightful marketing ideas and her friendship. Jacquie Ruderman, our daily check-ins keep me sane, always.

To my mom, Eva Gould, who came to this country as an immigrant, you taught me the power of hard work, and you continue to inspire every day. Thank you to my mom and my sister, Cynthia Berry, for your never-ending support. We may be a small pack, but we are fierce! Dad, I think you would have been proud.

To my extended family, thank you for always being there. I love you all. A special thanks to Judy Waitz, mother-in-law extraordinaire, for her amazing dust jacket photo and her photos on my website.

Thank you to Gina DeVito, to John Lentini, to Rebecca Greenberg, to the lawyers for Rodricus Crawford, and to all the others who took time out of their busy lives to speak with me. Your generosity and assistance are much appreciated.

Thank you to Montclair State University for giving me time away from teaching to write this book.

To Israel Vasquez. You will always be remembered.

This book would not have been possible without the entire publication team at the University of California Press. To Maura Roessner, Madison Wetzell, Peter Perez and Katryce Lassle, I am thankful beyond measure that my first book was placed in such attentive, capable, and creative hands; and thanks to Steven Baker for copyediting and to Cindy Fulton for managing the book's production.

Finally, to the exonerees featured in the book: You serve as a persistent and painful reminder to the world that we can and must do better to prevent wrongful convictions from occurring in the first place. I hope that you find peace and contentment in your hard-fought freedom.

Introduction

PHANTOM CRIMES

IN 2012, RODRICUS CRAWFORD WAS WRONGLY CONVICTED and sentenced to death in Louisiana for the murder of his one-year-old son, Roderius.[1] Years later, it was revealed that Roderius had not been killed but rather had died from pneumonia and sepsis in his lungs.

How, then, did Crawford wind up on death row for a murder that never happened?

At the time of Roderius's death, Crawford was a nineteen-year-old African American man living in Shreveport, Louisiana, a mostly impoverished city whose population was largely African American.[2] Crawford lived at home with his mother and a number of other relatives in a house down the road from Roderius's mother, Lakendra Lott. A talented dancer, Crawford worked a number of odd jobs to make ends meet. Most important: by all accounts, Crawford adored his son.

One morning, Crawford woke to find Roderius unresponsive in the bed next to him. A relative frantically called 911, but responders were slow to answer. After yet another call to 911, the dispatcher contacted a third party to check on what was happening. She snidely commented: "They're acting a fool over there.... They ask for everything, but [the] baby's dead." An unknown male responded: "Probably slept on [the] damn baby. There'll be 100 folks in the house."[3]

When responders finally did arrive, they placed the baby in the ambulance, and shut the doors to his parents. They decided to wait until the police arrived to tell Crawford the terrible news that his infant son was dead. Family members began knocking on the ambulance doors to see why the vehicle had not yet left for the hospital. Instead of opening the doors, the paramedics panicked, believing the concerned family was a dangerous criminal mob.[4]

From the outset, the paramedics seemed to presume foul play. One responding paramedic designated normal fluid from the child's nose as abnormal, claimed to see bruising on the baby's buttocks that was not visible to the naked eye, and found petechiae (broken blood vessels) in the baby's eyes, even though none were not found in the autopsy.[5] Another responding paramedic reportedly described the home as a "crime scene."[6]

The police, too, appeared to consider Roderius's death as suspicious from the very beginning. When the ambulance left for the hospital, the police brought Lott and Crawford directly to the precinct. At the precinct, the police did not treat Crawford as a grieving father, but instead aggressively questioned him about bruises on the baby's lip. When Crawford explained the baby slipped in the bathroom just the day before (a fact also confirmed by Lott and one that entirely explained the bruised lip), the police pressed harder for a different explanation. None was forthcoming.

Later that morning, without waiting for the lab results, a forensic pathologist declared that Roderius died from homicide by intentional smothering, citing the bruises on the baby's lip as support for his finding.[7] When testing later revealed the presence of bacterial pneumonia in the baby's lungs, the pathologist dismissed the illness and accompanying sepsis as coincidence. He never even conducted basic tests that could have confirmed Crawford's timeline for the child's fall in the bathroom.

Enter Dale Cox. Cox was a formidable Louisiana prosecutor in Caddo Parrish, where Shreveport is located, and was an ardent and outspoken supporter of capital punishment. Between 2010 and 2015, eight out of twelve death sentences in Louisiana came from Caddo Parish, four of which were directly attributable to Cox.[8] When asked to respond to a story about an innocent black man in Louisiana who had been wrongly condemned to die, Cox unapologetically replied that he believed the death penalty should be used more frequently and that "we need to kill more people."[9]

Cox charged Crawford with capital murder for the intentional killing of Roderius.

Crawford was tried in a courthouse where a Confederate veterans monument dominates the front landscape. At the start of the trial, Cox eliminated black jurors from the case—improperly, as the Louisiana Supreme Court later ruled.[10] During the trial itself, Cox relentlessly questioned witnesses about Crawford's lack of steady employment and his prior marijuana convictions, as though being unemployed or using marijuana explained an otherwise inexplicable crime. Aside from these personal attacks, however, the case rested almost exclusively on the testimony of the state forensic pathologist who testified that the baby was smothered and that the bruises on the baby's lip were consistent with death by smothering. The pathologist also incorrectly testified that the baby's brain swelling was caused by smothering when, in reality, it was caused by pneumonia with sepsis.

A different forensic pathologist from Michigan, Daniel Spitz, flatly disagreed with the state's findings. Spitz concluded that the baby suffered from severe bacterial pneumonia, which entered his blood stream, causing septic shock and death. Spitz's opinion was ignored by the prosecution before trial, and the jury considering the case apparently credited the state pathologist's testimony over Spitz's. Later, Spitz would tell a reporter from the *New Yorker* that in his opinion, "there wasn't enough evidence to even put this before a jury. You didn't have anybody who thought this guy committed murder except for one pathologist who decided that it was homicide on what seemed like a whim."[11]

Despite the questionable evidence, the jury convicted Crawford and sentenced him to death. Cox later wrote in a letter to the state's probation department: "I am sorry that Louisiana has adopted lethal injection as the form of implementing the death penalty," because "Mr. Crawford deserves as much physical suffering as it is humanly possible to endure before he dies."[12]

On appeal, Crawford's lawyers had other pathologists review the file. Each agreed that the baby had died of pneumonia. News media outlets picked up the story, and a lengthy *New Yorker* article drew significant attention to his case.[13] Online petitions to overturn Crawford's conviction were circulated around the country. National advocacy groups like the ACLU took up his cause. Four years after he was sentenced to death, Crawford's murder conviction and death sentence were overturned by the Louisiana Supreme Court because Cox had improperly excluded black people from the jury pool in violation of the U.S. Constitution.[14] At least two of those Louisiana Supreme Court judges seemed entirely perplexed as to how Crawford had ever been charged with capital murder in the first place, let alone convicted. As one judge wrote: "No rational trier of fact could have concluded that the State presented sufficient evidence to prove beyond a reasonable doubt that the defendant had the specific intent to kill his one-year-old son."[15]

In 2017 the state declined to retry Crawford and he became the 158th innocent person exonerated from death row since 1973.[16] The years he spent at Angola on Louisiana's notorious death row left their mark. At Angola, Crawford was kept in solitary confinement in a tiny, windowless cell for twenty-three hours day.[17] Three times a week, he was allowed outside for one hour in a small outdoor cage similar to a dog pen. Although the heat index easily rose above 90 degrees, Crawford had no access to air conditioning, ice, or even fans.[18] When asked to reflect on his experience, Crawford described it this way:

> You feel like an animal, period. . . . It's all a mind game. . . . You can go crazy. Not can—you're going crazy. . . . [The experience] messed with me. . . . Who can imagine an innocent person being on death row, and they talk about killing you, and you wake up in a little cell every day? I can't explain it. That's a feeling I hope nobody could feel.[19]

It is certainly a feeling Crawford should never have experienced.

Crawford's wrongful conviction was based on the premise that a crime had been committed, when in reality no crime had ever occurred. Because a death by illness was wrongly labeled a death by murder, Crawford wasted years of his life on Louisiana's notorious death row. Crawford's conviction and death sentence devastated his family and his extended community, who were left to deal with his absence and to make sense of the state's insistence that Crawford had committed a senseless act of violence. The community expended countless resources in investigating, prosecuting, defending, convicting, and incarcerating Crawford—for a case where no crime occurred at all.

Crawford was convicted because of a number of interrelated factors. He was black and poor in a city rife with racial division. Responders arrived with biased expectations about what had likely occurred in Crawford's home, and ignored evidence suggesting that the infant's death was caused by illness. The police investigated with tunnel vision, anticipating from the outset that Crawford had engaged in wrongdoing. The medical examiner prematurely committed to homicide as a cause of death and disregarded and minimized clear medical evidence that pointed to quite a different conclusion. The prosecutor was gung-ho to secure yet another capital conviction, and the judge went along for the ride.

It would be easy to dismiss Crawford's experience as bad luck or as a strange anomaly in the criminal justice universe. But that would be a mistake. As crazy as it sounds, potentially thousands of innocent people have been wrongly convicted of crimes that simply did not occur. In fact, nearly *one-third* of all known exonerations of innocent people involve no-crime wrongful convictions.[20] And those are only the cases that we know about. The actual number of no-crime wrongful convictions that have occurred throughout history is unknown and perhaps unknowable.

History is replete with examples of no-crime wrongful convictions. In fact, the first wrongful conviction ever recorded was a case involving a murder that never happened.[21]

In 1812, Richard Colvin vanished without a trace from his home in Manchester, Vermont. Colvin's brothers-in-law, Jesse and Stephen Boorn, were suspected of playing a role in his disappearance. Years later, in 1819, a man claimed that the ghost of Colvin appeared in his dream and directed him to dig up Colvin's murdered body from the Boorns' cellar. Armed with this spectral mandate, the townspeople dug through the Boorns' cellar floor. They found items belonging to Colvin, but no body. Soon after, a boy found bones under a tree near the Boorn farm. Triumphantly touting the bones as proof that Colvin had been murdered, the town arrested the Boorn brothers.

While in custody, Jesse Boorn confessed that Stephen, with Jesse's help, had killed Colvin. What prompted that confession is unknown, but he recanted shortly after making his statement. Later, but before the trial began, the bones were reexamined and determined to be of an animal—and not human—origin. The town nonetheless pursued its case, relying heavily on Jesse's confession and the new testimony of a jailhouse informant who had shared Jesse's cell. The informant claimed Jesse had told him about the murder and further claimed that the Boorns' father was involved. Soon after, Stephen provided a written statement in which he confessed to the crime but denied that his father and brother participated. Why Stephen confessed is also unknown, but whatever the reason, his confession shored up a case otherwise thin on evidence.

With Stephen Boorn's confession and the informant's testimony (but no body or bones), the prosecution proceeded to trial. Both Boorn brothers were convicted of murder and sentenced to death on the gallows. Jesse's sentence was later commuted to life in prison. With Stephen's life literally hanging in the balance, a minister read a newspaper article about Richard Colvin and recognized him as a man *who was alive and well in New Jersey*. With Colvin identified, the Boorn brothers were released from prison. There had been no murder.[22]

More than sixty years later and a few states to the west, William Jackson "Jack" Marion was not so lucky. In the earliest days of Nebraska's statehood, Marion eked out a living delivering goods from town to town in his horse-drawn wagon.[23] Marion and his friend John Cameron left Nebraska for Kansas to look for work on the railroad. Only Marion returned. A dead body was later discovered, wearing clothing believed to have been Cameron's. Marion was charged and convicted of Cameron's murder, and died by hanging in 1877. Four years after Marion's public execution, Cameron returned to Nebraska, very much alive. He'd left Marion seeking adventure on a trip that took him across Alaska, Colorado, and Mexico—and had no idea that he was thought to be dead or that Marion had been held responsible for his supposed murder. One hundred years after Marion's execution, the state of Nebraska issued a posthumous pardon.[24]

Of course, not every no-crime conviction in our early history involved a living person reappearing from the dead. The Salem witch trials of 1692 marked a time of mass hysteria.[25] When girls fell sick and could not be cured by the local doctor, witchcraft was blamed for their symptoms. In Salem, Massachusetts Bay Colony, the town moved swiftly to control the perceived forces of evil by accusing innocent people of being witches and holding witchcraft trials. All told, twenty people were wrongly condemned and executed for being witches, nineteen by hanging and one who was pressed to death, while another five people died in prison. The colonial American experience of convicting and punishing so-called witches for the harm that their fictive spells allegedly caused in their community serves as a stark reminder of how easy it is to scapegoat and convict innocent people for crimes that never happened.

CONTEXTUALIZING NO-CRIME WRONGFUL CONVICTIONS

The Very Big Picture

The subject of wrongful convictions—of innocent people being wrongly convicted of crimes they did not commit—has entered today's mainstream consciousness. Wrongful convictions have captured the attention of the public and media alike, as shown by the recent breakout successes of season one of *Serial* on National Public Radio, television shows such as *Making a Murderer* and *False Confessions,* and scores of books and Hollywood movies. Increased public awareness of wrongful convictions is a good thing, because it illuminates what defense practitioners and scholars have long known: the system is more prone to error than anyone ever imagined.

Most cases brought to the public's attention involve "actual-crime wrongful convictions," where an innocent person is convicted of a crime committed by someone else. A woman is raped, a man is murdered, or a building is intentionally burned to the ground. In these actual-crime wrongful conviction scenarios, a crime is committed, but the wrong person is identified as a suspect. The accused is dragged through the criminal justice system and is prosecuted, convicted, and punished for actions committed by someone else. Years later, sometimes decades later, the wrongful conviction is uncovered and the innocent person is cleared of wrongdoing. In the best-case scenario, the real offender is identified and the crime is finally and correctly solved.

This book focuses on no-crime wrongful convictions, which are different from actual-crime convictions in that no crime ever happened. A natural or accidental event might be mislabeled a crime, as when an illness-related death is wrongly attributed to murder, or an accidental fire is mislabeled as arson. A supposed victim might invent a false accusation. Corrupt police might plant evidence on a suspect and then lie about a crime's occurrence.

Once an event is mislabeled a crime, forward momentum often fueled by circular reasoning takes over. If a crime was committed, then someone must have committed the crime; therefore, the police have to find the perpetrator of that crime. Once the police identify the perpetrator of the crime, the existence of the crime is solidified. The prosecutor, in cooperation with the police, push forward to build a case against the alleged perpetrator. The initial, erroneous designation of a crime sets in motion a process that almost inexorably leads to a wrongful conviction.

It's the stuff of nightmares. But it is all too real. The old saying "Where there's smoke, there's a fire" is wrong. Sometimes, there's just smoke.

Systemic Weaknesses That Enable No-Crime Wrongful Convictions

The possibility of error—of convicting an innocent person of a crime they did not commit—is built into our criminal justice system. Under the United States Constitution, the prosecution need only prove a defendant's guilt "beyond a reasonable doubt." This standard of proof does not mean guilt beyond any doubt or beyond all error. Nor does it require proof of guilt to an absolute certainty. Stated another way, the reasonable doubt standard permits the possibility that an innocent person will be convicted of a crime.

Courts of appeal are charged with detecting and correcting errors made by trial courts. Yet appellate courts are not well suited to responding to claims of innocence, for reasons discussed in greater detail in chapter 7. But we do know that appellate courts reverse criminal convictions infrequently,[26] even when defendants raise compelling claims of actual innocence. It is an unfortunate truth that although our system permits the possibility of error, it is poorly equipped to respond to the errors that inevitably occur.

It is not the standard of proof alone that creates the possibility of a wrongful conviction. It is also the reliability of the evidence presented in court. If a prosecutor presents evidence that is inaccurate, exaggerated, or simply false, or a judge admits evidence that is unreliable, that evidence will skew an otherwise seemingly fair process. In cases involving a jury trial, for instance, jurors work diligently to evaluate the evidence against a defendant and to reach an accurate and fair outcome. Perhaps it can even be said that jurors do a good job of reaching a verdict based on the quality of the evidence presented to them. When system processes are subverted through, for instance, the presentation of faulty forensic science or lying witnesses, the jury is bound to get it wrong. The decisions they make are only as reliable and accurate as the evidence presented to them.

The Scope of Innocence

The total number of wrongful convictions, both actual and no-crime, is unknown. That hasn't stopped scholars from trying to figure out their frequency. Perhaps the best estimate was offered by Samuel Gross, a leading innocence scholar, who conducted a study of wrongful convictions in death penalty cases. Gross found that if all death-sentenced defendants remain under sentence of death indefinitely, at least 4.1 percent would be exonerated.[27] That's roughly one innocent person for every twenty-five death sentences.

Can we extrapolate from Gross's study that 4.1 percent of *all* convictions are wrongful? Maybe not. On the one hand, death penalty cases receive the most legal attention and postconviction scrutiny by courts and lawyers because of the seriousness of the penalty and the fact that an execution cannot be undone. This may mean that we are much more likely to uncover errors in death penalty cases than in any other kind of cases. On the other hand, there might be more errors in death penalty cases because there is so much pressure on the police to solve the types of crime that usually result in capital charges, and so much pressure on the prosecutors to get convictions. In other words, it may be that a 4.1 percent error rate is accurate only in cases involving a death sentence, and not in non-death-penalty cases. It is hard to know.

But we can estimate. In 2016, more than 6.6 million people were under the supervision of adult correctional systems.[28] An even greater number of people had been convicted of a crime but were no longer under correctional supervision. Even a conservative error rate of 1.0 percent (or even 0.1 percent) means that *thousands* of innocent people have been wrongly convicted whose innocence has never been uncovered.

Although we can offer only best guesses when it comes to the number of people who have been wrongly convicted, we know a little bit more about exonerations, or cases where innocent people convicted of crimes were officially declared innocent by someone in a position of authority to do so. Even those exoneration data are cautionary rather than conclusive. They capture only the very tip of the much larger innocence iceberg: the lucky few who were able to clear their names. Exoneration data, by their very definition, do not include innocent people whose innocence has not been (and may never be) proven.

The best information about known exonerations comes from the National Registry of Exonerations (NRE), which has tracked known exonerations since 1989. As of June 30, 2019, the NRE had recorded 2,468 exonerations. Of these, nearly *one-third* of all known exonerations (910) involved no-crime wrongful convictions. This means that in nearly one-third of all known exonerations, a person was convicted of a crime that never happened.

But even on their face, the NRE data undercount all wrongful convictions generally, and no-crime wrongful convictions specifically. That's because the compilations are only as good as the exoneration cases the Registry knows about and because of NRE data classification decisions. In its data the NRE does not count defendants who were part of "group exonerations," which happen when multiple people, some of whom are innocent and some of whom might well be guilty, have their convictions overturned because of police misconduct or other system errors.[29] More than 2,500 people were cleared of wrongdoing in the group exonerations that took place between 1989 and April 2018,[30] and at least some of those cases involved innocent people in no-crime convictions, such as when the police planted evidence or falsified charges as part an uncovered police scandal (see chapter 4). Obviously, if even a portion of the group exoneration data was included in the NRE count, there would be many more no-crime cases.

Exoneration data are also limited in the context of no-crime misdemeanor cases. Misdemeanor cases are the bread and butter of the criminal justice system. The court system processes roughly 10 million misdemeanor cases each year.[31] Courts, prosecutors, and public defenders are drowning in cases involving people facing low-level criminal charges. As discussed in more detail in chapter 8, thousands of innocent people are convicted of misdemeanors, often after they enter a plea of guilty, based on crimes that never actually happened. We know very little about these cases, except that few innocent people are ever exonerated from misdemeanor convictions.

Plea bargaining is another obstacle to capturing the full scope of wrongful convictions. Innocent people plead guilty to all kinds of cases, felonies and misdemeanors alike. This should come as no surprise: nearly 95 percent of cases in the criminal justice system are resolved by a plea bargain.[32] Of all known exonerations, nearly 20 percent come from innocent defendants who were convicted after a guilty plea.[33] My students cannot believe that innocent people plead guilty in cases where no crime occurred. I have heard students say time and again that they "would never plead guilty to a crime they didn't commit, let alone a crime that never happened."

In reality, however, a guilty plea is often the most reasonable option presented to a defendant. Innocent defendants who insist on asserting their constitutional right to a trial risk sitting in jail for weeks, months, or even years while awaiting their day in court because they are too poor to make bail. A guilty plea may provide them with the quickest route home to their children, employment, and other responsibilities. In addition, innocent defendants may plead guilty to avoid the risk of receiving a more severe sentence if they are convicted after trial. Informally called a "trial penalty," defendants receive harsher and lengthier sentences after a jury trial than if they plead guilty.[34] In the warped world of the criminal justice system, it is rational for innocent people to choose to plead guilty.

Consider what happened in Tulia, Texas, in 1999. Forty-eight defendants, almost all of whom were black and poor, were charged with drug crimes.[35] Several defendants went to trial, insisting on their innocence, and were convicted by a jury that credited the sworn testimony of a law enforcement officer over the word of the charged defendants. The resulting prison sentences were astonishingly long: from 20 years to a high of 361 years in prison. The remaining Tulia defendants received the message loud and clear, and quickly pled guilty despite their innocence to avoid similarly harsh penalties. As chapter 4 discusses in greater depth, it was later discovered that the charges against all forty-eight defendants were entirely fabricated; the defendants, including those who pled guilty, had been wrongly convicted of drug crimes that never happened.

No-Crime Wrongful Conviction Exoneration Data

Scholars have identified a set of the most common factors that contribute to wrongful convictions either singularly or, more often, in combination: eyewitness misidentification, false confessions, official misconduct, forensic error, perjured testimony, and ineffective legal counsel.[36] These contributing factors have remained fairly constant since 1932, when Yale law professor Edwin Borchard first began studying wrongful conviction cases and their causes.[37]

Because no-crime convictions are a subset of wrongful convictions, it is not surprising that they are in general caused by the same factors as wrongful convictions or that there are some similarities between actual-crime and no-crime wrongful conviction exoneration data. As demonstrated in table 1, the top two contributing factors in no-crime convictions are perjury or false accusations (61%) and official misconduct (42%). In actual-crime wrongful convictions, the top two prevalent factors remain the same but in inverse order: official misconduct (60%) is the primary contributing factor in actual-crime wrongful convictions, followed by perjury or false accusation (56%). In addition, both no-crime wrongful convictions and actual-crime wrongful convictions demonstrate a similar occurrence of inadequate legal defense (25% versus 26%).

But no-crime exoneration data differ from that for actual-crime convictions in ways that highlight unique characteristics of no-crime wrongful convictions. For instance, as illustrated in table 1, within the NRE exoneration data, mistaken eyewitness identification is present in *less than 1 percent* of no-crime exonerations (0.02%), but it is the third most prevalent factor in all exonerations (28%) and the third most prevalent factor in all actual-crime exonerations (45%). Innocence Project research also demonstrates that eyewitness misidentification is the most prevalent contributing factor where innocence was proven by DNA evidence.[38] That no-crime exonerations almost never involve mistaken eyewitness testimony likely reflects the fact that in many no-crime wrongful conviction cases, eyewitness identification is not at issue, either because a police officer is the main witness or because the "victim" in false accusation cases often knows the wrongly accused.

While DNA played a significant role in actual-crime exonerations (30%), it played almost no role in no-crime exonerations (2%). The absence of DNA

TABLE 1 Exonerations by factor contributing to conviction (percentage)

	All exonerations	No-crime exonerations	Actual-crime exonerations
DNA	20	2	30
False confession	12	5	16
Eyewitness misidentification	28	0	45
False/misleading forensic evidence	23	29	19
Perjury/false accusation	58	61	56
Official misconduct	54	42	60
Inadequate defense	26	25	26

NOTE: All figures have been rounded.

evidence in the overwhelming majority of no-crime exonerations makes sense. In no-crime wrongful convictions, DNA evidence is unlikely to be present, since no crime, and therefore no perpetrator, existed in the first place.

Another significant difference in contributing factors between no-crime and actual-crime cases is the prevalence of forensic error. Forensic error appears more frequently as a contributing factor in no-crime convictions (29%) than in actual-crime convictions (19%). This may well reflect the nature of no-crime wrongful convictions, some of which rely on expert testimony for diagnosis and for exoneration. In cases involving wrongful allegations of arson or shaken baby syndrome, for instance, forensic error was central to the conclusion that a crime was committed. Or, as later chapters show, bad forensic science was used to shore up weak cases where it would have been difficult to prove that a crime was ever committed.

As the data in table 2 demonstrate, drug possession or sale cases constitute 30 percent of all no-crime exonerations in the NRE data set, followed by child sex abuse cases, which make up 24 percent of no-crime exonerations. This contrasts starkly with actual-crime exonerations, of which drug cases make up only 3 percent of cases, and child sex abuse only 4 percent. Conversely, in actual-crime cases, murder is the most prevalent category of exoneration (56%), followed by sexual assault (16%); these categories appear less frequently in the no-crime exoneration data: murder accounts for 8 percent of no-crime exonerations, and sexual assault in 9 percent.[39]

In terms of no-crime exonerations in drug cases, the NRE data have limitations. The data reflect a significant number of exonerations that came out

TABLE 2 Exonerations by type of crime (percentage, rounded)

	All exonerations	No-crime exonerations	Actual-crime exonerations
Drug possession or sale	13	30	3
Child sex abuse	11	24	4
Sexual assault	13	9	16
Murder	38	8	56

of the Conviction Integrity Unit (CIU) in Harris County, Texas, where people pled guilty based on positive field tests conducted on site that indicated the presence of illegal drugs but that were later proven wrong by lab results.[40] The number of drug exonerations may soon begin to decline as Harris County completes its review of backlogged cases. As explored in chapter 4, Harris County was unique in that it sent out field tests for lab confirmation even after a plea conviction was reached. Most jurisdictions do not confirm field tests once a case is resolved; innocent people who plead guilty to drug possession based on a faulty field test are unlikely to be exonerated. In addition, the NRE excludes from its data "mass exonerations" that result in large-scale dismissal of cases due to police or forensic science misconduct. It does so because the exonerations are not based on the guilt or actual innocence of the person convicted per se, but rather reflect decisions by a particular jurisdiction that the convictions are so tainted that they cannot be permitted to stand. As a result, the data involving exonerations in no-crime drug cases may overrepresent the efforts of Harris County's CIU, while they may undercount the innocent people convicted for drugs that were planted on them by the police or that were not drugs in the first place.

The higher prevalence of no-crime exonerations in child-sex abuse cases may be fueled in part by the exonerations that occurred in the wake of the child sex abuse hysteria of the 1970s. The exoneration numbers in this category may level off, or increase at a diminishing rate to include cases outside the hysteria-induced cases.[41]

Although the factors that contribute to actual-crime wrongful convictions are similar to those that cause no-crime wrongful convictions, this book examines how those contributing factors play out specifically in no-crime cases. It also specifically examines what triggers no-crime cases in the first place. In this way, the book positions no-crime wrongful convictions squarely within the scholarly literature and demonstrates that they are a subject worthy of examination in their own right.

Why We Should Care about No-Crime Wrongful Convictions

All actual-crime and no-crime wrongful convictions are tragedies—the perfect storm of a system gone terribly awry. The fallout is disastrous for the innocent person who is wrongly convicted, for their families and extended communities, and for society at large.

All innocent people accused of crimes they did not commit experience trauma the likes of which we can only imagine. They experience the humiliation and indignity of being arrested, of being portrayed as a criminal and sometimes as a monster, of seeing their marriages and partnerships fray or disintegrate, of having their minor children placed in foster care, of watching family and friends turn on them in the face of criminal accusations, and of having their protestations of innocence ignored by police, prosecutors, and sometimes their own lawyers. They are dragged through an indifferent court system where they reluctantly enter guilty pleas, or expend tremendous time, energy, and resources fighting the charges against them. If they decide to go to trial, they may be held in pretrial detention, unable to make bail. When their day in court finally arrives, they are forced to endure day after day of court proceedings, listening to people testify under oath to inaccurate, incorrect, or false evidence. And they are forced to hear the judge or jury pronounce their guilt.

Once found guilty, whether after a trial or after a plea, the wrongly convicted person may be sent to prison. The correctional system makes no distinction between incarcerated people who are factually guilty and those who are factually innocent. The innocent experience the same treacherous and dehumanizing conditions as anyone confined to prison. They sit in overcrowded cells, receive equally poor health care, and experience the same cacophony of sounds and lack of privacy as those who are guilty. For the innocent, prisons are particularly traumatic, though, because they are forced to suffer extreme conditions of punishment and deprivation all the while knowing they did nothing criminal. They may even spend time in solitary confinement (a form of punishment that can cause permanent psychological trauma),[42] not because they are "dangerous" but perhaps because they did not follow exacting and arcane prison rules, or because they needed to be protected from others, or because they could not control their own outrage and frustration at the injustice of their situation.

Sometimes an innocent person is exonerated, but most of the time their innocence remains undetected, leaving the wrongly convicted to serve their time slowly, painfully, and alone. Separated from their families, sometimes for years, and painted as criminals, people who are wrongly convicted may complete their prison terms only to find their lives and dreams in tatters after their release. Tainted by a criminal record, they may be barred from obtaining work and housing and from exercising the right to vote. Importantly, even the wrongly convicted who receive probationary sentences or time served for more minor offenses still suffer the stigma of a criminal record for a crime that only they (and perhaps their loved ones) know they did not commit.

But if the experiences of all wrongly convicted people are similar in certain respects, there are significant differences between actual-crime and no-crime convictions.

When an actual-crime wrongful conviction occurs, the wrong person was held responsible. This means that the real perpetrator remains at large.[43] In no-crime conviction cases, however, there is no perpetrator. An innocent person can never hope to be exonerated by establishing the identity of the actual perpetrator, because there is none. This leaves the no-crime wrongly convicted defendant in the nearly impossible position of having to prove that no crime ever occurred. As they say, it is awfully hard to prove a negative. Yet that is exactly what a person in a no-crime wrongful conviction case must do if they ever hope to prove their innocence.

What is repelling and astonishing about no-crime cases is that unbelievable quantities of time, energy, and human capital, not to mention taxpayer dollars, are wasted investigating, prosecuting, convicting, incarcerating, and in some cases, supervising people (whether on probation, parole, or a sex offender registry) for events that were never criminal and should never have been pursued by the criminal justice system. In no-crime conviction cases, the state needlessly expends taxpayer resources pursuing convictions against its own citizens for fictional crimes. Think about that. The state seizes innocent people and builds cases against them using inaccurate, unreliable, and at worst, completely manufactured evidence, to gain convictions for crimes that did not happen. In a no-crime conviction case, every single strand of evidence introduced by the state to "prove" the defendant committed the crime is patently invalid because, in reality, no crime ever occurred. Kafka could not have invented a more bizarre and terrifying scenario. When the state prosecutes an innocent person even though no crime occurred, it loses all semblance of legitimacy.

No-crime convictions are important to talk about because they shine a light on the depths of dysfunction within our ever-increasingly indifferent and overwhelmed criminal justice system. No-crime convictions say something about the willingness of criminal justice actors to prioritize securing convictions over justice. We allow police to manufacture evidence, to create evidence when none exists. We allow prosecutors to pursue weak cases based on bad or flimsy or inconsistent or false evidence, and to demand lengthy sentences to induce defendants to plead guilty. We allow judges to blindly acquiesce in this process by admitting evidence that lacks reliability or by allowing guilty pleas and convictions in cases that have weak (or no) factual predicate. We allow a steady stream of poor people and people of color to be processed through our court system, represented by overwhelmed defense attorneys, without asking why so many have been caught in the criminal justice net, accused of crimes for which the proof is lacking. We have stopped holding our criminal justice actors to the highest of standards that should always accompany a loss of liberty, and sometimes life. In doing so, we have enabled no-crime wrongful convictions to exist in the first place.

No-crime convictions start with the fictional narrative that a crime occurred. That fiction can be based on honest error, tunnel vision, lies, or corruption, but in every case it is an illusion manufactured from whole cloth. The entire criminal justice system then steps in to process an innocent person where no wrongdoing occurred—and somehow, the error is undetected at every stage of the proceedings. Society has no recognizable interest in spending the time, energy, and resources in identifying, prosecuting, convicting, and punishing a criminal suspect for a crime that never happened. Yet we do. More often than anyone could have imagined.

No-crime convictions are based on phantom crimes. But for the wrongly convicted in no-crime cases, they are all too real.

HOW THIS BOOK IS ORGANIZED

This book is the first to identify and explore no-crime wrongful convictions, how they happen, and what can be done to reduce their occurrence. Chapter 1 looks at no-crime convictions that result when events are mislabeled as crimes. Sometimes the police mislabel a suicide as murder, or medical personnel mislabel a natural death as one caused by abuse or intention, or forensic scientists mislabel an accidental fire as an arson. Chapter 1 examines the mislabeling process and considers a range of factors from tunnel vision to bad forensic science. It seeks to demonstrate that once an event is initially labeled a crime, a self-fulfilling prophecy begins: if a crime was committed, then someone must have committed the crime. The initial criminal misdesignation sets into motion a process that ends with the conviction of an innocent person for a crime that never occurred.

Sometimes, however, the forensic error is based on deliberate misconduct. Chapter 1 also considers the role of forensic corruption in fostering no-crime wrongful convictions. Forensic analysts have been known to fabricate test results. In 2018 in El Paso, Texas, for example, a former forensic analyst, Ana Lilia Romero, had failed to conduct blood alcohol tests but fabricated the results in at least twenty-two cases.[44] In many of those cases, people pled guilty based solely on the false lab reports. As discussed in chapter 1, when forensic analysts engage in wholesale corruption and manufacture testing outcomes, innocent people suffer.

It is not only official mislabeling that sparks no-crime convictions. Chapter 2 demonstrates that no-crime convictions can also result from the false accusations of private citizens against innocent people. In cases involving rape or assault, such false allegations may be motivated by the need for an alibi, by revenge, or by emotional or financial gain. Their lies are accepted as truth by the police, then the prosecution, and then the judge and jury, causing innocent people to be convicted of falsehoods.

On May 7, 2018, Gregory Counts and VanDyke Perry were exonerated from a 1991 gang rape and kidnapping in New York City after spending a collective thirty-seven years in prison.[45] The men were cleared, in large part, after their accuser admitted that she completely fabricated the charges to help her then-boyfriend, who owed money to Counts and Perry. She explained that if Counts and Perry were incarcerated, they could not collect the debt. Based on her account of a terrible but invented crime, Counts spent twenty-six years behind bars, and Perry served eleven years in prison before being released on parole as a registered sex offender. No assault, rape, or kidnapping had occurred.

Chapter 3 focuses on deliberate police misconduct where police fabricate evidence, tamper with witnesses, and falsely arrest people for crimes that range from petty offenses to serious felonies. It addresses deliberate wrongdoing by the police, as when rogue police officers or whole corrupt units within police departments frame innocent defendants while often committing crimes themselves. They plant evidence, falsify charges, and fabricate crimes that did not actually happen. They also cause innocent people to falsely confess, a particularly difficult feat in cases where the crimes did not occur.

Police motivations for this misconduct vary widely. Some officers engage in misconduct to cover up their own wrongdoing or for personal monetary gain or career advancement, while others operate from a misguided sense of justice, otherwise known as noble cause corruption. Whatever the rationale, officers plant evidence, coerce defendants into falsely confessing, bribe or otherwise strong-arm so-called witnesses to tell falsehoods, and sometimes lie under oath, all to shore up arrests for crimes that never happened.

Chapters 1–3 present analytically distinct starting points on the path to no-crime convictions, whether it be the mislabeling of an event as a crime, false accusations, police misconduct, or aggressive policing policies. This last topic is revisited in Chapter 7, which examines how aggressive crime-policing policies trigger no-crime convictions in low-level offenses. While each trigger may be different, there is overlap between them. No-crime wrongful convictions may begin with police misconduct but be "proven" with the assistance of a prosecutor and the false testimony of an informant. A scientific expert may erroneously label a death as a homicide, and the police may falsify evidence to bolster that claim.

No-crime wrongful convictions have various catalysts, but they share a common thread of inequality, particularly in cases involving police misconduct and aggressive policing practices. The criminal justice system disparately impacts the poor and people of color. Perhaps it should come as no surprise that many no-crime convictions like those discussed in chapters 3 and 7 often involve stories about poverty, racism, and the ways we mistreat members of society who are most vulnerable to abuse. Racism and poverty leave their mark throughout the criminal justice system, and although this book does not do justice to these important subjects, themes of racism and classism are presented and discussed throughout.

Chapter 4 considers how prosecutors contribute to no-crime convictions. Rather than acting as a check on the process, prosecutors may double down on police allegations of criminality, even when the evidence is lacking. In addition, prosecutors may bring as many serious charges as possible against a defendant to induce a plea or keep trial verdicts flexible. The result, as noted earlier, is that innocent people plead guilty to avoid the risk of severe punishment if convicted after trial. Prosecutors also engage in more deliberate misconduct. They fail to turn over required discovery to the defense or knowingly present false and unreliable testimony by police, expert witnesses, or informants.

Chapter 5 examines the role of defense lawyers in no-crime convictions. Defense lawyers are often the best and only protection an innocent defendant has against a wrongful conviction, particularly in cases where no crime occurred in the first place. Defense lawyers should work tirelessly for their clients, investigating evidence and building a defense.

Of course, not all defense lawyers do their jobs well. They fail to file motions, conduct investigations, or even understand the charges against their clients. But it is hard for a defendant to do much about such negligence. The U.S. Supreme Court has set such a low bar in evaluating counsel's competence under the Constitution that some experts sarcastically claim that the "mirror test" governs whether courts will decide that a lawyer was competent: if a mirror held under a court-appointed lawyer's nose fogs up, then there is adequate counsel. This is not far from the truth. Chapter 5 documents cases where sleeping lawyers, intoxicated lawyers, and stunningly ill-prepared lawyers were all deemed by courts to have provided constitutionally adequate representation.

But even the most committed lawyers face structural impediments to doing their jobs effectively. As defense lawyers often complain, caseloads are overwhelmingly heavy and funding is limited, particularly for hiring experts to debunk prosecutions based on forensic testimony. And defense lawyers are often powerless when officials hide evidence or persuade witnesses to lie.

Chapter 6 considers the roles that trial and appellate judges may play in no-crime wrongful convictions. It begins with an examination of how judicial biases, both unconscious and intentional, influence judging and how those biases contribute to no-crime wrongful convictions. When judges fail to do their jobs, innocent people suffer. Judges, for instance, serve as gate keepers for forensic evidence. When they allow junk science into the courtroom, innocent defendants are forced to counter "expert" testimony more akin to magic than to science. In addition, judges accept guilty pleas without ensuring an adequate evidentiary basis and acquiesce to bad lawyering and prosecutorial misconduct. Judicial contributions to no-crime wrongful convictions extend to appellate courts, which often fail to robustly enforce existing legal standards.

Chapter 7 takes on misdemeanors. Misdemeanors are often dismissed as "petty." Misdemeanor convictions, however, have serious consequences for the defendant, including the creation of a criminal record that can lead to a ban on public housing and benefits, and dampen educational and employment prospects. This chapter considers no-crime misdemeanors produced by aggressive policing policies. When police officers engage in a "war on crime" or "broken-windows policing," innocent people are often caught in their net, resulting in hundreds of people being wrongly arrested for crimes that never happened. Even worse, many innocent people plead guilty to these so-called offenses. Having spent hours, and sometimes the night, in a holding cell waiting to appear before a judge, many innocent people in lower-level cases opt to plead guilty to avoid having to return to court or because they cannot make even relatively low bail. Poor people and people of color often bear the brunt of misdemeanor processing. Prosecutors, defense lawyers, and judges alike contribute to these no-crime convictions by participating in assembly-line justice that affords little time for careful scrutiny of routine cases or their evidentiary basis.

This book concludes with important policy recommendations that can reduce the prevalence of no-crime convictions. These recommendations include proposals to improve forensic science used in courtrooms, reform police practices, improve training about cognitive biases, reevaluate the plea-bargaining process, improve discovery in criminal cases, change prosecutorial cultures and priorities, support defense lawyers, and hold bad actors accountable. Each proposal includes concrete actions that can be implemented to reduce the incidence of convictions for crimes that did not occur.

No-crime wrongful convictions exist beyond the mainstream understanding of wrongful convictions. When most people think of a wrongful conviction, they think of a case where the wrong person was convicted of a crime committed by someone else. Whenever I share the subject of this book, people are stunned to learn that there is even such a thing as a no-crime wrongful conviction. It never occurred to them that innocent people could be convicted of crimes that did not happen.

No-crime wrongful convictions make-up one-third of all known exonerations, but occur with greater frequency than captured by the exoneration data. They can be caused by bad forensic science, by lying civilians or lying police, or by aggressive police practices. They occur because the system does not function as it should. Prosecutors fail to serve as a check on the police, judges fail to serve as a check on the prosecutors, defense attorneys do not have the resources (and sometimes the skills) to properly do their jobs, and jurors can only evaluate the evidence put before them.

When the system goes this terribly wrong, innocent people are convicted of crimes that were never crimes in the first place. In the chapters that follow, we will explore how crimes that never happened become actual criminal convictions with real-life consequences.

Forensic Error

MISCLASSIFIED MURDERS AND
MISLABELED CRIMES

Things are not always what they seem; the first appearance deceives many.

PHAEDRUS

IN 1992, BEVERLY MONROE WAS A FIFTY-FOUR-YEAR-OLD mother of three with a master's degree in organic chemistry.[1] She had never been in legal trouble before, not even for a speeding ticket. Then she was convicted of murder.

Monroe first met Roger Zygmunt Comte de la Burde in 1979 while she was working in the patents department at Philip Morris Inc. They began an affair, and their marriages to other people soon ended.[2] Yet, as Monroe would eventually learn, Burde was not what he appeared to be. He boasted that he was descended from Polish royalty, a claim as questionable as his suspect real estate and art dealings. Burde also was a notorious philanderer who had numerous affairs throughout his and Monroe's thirteen-year relationship.

In the early hours of March 5, 1992, Burde's groundskeeper discovered Burde's body lying on a couch in the library of the main house of his Powhatan County, Virginia, estate. Burde had died from a single gunshot wound to his forehead; the shot had been fired from his own handgun. He left no note, but had gunshot residue on his fingers. The Powhatan County Sheriff's Office and medical examiner originally declared Burde's death a suicide. But David M. Riley, a senior special agent from the Virginia State Police, suspected foul play. His single suspect was Monroe, who Riley believed had both motive and opportunity to commit murder. The motive? Burde was seeing another woman, who was allegedly pregnant with Burde's child. The opportunity? Monroe had been with Burde on the evening of his death, a fact that Monroe readily admitted. Even though only Burde's fingerprints were on the gun, Riley concluded that Monroe had killed Burde and was trying to cover it up by making his death appear to be a suicide.

Riley relentlessly pursued his theory of the case, summoning Monroe for unrecorded interrogation sessions in which he repeatedly insisted that she had been present in the library at the time of Burde's death. Finally, after Riley falsely told Monroe that she had failed a polygraph test, Monroe agreed to sign a number of statements—each written by Riley—that placed her in the library during the shooting. These statements also contained a convoluted story of what Monroe might have done if she had been in the room at the time of the shooting. Based on these signed statements, Monroe was arrested for murder.

At her trial, the prosecution presented a circumstantial but seemingly strong case against Monroe. There was evidence of Burde's affair with another woman, Monroe's so-called confession, and testimony that the position of the gun made it unlikely that he had shot himself. A witness also testified that Monroe had tried to buy an untraceable gun from her several months earlier.

In her defense, Monroe raised a compelling alibi. She explained that she had left Burde at home around 9:30 P.M., filled her car with gas and called her son, and arrived at a Safeway at around 10 P.M. This last statement was corroborated by a store receipt timed at 10:40 P.M., a canceled check, and an eyewitness who remembered seeing her there. She further presented evidence that Burde made a phone call from his home around 10 P.M., well *after* Monroe left his house and right around the time she was in the store. Monroe testified that Burde had been depressed, but also offered a roster of alternative suspects who stood to gain from Burde's death or who had a motive to want him dead. Finally, Monroe raised the fact that her fingerprints were not on the gun.

The jury took less than three hours to convict Monroe of murder. She was sentenced to twenty-two years in prison.

The story might have ended with Monroe serving out her time in a prison cell. But her daughter, Kate, a newly minted lawyer, devoted herself to proving her mother's innocence. She uncovered official misconduct, including the prosecution's failure to turn over critical exculpatory evidence to the defense.[3] The prosecution did not disclose (among other evidence): (1) that Riley had improperly and inappropriately manipulated Monroe during aggressive interrogation sessions, causing her to agree to statements that she later recanted; (2) documentary evidence that the medical examiner had initially ruled the death a suicide; (3) a laboratory request by a different doctor in the Medical Examiner's Office, who labeled the death a suicide, 4) statements from Burde's ex-wife to the medical examiner that Burde had been having personal problems and was taking an antidepressant; (5) a statement from the grounds-keeper that he had moved the gun when he found Burde's body; and (6) the fact that the witness who swore Monroe tried to purchase a gun was in fact a convicted felon and government informant who testified in exchange for a favorable deal in a pending gun case and in an unrelated open felony case.

Upon review of the undisclosed evidence, the Fourth Circuit Court of Appeals dismissed Monroe's case and Monroe was officially cleared of any wrongdoing.[4] Monroe served eleven years in prison for a suicide that had been mislabeled a murder.

This chapter considers the misclassification of noncriminal events as crimes, and how use of the term *crime* transforms the ways events are perceived and evaluated. Misclassification often occurs in difficult cases—the cases where what happened is unclear and is subject to multiple interpretations. This makes sense. Events that are clearly accidents do not result in prosecutions, while events that are clearly crimes and have an identifiable suspect are efficiently resolved by an arrest, prosecution, and typically a guilty plea. It's the gray cases, the hard cases, that require tough judgment calls.[5] It's in these gray cases that police officers, medical professionals, or forensic experts might misclassify a noncriminal event as a crime. When that misclassification takes root as truth, the criminal justice process is set in motion and an innocent person is pursued as a suspect for a crime that did not happen.

Gender also plays a role in no-crime wrongful conviction cases based on events misclassified as crimes. In the National Registry of Exonerations (NRE) database, females represent only 9 percent of all known exonerees, and only 4 percent of exonerees from actual-crime wrongful convictions. Yet they make up nearly 17 percent of all no-crime exonerees. Even more striking, of all the female exonerees in the NRE database, *70 percent were wrongly convicted of a crime that never happened.* Males, in contrast, are far more likely to be exonerated in actual-crime convictions (66%) than in no-crime cases (34%).[6] Andrea Lewis and Sandra Sommerveld, of the Center on Wrongful Convictions at Northwestern University, found that exonerated women, particularly in no-crime cases, were particularly susceptible to convictions involving the intentional killing or physical harming of a child or other loved one. They argue that gender stereotypes feed into no-crime wrongful convictions.[7] If women are "supposed" to be nurturers, then women who violate their "womanly" role or who are "flawed" mothers are blamed and condemned not only because they have been accused of a crime but also because they "shirk[ed] their duties as a woman and a natural caregiver."[8]

In this chapter, we look at several different types of noncriminal events that have resulted in no-crime wrongful convictions of innocent people: suicides mislabeled as murders, mechanical malfunctions misidentified as homicides, illnesses or natural deaths misdiagnosed as shaken baby syndrome or murder, and accidental fires misclassified as arsons. We will even examine murder convictions where the person was alive and, in one case, where the so-called victim was a "person" that had never been conceived. To shed light on how these mistaken beliefs take root in the first place, we begin the chapter with a brief look at cognitive biases and the ways in which they contribute to the misclassification of events as crimes.

COGNITIVE BIASES: AN OVERVIEW

Cognitive bias is an umbrella term, rooted in psychology, that explains the ways human judgments and decision making are influenced by unconscious thought patterns.[9] Cognitive biases reflect the brain's attempt to quickly process and organize a never-ending onslaught of information. They are a "byproduct of our need to process efficiently the flood of sensory information coming from the outside world."[10] Cognitive biases prevent the brain from overloading by helping it to make sense of the world quickly and efficiently.

The problem, however, is that cognitive biases reflect heuristics, or mental shortcuts, that can lead to unconscious errors in judgment and reasoning.[11] Because cognitive biases are unconscious, we rely on them without realizing that we are engaging in a flawed or distorted thought process that can result in inaccurate, irrational, or biased conclusions or beliefs.

In subtle but pernicious ways, cognitive biases have a tremendous impact in no-crime wrongful convictions and help explain how noncriminal cases are transformed into crimes. Criminal law scholars Keith A. Findley and Michael Scott provide insight into how "tunnel vision," a form of cognitive bias, contributes to the creation of a criminal case against an innocent suspect. When police have tunnel vision, they "select and filter the evidence that will build a case for conviction while ignoring or suppressing evidence that points away from guilt."[12] As Findley and Scott explain, the police focus on a particular conclusion—that a crime was committed or that a particular suspect committed that crime—and then "filter all evidence in a case through the lens provided by that conclusion. Through that filter, all information supporting the adopted conclusion is elevated in significance, viewed as consistent with the other evidence and deemed relevant and probative. Evidence inconsistent with the chosen theory is easily overlooked or dismissed as irrelevant, incredible, or unreliable."[13] Once the police decide a crime has occurred, they view the available information through a lens that confirms that belief and they disregard evidence to the contrary.

Tunnel vision is not the only cognitive bias prevalent in no-crime convictions. Confirmation bias, for example, reflects the unconscious tendency to interpret information in ways that confirm preexisting beliefs or hypotheses,[14] while belief perseverance occurs when a person firmly maintains a belief despite being presented with new information that firmly contradicts it. In no-crime wrongful convictions, these cognitive biases prevent authorities from reexamining their initial determination that a crime occurred, even in the face of evidence that suggests another outcome. Instead, they ignore, minimize, or dismiss evidence that does not support the crime theory of the case.

Various theories of cognitive bias appear throughout this book. That's because unconscious biases have profound and indelible consequences in many no-crime wrongful conviction cases. As seen throughout this chapter, one error—the initial misclassification of an event as a crime—is reinforced by criminal justice actors who uncritically accept the claim that a crime occurred and who then work to solve and prosecute that crime. The result is the conviction of an innocent person for a crime that never happened. While this may seem an unlikely occurrence, it happens more frequently than might first be imagined.

Suicides Mislabeled as Murder

In popular depictions of suicide, a person who takes their own life leaves a detailed note explaining their action and saying good-bye to their loved ones. In reality, however, only 20 to 30 percent of people who commit suicide leave behind a note.[15] In the wrongful conviction of Beverly Monroe, for instance, Burde was in the majority of people who committed suicide without leaving behind an explanation. Absent conclusive evidence that a suicide has occurred, police and the medical examiner typically base the determination that suicide was the cause of death on context and on a finding that the death was self-inflicted and intentional.[16] Whether a death was self-inflicted is determined "by pathological (autopsy evidence), toxicological, investigatory, and psychological evidence, and statements of the decedent or witnesses."[17] Intentionality can be gauged by explicit or implicit evidence that the decedent intended to kill themselves, such as preparations for death, expressions of good-bye or extreme hopelessness, previous suicide attempts or threats, or serious depression or mental disorders.

In the absence of clear evidence, investigators and medical examiners decide whether a suicide occurred. Vernon Geberth, author of *Practical Homicide Investigation: Tactics, Procedures, and Forensic Techniques,* a leading police handbook now in its fifth edition, urges investigators always to arrive at a death scene with the premise that the death was a homicide: *"All death inquiries should be conducted as homicide investigations until the facts prove differently.* The resolution of the mode of death as Suicide is based on a series of factors which eliminate Homicide, Accident and Natural Causes of death."[18] In other words, the conclusion that a death was by suicide should occur only once other causes of death have been ruled out.

That all death investigations should be pursued as a homicide is telling, because it provides a mandate to first look for criminal activity. This mandate can greatly influence how a crime scene is evaluated and processed. Research has consistently shown that law enforcement personnel tend to have "tough on crime" worldviews, with an overall orientation that focuses more on crime control and crime solving than due process and the rights of suspects.[19] When an investigator arrives at a death scene prepared to find a homicide, that perspective may cause the investigator to create evidentiary inferences that lean away from suicide and toward homicide.

Consider Detective Riley's approach to Burde's death. He jumped to the conclusion that a murder had occurred and that Monroe was the killer even though the medical examiner initially ruled the death was a suicide and Burde's were the only fingerprints on the gun. Blinded by severe tunnel vision, Riley followed his gut instinct and ignored, devalued, or rejected all evidence that pointed away from Monroe's guilt.[20] He simultaneously overvalued Monroe's possible motives to commit murder and failed to pursue other leads or potential suspects in his homicide investigation. He also did whatever he could to secure a conviction. He coerced a confession from Monroe to build his case, using aggressive interrogation techniques that model what *not* to do during questioning, and then hid notes taken by his own secretaries that documented his manipulations.[21] He found a female "professional snitch" to tell a story that Monroe had approached her about buying a gun, but failed to share the informant's prior criminal history or the inconsistent statements she gave about the alleged gun purchase request.[22] In short, Riley's laser focus on Burde's death as murder and Monroe as the perpetrator led to a biased and tainted investigation, and ultimately to Monroe's wrongful conviction.[23]

Monroe's story and subsequent exoneration from a murder that was in fact a suicide is incredible, but not singular. As of this writing, the NRE database contains at least six additional exonerees who were wrongly convicted of murder in cases of suicide.[24] These were the lucky ones. The Wrongly Convicted Group, described on its website as "a grass-roots group of advocates working to obtain justice for innocent people on death row or serving long prison sentences due to wrongful convictions," identifies seven additional cases where individuals are fighting to prove their innocence in murder cases that they say were a suicide.[25] The true number of people wrongly convicted of intentional murder for someone else's suicide is unknown. But when this miscarriage of justice happens, a trail of wreckage is left in its wake.

Mechanical Malfunctions Mislabeled as Homicide

Then there are people who are convicted of homicide when, in reality, the death was entirely due to mechanical or other technical failures. In these cases, cognitive biases lead law enforcement officials to wrongly conclude that a crime has occurred and to filter the evidence in ways that confirm that theory.

In 2004 Candice Anderson was driving her Saturn Ion when she was involved in a fatal car accident in which her boyfriend died.[26] The officer who arrived at the scene noted the lack of skid marks or other evidence of evasive action, Anderson's confused and disoriented demeanor, and her history of recreational drug use. He concluded that Anderson had been intoxicated at the time of the accident and that her intoxication caused her boyfriend's death. Toxicology reports later revealed small amounts of the prescription sedative Xanax in Anderson's system. The prosecution moved ahead with a criminal case, and in 2007 Anderson pled guilty to criminally negligent homicide.

In 2014, General Motors recalled 2.8 million cars with possible ignition switch defects, including the Saturn Ion.[27] Cars with the defective ignition switch would sometimes shift into the "accessory" mode, shutting off the engine and disabling the airbags and brakes. Although GM had known about the defect at least several months *before* Anderson pled guilty, the police and the prosecution did not.

Instead, Anderson fell prey to the responding police officer's expectation biases. "When people are led by circumstances to expect some fact or condition (as people commonly are)," Findley and Scott explain, "they tend to perceive that fact or condition in informationally ambiguous situations. This can lead to error biased in the direction of the expectation. . . . [T]he personal investment in those hypotheses will reinforce the tendency to perceive or overvalue confirming information and to miss or irrationally undervalue disconfirming information."[28] When the police officer arrived at the scene of the car accident, he expected to see skid marks or other evidence of defensive driving. In the absence of that evidence, he assumed Anderson had not attempted to brake or avoid the accident, and he locked onto the hypothesis that she was criminally liable because she was intoxicated. He then interpreted the scene in ways that conformed to his hypothesis. Anderson's demeanor, which the officer described as "confused," was attributed to intoxication rather than to shock from the accident or the severity of her own injuries, which included a lacerated liver for which she received treatment at the hospital. The small amount of prescription medication in her system was deemed an intoxicant, rather than an ancillary medication unrelated to her driving competence.

The police and prosecutor involved in the case later admitted that if they had known about the ignition switch defect at the time of the accident, the crime scene evidence would have been understood differently. As the prosecutor wrote to the court in an unusual letter of support of Anderson: "At the time, unbeknownst to Ms. Anderson or my office, there were issues regarding her 2004 Saturn Ion. Had I known at the time that G.M. knew of these issues and has since admitted to such, I do not believe the grand jury would have indicted her for intoxication manslaughter."[29]

Had the authorities known about the GM recall and ignition switch defect, they would have had different expectations and likely would have interpreted the same evidence that they said proved Anderson's guilt as evidence supporting a finding of an accident. Anderson would not have been prosecuted for and convicted of causing a fatal car wreck that was actually the result of her car's defective design.[30] Anderson was eventually exonerated of all criminal wrongdoing, and she sued and settled with GM for an undisclosed amount of money.[31]

Candice Anderson and Beverly Monroe are two women convicted of homicide in two different states under vastly different circumstances. Yet their no-crime wrongful convictions are unified by one common denominator: they were each the victim of cognitive biases that inexorably shaped the outcomes of their cases.

MEDICAL MISDIAGNOSES OF MURDER

The police are not the only ones with unconscious cognitive biases that influence their perceptions. Medical personnel also experience cognitive biases, and these lead them to reach the flawed conclusion that a crime occurred in a death or injury that was accidental or the result of an undiagnosed illness. They share their mistaken belief that a crime occurred with law enforcement, which in turn frames the case for investigators tasked with solving the "crime" before them.

Shaken Baby Syndrome, or Abusive Head Trauma

Shaken baby syndrome (SBS), now more frequently referred to as abusive head trauma (AHT), is a medical-legal diagnosis used to identify the cause of severe injury or death in infants who present with a triad of symptoms: subdural hematoma, retinal hemorrhage, and encephalopathy (brain abnormalities or neurological symptoms, or both).[32] For decades, the medical and legal establishments endorsed the belief that SBS was, in the absence of extraordinary blunt force trauma such as that found in an automobile accident, the cause of the triad. The American Academy of Pediatrics (AAP), which embraced the SBS hypothesis as early as 1993,[33] explicitly called for the "presumption of child abuse" when a child presented with the triad of symptoms.[34]

In case after case, experts testified that the triad of symptoms was produced by abuse that occurred immediately before the first signs of distress appeared.[35] Prosecutors then needed only to prove that the defendant was the last person in the presence of the infant before the symptoms appeared.[36] If they were, then, ipso facto, the defendant was the abuser. In essence, expert testimony relating to the diagnosis of SBS based on the triad of symptoms provided the criminal intent, the *actus reus* (criminal act), and the identity of the perpetrator in one fell swoop.

In 1995, Audrey Edmunds was a stay-at-home mother who also watched other children in the neighborhood.[37] On October 16, Cindy Beard dropped her six-month-old daughter Natalie off at Edmunds's home. Beard warned Edmunds that Natalie was being fussy and had taken only half her bottle, but that otherwise the baby seemed fine. One hour later, Edmunds called 911 after she saw that Natalie appeared to be gasping for air. The baby died later that evening. The autopsy showed that Natalie had suffered from severe brain trauma, and the forensic pathologist determined she had died from shaken baby syndrome. Because it was believed that a shaken baby would immediately exhibit symptoms of injury, the last person to care for the baby—Edmunds—was presumed to be the source of the injury.

Edmunds was charged with homicide for Natalie's death.

At trial, the prosecution presented multiple experts, each of whom testified that Natalie had died of SBS. Because the child would have suffered the fatal injuries immediately after being violently shaken, and because Edmunds was the last person in the presence of the baby, she must have been the abuser.

In her defense, Edmunds vehemently denied ever harming Natalie. Character witnesses took the stand to extol Edmunds as a patient, caring, and kind person. A defense expert suggested that the baby's brain injuries could have occurred earlier; in fact, Natalie had been treated by a doctor on multiple occasions for lethargy and other symptoms consistent with brain injury. But the prosecution in its closing argument brushed that defense expert aside, arguing that prior medical history was not relevant: since Natalie died from SBS, the abuse must have occurred immediately before she exhibited symptoms, leaving Edmunds as the only likely culprit.

The jury agreed and convicted Edmunds of murder. She was sentenced in 1996 to eighteen years in prison. After eleven years behind bars, Edmunds was finally exonerated by scientific evidence that disproved the SBS diagnosis. She has since written a book about her harrowing ordeal, *It Happened to Audrey: From Loving Mum to Accused Baby Killer*.[38] It's a tough title to process, and one that captures an even tougher experience that Edmunds had to live through.

Today, the so-called science behind the SBS/AHT diagnosis has largely been rejected by the scientific community. In 2009, the AAP reversed its earlier stance that the triad of symptoms warranted a presumption of abuse, and recognized the ongoing controversy surrounding the SBS diagnosis.[39] In 2016, the Swedish Agency for Health Technology Assessment and Assessment of Social Services issued a groundbreaking report which determined that studies supporting the SBS hypothesis were insufficient and not rooted in reliable methodologies.[40] In fact, it has been scientifically established that the triad of symptoms can be produced by a variety of noncriminal occurrences, including illnesses, short falls, or other accidental injuries.[41] Real questions have been raised as to whether violent shaking could ever produce enough force to create the triad of symptoms without also causing other injuries that are often not present in these cases.[42] SBS/AHT as a tool for diagnosing both the crime and the criminal has been discredited and questioned by doctors, scientists, legal scholars, and courts.[43]

Despite its unreliability, SBS/AHT has served as the basis for "thousands of cases in which children have been separated from their parents, and parents and caretakers have been sent to prison or even sentenced to death." The Innocence Network has collectively reviewed more than one hundred criminal convictions resulting largely from expert testimony about SBS based on the presence of the triad of symptoms.[44] At the time of this writing, the NRE includes seventeen exonerations in cases involving an SBS misdiagnosis.[45] Prosecutions based on the SBS/AHT theory continue to occur,[46] and it is likely that other people wrongly convicted under SBS theories have yet to be identified, let alone exonerated.

Other Medical Misdiagnoses of Murder

Even without the SBS/AHT label, medical personnel sometimes misdiagnose a sudden unexplained death as a crime when in fact the death was caused by an overlooked illness or disease.

In 1989 in Columbus, Mississippi, seventeen-year-old Sabrina Butler found her nine-month-old son lifeless in his room.[47] She called the hospital, frantically performed CPR, and then raced with him to the emergency room. Emergency medical personnel were unable to revive him. The emergency personnel contacted the police with their suspicions about the baby's death and specifically cited the baby's swollen abdomen and bruises.

The police aggressively interrogated a shocked and grieving Butler as if she were a murder suspect. In response to intensive questioning, Butler gave a number of inconsistent and contradictory stories before finally and falsely stating that she had punched her baby in his stomach. The Mississippi prosecutor, armed with Butler's false confession and the medical expert's testimony that the baby appeared to have been abused, charged Butler with capital murder.

At trial, the prosecutor relied on expert testimony that the baby's death was caused by internal injuries consistent with abuse, and introduced Butler's false confession to the jury as proof of murder. Butler's lawyers did not present any witnesses or evidence in Butler's defense, and Butler did not testify in her own defense.

Perhaps not surprisingly, Butler was convicted and sentenced to death. For the next five years, she was the only woman on Mississippi's death row.

A Mississippi appellate court reversed Butler's conviction based on prosecution error.[48] At her retrial, Butler's new defense counsel presented testimony from a neighbor that Butler had attempted CPR on her infant while she waited for the ambulance. An expert testified that the baby's bruising could have been caused by Butler's attempts to revive her child. And, perhaps most importantly, the medical examiner testified that he now believed the baby could have died from a kidney disorder. After a brief deliberation, on December 15, 1995, the jury acquitted Butler and she was fully exonerated from any wrongdoing.[49]

Patricia Stallings also suffered a wrongful conviction for murder based on a misdiagnosed medical condition.[50] In 1989 Stallings rushed her son Ryan to the hospital in St. Louis, Missouri, because he was vomiting and having difficulty breathing. Ryan was placed in the pediatric intensive care unit, where doctors found elevated levels of ethylene glycol in his blood. The doctors suspected that Ryan had been poisoned with antifreeze. Ryan seemed to recover in the hospital and was released from the hospital into foster care through protective services. A few weeks later, Stallings was permitted a short visit with her son. Ryan again exhibited symptoms and, shortly afterward, died.

The prosecution charged Stallings with first-degree murder. Pregnant at the time with her second child, Stallings was incarcerated pending the murder trial. While incarcerated, Stallings gave birth in 1990 to a son, David, who was promptly placed in foster care. Soon after, David exhibited symptoms similar to those experienced by Ryan and was found to have elevated ethylene glycol levels in his blood, even though Stallings had had no contact with him. Unlike Ryan, however, David was diagnosed with methylmalonic acidemia (MMA), a rare and sometimes fatal genetic disorder that can cause elevated ethylene glycol levels.

At Stalling's 1991 murder trial, the prosecution presented expert medical testimony relating to the presence of elevated ethylene glycol levels in Ryan's blood and brain, which was consistent with antifreeze poisoning. Counsel for the state also established that Stalling had antifreeze in her home. Stallings's defense lawyer sought to introduce the theory that Ryan may also have had MMA, but failed to offer any evidence or expert testimony to support that theory. Without evidence, the judge refused to allow Stallings to offer MMA as an alternative, noncriminal explanation for Ryan's death. Stallings was convicted and sentenced to life in prison.

Stallings then got a lucky break. The television show *Unsolved Mysteries* filmed and aired a segment on Stallings's conviction for Ryan's death. A biochemist from St. Louis University saw the episode and arranged for another scientist to reexamine Ryan's blood. The bloodwork demonstrated Ryan had MMA. A second researcher from Yale University also examined the bloodwork, and confirmed that Ryan had MMA. The trial prosecutor learned about the test results, and personally requested a new trial for Stallings based on inadequate defense counsel. Stallings was released from prison after serving two years of her sentence, and later was fully exonerated.[51]

In each of these cases, presumably well-intentioned medical personnel believed there was a suspicious death and contacted the authorities. Once a criminal cause of injury or death was fixed in the treating physician's mind, that diagnosis was passed along and reaffirmed to colleagues, the police, and prosecutor, all to the exclusion of other, noncriminal explanations. The police pursued an investigation based on the initial misdiagnosis that a crime was committed, rather than proceeding inductively, wherever all the evidence leads them.

The problem is that medical personnel are not criminal investigators. They lack training and expertise in crime identification. When the police uncritically rely on a medical professional's diagnosis of a crime, they abdicate their responsibility to objectively investigate the evidence. A medical misdiagnosis can lead the police and prosecutors to believe that a crime occurred, to approach the "crime scene" with preconceived theories about what happened, to reject evidence (including statements of innocence) that does not conform with a theory of guilt, and to engage in guilt-presumptive interrogations that result in false admissions and confessions. The combination of a medical misdiagnosis of a crime with a guilt-presuming investigation can lead to the arrest and eventual conviction of innocent people for deaths that were certainly tragic but not criminal.

FIRE MISLABELED AS INTENTIONAL ARSON

After a 1980 fire swept through a Brooklyn townhouse killing a woman and her five young children, William Vasquez, Amaury Villalobos, and Raymond

Mora were charged with six counts of arson murder.[52] Hannah Quick, the building's owner and a drug dealer, called the authorities to report the fire. She told Fire Marshall Donald Clark, before he ever set foot on the site of the fire, that Vasquez, Villalobos, and Mora had been in the building and that they intentionally set the fire.

Despite their protestations of innocence, the three men were arrested.

At the 1981 trial, Fire Marshal Clark testified for the prosecution and claimed that the fire had two points of origin. This was extremely persuasive evidence that the fire was intentionally set, because accidental fires typically have only one point of origin. He also described finding "pour patterns" on the floor that he claimed was proof the fire had been deliberately enhanced by a person who poured flammable liquids throughout the area. Hannah Quick also testified. Based primarily on the testimony of these witnesses, the jury convicted the three men. They were sentenced to life imprisonment.

Decades later, John J. Lentini, a nationally recognized fire science expert and author of the book *Scientific Protocols for Fire Investigation,* was asked to reexamine the fire using modern fire science principals.[53] In his 2014 report, Lentini concluded that the arson convictions were based on outdated and unreliable fire science, and that what Clark had presented as evidence of an intentional fire had no validity in light of the modern scientific understanding of fire behavior. Instead, Lentini determined that a "flashover" had occurred, causing the fire to spread between contiguous places from a single point of origin. The flashover also explained the discoloration on the floor: what Clark had described as pour patterns were actually substances that melted from the intense heat. Lentini's findings supported a theory that the fire was accidental.

Lentini further concluded that Clark's analysis was likely tainted by expectation bias. Clark was both the criminal investigator and the person tasked with evaluating the fire, and he interviewed Quick *before* he went to the fire scene. Quick told Clark not only that the fire was intentionally set but also who set the fire. As Lentini noted in his report: "This 'wearing of two hats' unduly prejudices a fire scene investigator, and as a result, it is very unlikely that if there had been an accidental cause for this fire, Fire Marshal Clark would have been able to recognize it."[54]

Brooklyn prosecutors agreed to review the case. In addition to the outdated science on which the conviction was based, it was also discovered that Quick on her deathbed had confessed to family members that she lied to investigators, perhaps to cover up her own liability for the fire or to receive insurance money.[55]

After careful examination of the evidence, the prosecution agreed that a manifest injustice had occurred and that the three men had been wrongly convicted. Vasquez and Villalobos served thirty-three years in prison before their release and eventual exoneration in 2015; Mora died in prison of a heart attack years earlier. Vasquez went blind because of glaucoma that was left untreated during his incarceration.[56] All for a fire that was erroneously labeled an arson.

Forensic scientists are supposed to collect, preserve, and analyze evidence in a neutral and objective manner, using reliable, up-to-date scientific methods that result in accurate, evidence-based conclusions. In fire investigations, however, the neutrality of forensic scientists is often compromised because they typically also serve as the lead criminal arson investigator.[57] As a result, forensic experts typically do not come to the investigation with a neutral outlook and true independence from law enforcement. Indeed, they are often part of the law enforcement apparatus itself. This does not mean that fire scientists deliberately or intentionally misinterpret evidence, but simply that they experience unconscious cognitive biases that stem from their dual roles as scientist and investigator.

Fire scientists who also assume the role of criminal investigator may be particularly susceptible to unconscious bias.[58] The National Research Council cautions that "forensic investigations should be independent of law enforcement efforts either to prosecute criminal suspects or even to determine whether a criminal act has indeed been committed."[59] Yet fire scientists may well adopt the perspective of other witnesses and law enforcement investigators instead of engaging in an objective evaluation of the evidence. Fire scientists' conclusions may also be contaminated by information not relevant to the objective, science-based determination of the origin and cause of the fire.[60] This is what occurred when Quick told Marshall Clark that the fire had been intentionally set and that the three men set it.

Further complicating arson investigations is fire itself, which usually damages or destroys evidence such as DNA or fingerprints. As a result, fire experts often resort to examining evidence created by the fire, such as fire patterns. Fire pattern analysis, when performed correctly, can help determine where a fire started and its cause (the goal of fire science). It cannot, however, identify a suspect or shed light on a possible motive (the goals of an arson investigation).[61] When the two are conflated, information about the investigation may bias the investigation.

Cameron Todd Willingham was executed in Texas in 2004 for the arson murder of his three young children, who died in a house fire.[62] Willingham was the sole survivor of the terrible blaze. Arson investigators claimed to have found "pour patterns" indicating that someone had deliberately poured accelerants throughout Willingham's home. Although there was other, highly circumstantial evidence, the crux of the case against Willingham was the fire science. After the jury deliberated for just one hour, Willingham was convicted and sentenced to die. By the time the fire evidence was debunked, Willingham had been executed by lethal injection at the hands of the state of Texas. His last words at his execution are worth repeating here: "The only statement I want to make is that I am an innocent man convicted of a crime I did not commit. I have been persecuted for twelve years for something I did not do. From God's dust I came and to dust I will return, so the Earth shall become my throne."[63]

MISLABELED CRIMES BASED ON FALSE ASSUMPTIONS: WHEN THE VICTIM EMERGES FROM THE DEAD

No-crime convictions also occur when false assumptions become realities. Recall from the introduction the Boorn brothers, convicted of killing their brother-in-law Richard Colvin, who emerged from New Jersey just days before Stephen was scheduled to be hanged. Although rare, modern examples of murder convictions where the victim turned out to be alive and well still occur.

In China in 2000, Zhao Zuohai, was sentenced to twenty-nine years in prison for the murder of a local man named Zhao Zhenshang.[64] Zuohai had been in a fight with his so-called victim, Zhenshang, immediately before the latter disappeared. The police decided that Zhenshang had been murdered and that Zuohai was the culprit. After a decomposing, headless body turned up, pressure on the police to solve the crime mounted. The police arrested and tortured Zuohai until he finally confessed to the supposed murder. Relying solely on Zuohai's coerced confession, the Chinese authorities secured Zuohai's conviction.

In 2010, ten years into his prison sentence, Zuohai was exonerated after Zhenshang suddenly reappeared in his village to collect welfare support. Upon his return, Zhenshang explained that he had fled the province because he feared that *he* had killed *Zuohai* in the fight. Zuohai was released and his name was cleared, but his preprison life was now in tatters. His wife had left him for another man, and his children had been adopted by other families.

Australian teenager Natasha Ann Ryan was fourteen-years-old when she went missing in 1999.[65] After years of futile searching, her family believed Ryan dead and continued to pressure the authorities to solve the case. This belief was bolstered by the later confession of Leonard John Fraser, an Australian serial killer, who claimed to have killed Ryan along with three other young women. When Fraser confessed, the prosecution leaped at the chance to hold someone accountable. During Fraser's trial for her murder, Ryan was found hiding in her boyfriend's cupboard. She had been living with him the entire time. The Ryan murder charges against Fraser were promptly dismissed.

There are also murder convictions for the deaths of people who never existed.

Victoria Banks, Medell Banks, and Diane Tucker—sometimes called the Choctaw Three—were poor, black, intellectually disabled people charged in Alabama with capital murder for the killing of an infant who never existed.[66] Victoria Banks was in an Alabaman jail in 1999 when she decided to feign a pregnancy in an effort to obtain an early release. She refused a pelvic examination, and no pregnancy test was ever performed. Two doctors met with her. Although one doctor found no evidence that she was pregnant, the other claimed to hear a fetal heartbeat. Banks's plan proved effective: she was released on bond after she threatened to sue the jail for inadequate prenatal care.

When the local sheriff later encountered Victoria, he asked about the baby. She claimed to have had a miscarriage. Thinking that assertion suspicious, the sheriff brought Victoria, her estranged husband, Medell Banks, and her sister, Diane Tucker, into the station for questioning. The three were interrogated over the course of several days about the "missing baby." They initially protested that no baby had been born, repeating time and again that Victoria had undergone a complete tubal ligation in 1995 and could never have been pregnant. They also explained that Victoria had lied about being pregnant in a desperate ploy to be released from jail. Exhausted and drained after days of questioning, the three eventually confessed to murder. To avoid the death penalty, each defendant pled guilty to manslaughter.

Medell Banks recanted his confession and later challenged his guilty plea. He was exonerated after it was proven that Victoria Banks had indeed had a tubal ligation, which would have prevented her from ever being pregnant. The Alabama Court of Criminal Appeals threw out his case, noting that a "manifest injustice" had been done.[67] The two women, however, did not withdraw their pleas, and continue to be guilty in the eyes of the law for the killing of a baby that was never conceived.[68]

Beyond forensic error, forensic scientists and other experts involved in foren-sic testing may engage in deliberate corruption and misconduct that results in the conviction of innocent people for crimes that simply did not happen. This phenomenon occurs in forensic laboratories across the country, with wide-sweeping implications for thousands of criminal defendants and the taxpayers who fund their wrongful prosecutions.

In Massachusetts, more than 47,000 convictions were vacated based on forensic misconduct by two different scientists in two different labs.[69] Annie Dookhan, a forensic lab scientist, was arrested in 2012 after admitting that she falsified drug tests in at least 24,000 cases. It was later discovered that Sonja Farak, a forensic scientist with a drug problem, faked lab results in more than 11,000 cases. Nearly all the Dookhan and Farak cases were dismissed. In Texas, Jonathan Salvador, who worked on thousands of cases, was suspended for falsifying lab results in drug cases.[70] Also in Texas, Ana Romero was accused of dry-labbing alcohol samples, resulting in the wrongful conviction of at least twenty-two people for intoxication-related offenses based on those falsified lab results.[71]

In New Jersey in December 2018, the corruption of one officer led to the review of 20,000 drunk-driving cases.[72] Sergeant Marc W. Dennis was a coordinator in the Drug and Alcohol Testing Unit of the New Jersey State Police. As part of his responsibilities, Dennis was required to conduct twice-a-year tests to confirm the accuracy of the Alcotest machines and to recali-brate them as needed. Dennis, however, did not perform the required calibra-tions, but instead falsely certified the accuracy of the machines in papers he filed with the state. Once Dennis's misconduct was revealed, the New Jersey Supreme Court determined that more than 20,000 breath tests used in drunk-driving cases had been called into question.[73]

Some of the people convicted based on these false lab results were in fact guilty. But undoubtedly a sizable number of people ensnared in the forensic misconduct scandals were factually innocent of crimes that never happened.

Then there was Fred Zain, a forensic scientist consistently promoted and praised for his work. He also blatantly made up forensic results. Gerald Davis and his father, Dewey Davis, were among Zain's victims. In 1986, Gerald and Dewey were convicted of sexual assault in West Virginia.[74] The alleged vic-tim, who knew both Gerald and Dewey and considered the Davises to be "family friends," went to their home to do laundry. She claimed Gerald raped her on his bed and that Dewey allowed it to happen. The case seemed strong, as the alleged victim knew both accused men. But it was the testimony of Fred Zain that sealed their fate. Both the victim and Gerald Davis were Type O secretors, yet Type A antigens were present in the DNA testing, which means that Gerald Davis should have been excluded as a contributor. Yet, during Gerald Davis's trial, Zain concocted a theory that bacteria explained the presence of Type A antigens. He also exaggerated the likelihood that Davis was the perpetrator, claiming that only Davis and 3.5 percent of the male population could have perpetrated the crime. In truth, the victim and the entire male population of the world could have deposited the semen.[75]

Both Gerald and Dewey Davis were convicted.

After their convictions, accusations against Fred Zain, the former director of the West Virginia crime lab, began to surface in unrelated cases. It soon became apparent that Zain had fabricated lab results, omitted evidence from his reports, overstated scientific conclusions, and lied under oath about test results. The scope of Zain's misconduct was so egregious that the West Virginia Supreme Court, after a review of 189 of the cases in which he was involved, warned that "any testimony or documentary evidence offered by Zain at any time should be deemed invalid, unreliable and inadmissible."[76] The same court called for DNA retesting in all of Zain's cases.

Gerald and Dewey Davis were among them. The Center for Blood Research reported the rape kit samples indicated a male and a female presence, but that Davis was not a contributor to the sample. Testing on Davis's sheets and underwear also failed to find any evidence of the victim's DNA profile. Both Davises were exonerated, but not before they spent eight years in prison for a fictive crime based on Zain's false testimony and the weight given to a false accusation (more about the latter in chapter 2).

Our criminal justice system relies on forensic experts to do their jobs honestly and with integrity, because jurors look to those experts to explain scientific principals outside their knowledge. Forensic misconduct fundamentally undermines the integrity of the criminal justice system because fact finders have no way to distinguish forensic truths from forensic lies. When experts lie, the criminal justice system is bound to fail, causing the guilty to go free and the innocent to be convicted.

As shown in this chapter, no-crime convictions can result from the mislabeling of an event as a crime. The psychology of cognitive bias helps provide a lens with which to explain, at least in part, how these miscarriages of justice occur. After an accidental, natural, noncriminal, or fictive event is labeled a crime, the erroneous label is often embraced as reality. The police, working with forensic experts and the prosecution, engage in a guilt-presumptive investigation to find evidence that will "prove" the guilt of the suspect. Prosecutors and judges fail to objectively examine the evidence and instead close ranks to secure a conviction, while defense lawyers fail to ask whether a crime in fact happened in the first place.

No-crime wrongful convictions can be based on the misclassification of a noncriminal event as a crime. The following chapter considers a different source of no-crime wrongful convictions: when civilian witnesses make false accusations that authorities accept as true.

TWO

False Accusations

WHEN LIES BECOME COURTROOM TRUTHS

ON THE NIGHT OF JULY 9, 1977, a patrol officer came upon sixteen-year-old Cathleen Crowell standing on the side of a road near a suburban shopping mall outside Chicago where Crowell worked at a seafood restaurant.[1] Crowell tearfully told the officer that as she was walking through the mall parking lot after work, a car with three young men pulled next to her. Two of the men grabbed her and threw her in the back seat. One of them raped her. They then pushed her out of the car and sped away.

The police took Crowell to a nearby hospital, where medical personnel conducted a rape examination. Seminal fluid was found in her underwear and in her vagina; the underwear, several hairs, and a vaginal swab were preserved as evidence. Three days later, Crowell went to the police station and provided a description of the perpetrator, who she said had long stringy hair and a clean-shaven face. From her description, a police artist created a composite sketch that closely resembled a photo of a man named Gary Dotson. Crowell picked Dotson out of a police mug shot book and a police lineup. Even though Dotson had a strong alibi and a full-grown, thick moustache that could not have grown in a few days, he was arrested and charged with the alleged rape and kidnapping.

At trial, Crowell positively identified Dotson. A prosecution police expert who presented false credentials incorrectly testified that there was a one-in-ten chance that Dotson had provided the antigens found in the seminal fluid. In his defense, Dotson claimed he was the victim of a mistaken identification, and presented four alibi witnesses who claimed he had been with them all night, hanging out and stopping at two parties. Dotson was nonetheless convicted and sentenced to twenty-five to fifty years in prison.

The problem with Dotson's conviction, however, is that it was based entirely on lies. Crowell had never been attacked. Instead, she invented the rape and the identity of her so-called assailant from whole cloth.

At the time she made her false accusation, Crowell lived in an Illinois foster home. She was worried that she would be kicked out if she were to become pregnant after having consensual sex with her boyfriend. Crowell invented a preemptive cover story—a rape—to explain any possible pregnancy. Crowell's vivid details of the attack were lifted from a romance novel that included a rape scene similar to the story she shared with the police.

Years later, Crowell married and became Cathleen Crowell Webb. She joined a church and became an active member. Haunted by having sent an innocent man to prison, in 1985 Webb came forward with the truth about her false allegation. She obtained a lawyer and told the Illinois State Attorney's Office that she had lied about the rape to cover up a consensual sexual relationship with her then boyfriend. Prosecutors initially discounted her recantation, but Webb persisted and contacted the national media in an effort to secure Dotson's freedom. After her story was featured in numerous national media outlets, the governor of Illinois commuted Dotson's sentence. It was not, however, until 1988 that Dotson was finally and fully exonerated of any wrongdoing, becoming one of the first people in the country to prove his innocence through DNA testing.

This chapter is about false accusations. It begins by examining the science of lie detection and considering just how difficult it is for even the most seasoned professionals to detect lies. When accusations go undetected as false, they gain traction and viability among actors in the criminal justice system. Taken to their logical conclusion, their lies culminate in the convictions of innocent people for crimes that did not occur. The chapter then examines adult sexual assault and child sex abuse, the two types of cases in which false accusations lead most frequently to no-crime convictions.

THE LIE OF LIE DETECTION

People lie. A lot. By one estimate, people lie on average twice a day, every day.[2] Despite the prevalence of lying, however, we are not very good at detecting lies. Laypeople like you and me can identify the difference between truths and lies with no more accuracy than a coin toss, which means that around 50 percent of the time, we do not realize someone is lying.[3]

Astonishingly, professionals tasked with lie detection, such as police officers, do not fare much better. One meta-analysis of eight different research studies conducted between 1986 and 2005 comparing the lie detection abilities of police officers and laypeople found "not a single study that police officers are superior to laypersons in discriminating between truth tellers and liars."[4] Trained professional lie detectors fared slightly better. A 1991 study found that members of the Secret Service were better at detecting lies than laypeople, with a 64 percent accuracy rate,[5] and a 1999 study found members of the CIA had a 73 percent accuracy rate.[6] More recent studies, however, continue to suggest that most law enforcement professionals have a lie detection accuracy rate only marginally higher than chance alone.[7] Even highly trained lie detectors are only a bit better than "heads or tails" at ferreting out lies.

Lie detection is hard because there is no behavioral marker that conclusively reveals deception; no universal, consistent physiological or behavioral tell or sign marks an active liar. In the fairy tale *Pinocchio,* Pinocchio's nose grew long every time he told a lie, enabling his father, Geppetto, to catch him every time. In the real world, however, there is no Pinocchio's nose for identifying a lie.

But you'd never know it. Books and articles on lie detection abound, claiming that behavioral tells reveal a liar: liars are said to avoid eye contact, clear their throats, fidget, look up and to the right (or to the left), touch their noses, or play with their glasses.[8] While these behaviors may mean *something* about the person speaking, it may not mean that they are liars or are lying. Avoiding eye contact may reflect cultural differences for people from societies where looking a person of authority in the eye is considered disrespectful. Similarly, nervous gestures might reflect anxiety about any number of things, including being questioned, or the underlying situation that is the subject of the questioning, or something entirely unrelated to the issue at hand. Sometimes your nose might just be itchy.

Another popular method of lie detection is to track physiological changes in the presumed liar. This is not a new concept. In 1000 BCE China, people thought to be lying were forced to chew dry white rice and spit it out. Rice that was too dry "proved" the person was lying.[9] In reality, however, physiological changes do not always signify dishonesty, and tests to measure those changes are notoriously unreliable. Polygraph machines, popularly known as lie detectors, measure physiological changes exhibited by a person upon being asked a question by an examiner. The polygraph examiner interprets the results after a series of questions is completed. But there are many reasons an examinee might do poorly on the polygraph test. If the examinee responded with anxiety to the test conditions, the examiner, or even the test itself, the examiner might incorrectly find deception.[10]

Racial, ethnic, and class biases may also impact the efficacy of polygraph examinations. In a landmark report on polygraphs, the National Research Council warned of racial and socioeconomic biases: "[T]ruthful members of socially stigmatized groups and truthful examinees who are believed to be guilty or believed to have a high likelihood of being guilty may show emotional and physiological responses in polygraph test situations that mimic the responses that are expected of deceptive individuals."[11] In other words, the polygraph examiner and the test itself may be biased against specific racial or ethnic groups, thereby producing biased or inaccurate results.

Another problem with polygraph tests is that they can be manipulated. Liars can and do take countermeasures to defeat the polygraph.[12] Many of these techniques can be learned through a quick Google search. For instance, one authority on polygraph examinations suggests that you can skew the exam during the "probable lie" question—the baseline question that asks something like "Have you ever lied to your parents?"—by biting down hard on your tongue.[13] This will set off a host of physiological responses and cause the examiner to believe that you have stronger reactions to lying than you actually do. The same authority suggests day dreaming about something pleasant while you lie. The list of ways to beat the test goes on.

For these reasons, the National Research Council cautioned that although the polygraph was "better than chance" at detecting lies, it also had an unacceptably high rate of false positives.[14] Polygraphs fall short of reliability and accuracy because of human interpretative error, false positives from the test itself, and countermeasures that defeat its testing mechanisms. Given their unreliability, polygraph results are not admissible in court in many states, though they are used by some employers, including various federal government agencies for employment screening.

But it is not just the polygraph that yields questionable outcomes. Efforts to create new, more effective technologies for lie detection based on physiology have not fared particularly well. Functional magnetic resonance imaging (fMRI), for instance, evaluates changes in brain activity by measuring blood flow. The primary form of fMRI measures the blood oxygen level–dependent (or BOLD) response. Scientists hypothesized that fMRI could capture BOLD responses in the brain regions most closely related to the cognitive processes for lying and use it to detect falsities.[15] One lie detection company boldly proclaims that "[t]he technology used by No Lie MRI represents the first and only direct measure of truth verification and lie detection in human history!"[16]

The website's optimism may be quite unfounded. As a lie detection tool, fMRI has bumped up against the same reliability issues as the polygraph.[17] Courts have rejected the admission of fMRI results as unreliable for lie detection,[18] and significant questions have been raised in the scholarly literature as to what fMRIs actually measure, the accuracy of their stated outcomes, and the potential use of countermeasures.[19] Nor have other advanced technological attempts to measure lying through brain functioning—brain fingerprinting or positron emission tomography—yielded conclusive or reliable lie detection methods.

No one methodology or technique allows people—even professional lie catchers—to clearly and accurately detect liars or their lies. Yet professional lie catchers express a high degree of confidence in their ability to distinguish truth from lies.[20] Overconfidence unmoored from reality can be highly problematic in the context of the criminal justice system for any number of reasons. An overconfident, not particularly skilled or accurate professional lie detector may be quick to make decisions about a defendant based on heuristics (cognitive shortcuts), as by relying on inaccurate assumptions about nonverbal behavioral cues to determine truthfulness or by wrongly attributing truthfulness or falsity to certain traits and behaviors (fundamental attribution error).[21] As chapter 1 shows, the use of heuristics can lead to devastating errors.

Law enforcement personnel are on the front lines of lie detection in the criminal justice system. When a civilian witness alleges that a crime was committed, the police bear the responsibility of determining whether that witness is telling the truth. The police generally get it right. But if they assess a false accusation to be true, they may commit to a narrative that leads them to build a case against an innocent person for a crime that never happened. Once the police commit to a theory, tunnel vision may blind officers—and eventually the prosecutors to whom the case is referred—about who is telling the truth and who is lying. Cognitive biases cause the police to overvalue evidence that reinforces the lie, and to discard or minimize evidence that would otherwise indicate that something is rotten at the foundation of their case. When a wrongful conviction results, the lie becomes a legal truth, and a factually innocent person becomes a guilty one in the eyes of the law.

The rest of this chapter looks at two types of crimes where false accusations result in no-crime wrongful convictions: adult rape and sexual assault, and child abuse and sexual assault. False accusations and resulting no-crime wrongful convictions occur in the context of other crime categories including kidnapping, stalking, robbery, and burglary.[22] But because no-crime wrongful convictions based on false accusations occur most frequently in adult rape and child sexual abuse, they are useful in demonstrating the dangers of false accusations, the motivations behind the lies, and the processes by which the lies take root in the criminal justice system.

THE TRUTH ABOUT SEXUAL ASSAULT

In a chapter that is all about lies, let's start with a few truths. First, sexual assaults occur frequently. Statistics about sexual assault indicate that one in three women has been sexually assaulted in her lifetime.[23] Second, sexual assault is often not reported to the police. By some estimates, two out of every three sexual assaults are not reported.[24] The reasons survivors of assault do not report being attacked are varied, but include the belief that the police will not do anything to help.[25]

Therein lies the third and final truth. The police sometimes wrongly discredit victims' reports. As the following accounts illustrate, police inability to tell truths from lies can lead to no-crime wrongful convictions of sexual assault survivors for the crime of false reporting, when in fact the reports of sexual assault were very much true.

Fancy Figueroa was raped on her sixteenth birthday by a stranger who followed her into her home in Queens after school.[26] After the rape, she called the police and then was taken to a hospital, where a rape kit was taken. At the hospital, medical personnel determined that Figueroa was pregnant. The police, suspecting that Figueroa was faking her claim of rape to cover up the pregnancy, dismissed her repeated claims that the rape had occurred. Instead, detectives told the high school sophomore that they would help her find the perpetrator only if she admitted in writing that she was lying about the rape. They then used her written statement to charge her with filing a false report. Figueroa pled guilty and was required to perform community service. Several years later, a serial rapist was caught in a different case, and his DNA was entered into New York's DNA database. It was a match for the DNA profile developed from Figueroa's rape kit. Figueroa was exonerated, and her rapist was eventually sentenced to twenty-two years in prison for his violence against her and other women. She had been wrongly convicted of false reporting when she had committed no crime at all.

In 2008, eighteen-year-old "Marie" was viciously raped by a man who bound her with shoelaces, blindfolded and gagged her, and took photos of the aftermath.[27] Marie reported the crime to the police. Her foster mother thought Marie had a flair for the dramatic, and so found it odd that Marie was acting unemotionally given her claimed trauma. After the foster mother shared her uncertainties with the police, the police subjected Marie to a guilt-presumptive interrogation, homing in on minor inconsistencies and threatening her with jail for lying. Marie was eventually prosecuted for filing a false report, and pled guilty to end the entire ordeal. Years later, the rapist, who had gone on to commit other rapes, was captured. Photos of Marie were found among his possessions during the investigation.

In these cases, the police erroneously determined that survivors of sexual assault were liars and subjected them to intimidating, humiliating, and degrading processes in which their credibility was torn apart. They were then prosecuted and wrongly convicted of filing a false report, a crime that never happened, and were exonerated only after the perpetrator of the assault was brought to justice after committing crimes against other innocent people. It is hard to determine exactly what went wrong in the initial stages of these cases, but had the police engaged in a more open-ended interview process, with a more objective evaluation of the evidence, there may well have been a different outcome.

And yet.

In this chapter about lies, there is another, uncomfortable truth. People make false allegations of sexual assault and rape. How frequently are false sexual assault allegations made? The most widely cited studies suggest that between 2 and 10 percent of all rape allegations made to the police are false.[28] These data, which have been criticized both for undercounting and for overcounting false reporting, capture only the instances when a false report was made and when the falsehood was detected.

Which begs the larger and perhaps more significant question: How often are false accusations of sexual assault *not* detected by the police? How often are innocent people arrested, prosecuted, and convicted for sexual assaults that did not occur? Rape and sexual assaults account for 9 percent of all known no-crime wrongful-conviction exonerations (see table 2, in the introduction). The number of innocent people who have been wrongly convicted of a rape or sexual assault that never happened is surely much higher.

Motivations for false accusations generally fall into broad, sometimes over-lapping categories. Here I use the lens of sexual assault cases to consider the motivations of people who make false accusations: to obtain revenge, to hide wrongdoing, to create an alibi, to obtain a financial benefit, to receive sympathy and attention, or because of the accuser's mental illness. In each instance, the accuser falsely alleges a sexual assault, the police incorrectly credit the claim and pursue the accusation, and the prosecution seeks and obtains what is later revealed to be a wrongful conviction.

Revenge. Revenge is an ancient and powerful motivation to lie. In Greek mythology, Hippolytus spurned the advances of his stepmother, Phaedra, who spitefully and falsely informed her husband, Theseus, that his son, Hippolytus, had raped her.[29] Phaedra's false accusation of rape led Theseus to arrange for his own son's murder.

Revenge as a motive to lie is as potent today as it was in ancient Greece. Then-nineteen-year-old Casey Ehrlick was accused in 2014 by his former girlfriend of rape.[30] The complainant, who had autism, claimed that Ehrlick raped her while she was sleeping, first with a bundle of sharpened colored pencils and then with his penis. Ehrlick insisted his ex-girlfriend was lying in retaliation for ending their relationship, and vehemently denied the charges. At trial, a sexual assault nurse testified that the complainant came to the hospital two days after the alleged rape and that she saw abrasions that were consistent with rape. A defense pathologist testified there were no abrasions and no evidence that the complainant had been raped.

Ehrlick was nonetheless convicted after a jury trial. While he was waiting to be sentenced, the complainant admitted to her counselor that she had lied and that the rape had not happened. The complainant also accused another man of raping her (and, somewhat bizarrely, of stealing her dog). After the prosecution reinterviewed the complainant, it dropped the charges against Ehrlick, and the court vacated his conviction. Ehrlick spent months in jail pending trial where he was beaten by other inmates, based on the lies of a scorned ex-girlfriend out for revenge.

To Cover Up Wrongdoing or to Obtain a Financial Benefit. Revenge is not the only reason for false accusations of sexual assault. As in the case of Gary Dotson and Catherine Crowell Webb, a person might bring a false allegation of rape to create a cover for their own behavior. In this situation, the accuser makes a false accusation because they believe it will help them avoid punishment or provide an alibi for their own questionable conduct.

William McCaffrey was convicted and sentenced to twenty years in prison after a woman claimed he had raped her while the two were on their way to a party.[31] The woman had bruises and scrapes on her arms, but there was no other evidence of rape and the only DNA evidence recovered from her person was female. She later confessed that she had invented the rape because her friends were angry at her for stranding them after she chose to go with McCaffrey to the party. The bruises came from an earlier altercation that had not involved McCaffrey at all. Once her lies were revealed, McCaffrey was exonerated in 2009, having served three long years in prison.

Sixteen-year-old Brian Banks, a high school student with professional football prospects, had been planning to attend the University of Southern California on a full football scholarship when he was accused in 2002 by a fellow student, Wanetta Gibson, of raping her in a stairwell at their high school.[32] Although he maintained his innocence, Banks knew he was facing a potential life sentence if convicted after a trial. Given this risk, his lawyer encouraged him to plead guilty. Banks reluctantly pled no contest to the charges and was sentenced to six years in prison. For five years after his release from prison, he was subjected to highly restrictive monitoring as a registered sex offender. Gibson eventually admitted no rape had occurred and that she had lied. This was of small comfort to Banks, whose college opportunities and best chance to play for the NFL had been left in ruins by her lies.

Gibson's false accusation against Banks highlights another motive for bringing and maintaining a false accusation: financial gain. After Banks's conviction, Gibson's family sued the Long Beach Unified School District, alleging that it had been negligent in failing to provide adequate security for one of its students.[33] The family settled for $1.5 million dollars. Gibson later admitted that one reason she had not come forward sooner to recant her story is that she was afraid her family would have to repay the money. In fact, after Gibson's lies were revealed, the school district won a $2.6 million default judgment against Gibson to recoup the settlement payout made to her. Banks, on the other hand, received a paltry $142,200 from the state of California for his wrongful conviction.[34] Banks's ordeal is now the subject of the movie *Brian Banks*.[35]

Attention, Mental Illness, or Sympathy. Alternatively, someone may make a false accusation to gain attention or sympathy. In the United Kingdom,

Jemma Beale claimed she had been raped by nine men and sexually assaulted by another six men in four different encounters over a three-year span.[36] Her motive for these "impulsive" lies was to gain attention and to make her girlfriend jealous. Mahad Cassim was one of Beale's victims. He was convicted of sexual assault based on Beale's false accusations and served nearly three years in prison. He was eventually exonerated, but said after his release from prison that the conviction damaged him, physically and emotionally: "I am working on the happiness . . . I have a long way to go."[37] Beale was prosecuted for multiple instances of perjury and was sentenced to ten years in prison.

Still others make false accusations because of mental illness or the accuser's difficulty in distinguishing between truth and reality. Amber Mundy claimed she had been raped on a freezing winter evening in upstate New York.[38] After she described her attacker, police homed in on Dan Lackey, a man with a learning disability and an IQ that bordered on the legal definition of intellectually impaired. Mundy claimed to have been bitten by her attacker, but the only DNA recovered was her own. The police obtained an unrecorded confession from Lackey, and even though there was no DNA or other evidence of a rape aside from his confession, Lackey was convicted and sentenced to eight years in prison. Three months after Lackey was incarcerated, Mundy again claimed that she had been raped by a different man. This time, the police determined she had invented the allegation, and she was convicted of filing a false report. Mundy later explained that she had been hearing voices and having trouble distinguishing what was real from what was not real. Perhaps that is why she pressed forward with the Lackey prosecution. Dan Lackey was exonerated by a judge who admitted he'd had real doubts about the case since the guilty verdict years before. Lackey spent more than three years in prison.[39]

The police typically bear the responsibility for detecting lies up front. Sifting what is true from what is false in an alleged sexual assault case is complex. If the police fail to detect a false accusation, an innocent person may well be convicted and sentenced to lengthy terms for a sexual assault that never happened. Conversely, if the police mislabel a true accusation as false, then the accuser may experience secondary victimization and even be wrongly convicted for filing a false report, while an actual rapist remains at large to commit additional crimes and harm other people. The stakes are high, and when law enforcement officers get it wrong, countless people suffer.

Accurate lie detection is hard. But the procedures by which the police approach credibility assessments can certainly be improved. No test or methodology for identifying liars and truth tellers is perfect, but as chapter 9 shows, there are policy reforms and recommendations that could improve lie detection and the investigative techniques the police use to deal with the very real challenge of distinguishing truths from lies.

FALSE ACCUSATIONS OF CHILD SEX ABUSE

Despite the real suffering of children who are sexually abused, false accusations of child sex abuse occur that result in wrongful convictions of innocent people who have done nothing wrong. Of exonerations in no-crime cases, 24 percent involve convictions for child sexual abuse that never happened (see table 2, in the introduction).

When a parent or a child makes a false accusation of child sexual abuse, there are terrible consequences for all involved. People who commit child sex abuse are reviled throughout society, and a mere accusation of such abuse can permanently damage a person's life and reputation regardless of the truth—or falsity—of the claims. Here we consider two contexts in which false accusations of child sex abuse have occurred. The first involves divorce or child custody battles. The second involves mass allegations, as occurred in the infamous child abuse hysteria cases that swept through the country in the 1970s and 1980s.

Divorce or Child Custody Disputes

Divorce marks the end of a legal and intimate partnership. Divorce may happen for a variety of reasons ranging from "irreconcilable differences" to some form of betrayal within the relationship. It can be amiable or extremely acrimonious. The parties involved in a divorce may experience a range of emotions from sorrow and grief to full-blown fury and unbounded bitterness. As emotionally charged as divorce can be, it also has important practical repercussions. It can lead to financial devastation for one or both of the parties, depending on the division of assets, such as the family home and other property. Issues relating to a child's primary residence, child support, and visitation can be so hotly and bitterly contested that it is hard to fathom the parties as a couple who ever liked, let alone loved, each other.

When a couple cannot agree to the terms relating to separation, divorce, and child custody, a court will set the terms for them. One party might seek an advantage in court by claiming that the party's ex-spouse is not responsible, or is a risk to the health and well-being of the children. Or one party might make false claims of abuse to ensure that the divorce or custody outcome is in their favor, or to inflict pain and suffering on their former spouse.

An extreme version of this advantage seeking occurs when one party makes false accusations of child sexual abuse, resulting in convictions for serious crimes that never happened. Anthony Cooper was embroiled in a bitter child custody dispute involving his and his ex-wife's seven-year-old son and an infant child.[40] In 1994, his ex-wife claimed that Cooper anally raped the seven-year-old child. At trial, a physician testified that there was no physical evidence of rape, but that the abuse could have happened despite the lack of physical evidence. In his testimony, Cooper denied the abuse. A jury convicted Cooper, and in 1995 a judge sentenced him to fifty years in prison. His conviction was overturned in 1996 for legal reasons relating to the role of the child's appointed attorney. At his second trial, in 1999, Cooper was acquitted after the jury learned about the bitter custody battle that had been going on and that his ex-wife had previously claimed, falsely, that she was sexually abused as a child.

In 1984, Joseph Elizondo and his wife, Mary Ann, were convicted of sexually abusing Mary Ann's two young sons, Robert and Richard (Joseph's stepsons).[41] After separate jury trials at which Robert testified graphically to sexual abuse, Joseph was sentenced to life imprisonment and Mary Ann was sentenced to twenty years in prison, plus thirty-four years on a plea of guilty to additional charges. The children had no further contact with the Elizondos, who were serving their sentences. When Robert turned seventeen, he found a letter from Mary Ann and learned for the first time that his mother and stepfather were in prison. Robert promptly recanted his trial testimony, explaining that his biological father (Mary Ann's ex-husband) had threatened the boys with daily spankings for the rest of their lives if they didn't make and maintain the accusation. Robert also explained that his father made them bring the accusations to retaliate against Mary Ann for marrying Joseph. A hearing was eventually held at which both boys swore the abuse did not happen. Joseph and Mary Ann were fully exonerated in 1997. Their marriage had ended while they were in prison, and their lives were mere shadows of what they once had been. Joe Elizondo's health had deteriorated in prison, and he died in 2003.

In each case, a parent manipulated a young child into telling a lie for custody purposes or to exact revenge. It was only after the convicted parents spent years in prison as child sex offenders and endured endless court proceedings that they were finally exonerated.

It is usually a parent or guardian who drives the lie telling, but not always. After a divorce, children may have their own agenda—and invent stories to further it. They might want their parents to get back together, or they might prefer to live with the noncustodial parent. In 2006, Josh Horner divorced his wife, with whom he had a five-year-old daughter named "A." In 2014, Horner became engaged to a woman that A., now thirteen, did not like. Around the same time, A. was told that she would be living with her father every other week. A. told her mother that Horner had been abusing her. Horner was arrested and charged with sexually molesting his daughter, allegations that he vehemently denied. At the 2017 trial, A. claimed that Horner had shot their family dog in front of her as punishment after A. refused his advances. Horner testified in his own defense, swore that he was innocent, and explained that he had given the dog away. He was nonetheless convicted by a non-unanimous jury (in Oregon, the jury does not need to be unanimous) on one count of sexual abuse of a minor, and was sentenced to fifty years in prison. The Oregon Innocence Project took his case shortly after Horner began serving his sentence and spent months tracking down the dog, who was living with new owners. With evidence that A. lied about the dog (and given a number of other material legal errors), Horner was fully exonerated in 2018.[42]

In 1994, Ricky Dale Harmon was sentenced to thirty years in prison after his stepdaughter falsely accused him of raping her. Years later, at a 2002 hearing, his stepdaughter admitted the accusations were false. She explained that she had believed that if she accused Harmon of sexual assault, he would be "out of the picture and my mom and dad would get back together."[43] A similar scenario played out in a child sex abuse case against Barry Byars, who pled guilty to sexually assaulting his niece based on her false accusation. He was sentenced to ten years in prison. The niece later recanted. At the time she made the false accusation, she was living with her mother and Byars. She invented the story because she wanted to live with her father.[44]

Mass Hysteria, Child Abuse, and False Memories

Mass hysteria can also fuel no-crime wrongful convictions. Among the first recorded incidents of mass hysteria leading to criminal charges occurred during the Salem witch trials in the late 1600s. In April 1692, Ann Putnam told her father, Thomas Putnam, that a minister named George Burroughs had appeared to her in a vision and tried to convince her to sell her soul to the devil. Ann Putnam also claimed that Burroughs was a mass murderer who had used witchcraft to murder two of his wives and two other people. Thomas Putnam had Ann write down her claims and sign the document. Other girls declared that they too had been afflicted by Burroughs's devil powers. An order was issued for Burroughs's arrest. At his trial that summer, the afflicted girls twitched and pointed as they repeated their allegations about his efforts to entice them to join forces with the devil. Burroughs was found guilty and, on August 19, 1692, was hanged alongside other convicted witches on Gallows Hill.[45]

In the 1980s, America was hit by another moral panic. In this one, hundreds of men and women were convicted of child sexual abuse that never happened. Their cases are eerily reminiscent of the Salem witch trials and were based on evidence as unreliable as the Salem devil himself. Societal acceptance of fantastical stories involving heinous, satanic sexual abuse in day care centers around the country was widespread and uncritical. Parents, prosecutors, and the popular media embraced wild stories of blood rituals, animal mutilation, naked story times, and brutal sexual assaults that were allegedly carried out in day care settings during normal business hours by evil preschool teachers.[46]

Consider the accusations made against Frances and Dan Keller, a married couple who ran a day care center in Texas:

> Among the atrocities that Frances and Dan Keller were supposed to have committed while running a day care center out of their Texas home: drowning and dismembering babies in front of the children; killing dogs and cats in front of the children; transporting the children to Mexico to be sexually abused by soldiers in the Mexican army; dressing as pumpkins and shooting children in the arms and legs; putting the children into a pool with sharks that ate babies; putting blood in the children's Kool-Aid; cutting the arm or a finger off a gorilla at a local park; and exhuming bodies at a cemetery, forcing children to carry the bones.[47]

Dismembered babies with no independent reports or evidence of any kind that a baby was missing or injured? Adults in pumpkin suits shooting children with no evidence of children with gunshot wounds? Baby-eating sharks? Mutilated gorillas at a park that housed no gorillas? These accusations were almost laughable, except they had real life consequences.

In 1992, the Kellers were convicted of sexual abuse and each sentenced to forty-eight years in prison. In 2013, *after twenty-one years behind bars,* the

Kellers were finally exonerated. In their seventies at the time of their release, the Kellers were wizened, gray-haired, and walking with assistance. They had been victimized and then left to languish in prison in the wake of a ritual abuse hysteria in their town, convicted of crimes that had never occurred.[48]

There was no shortage of innocent people swept up in the wave of this hysteria over ritual child sex abuse. Michele "Kelly" Michaels was exonerated in New Jersey after serving five years of her forty-eight-year prison sentence for 299 offenses against thirty-three children. Among the allegations against her were that she stabbed children in the genitals with plastic utensils, forced the children to eat cakes made from human feces, and made them play "duck, duck, goose" and sing "Jingle Bells" while naked. None of this happened.

In Kern County, California, between 1984 and 1986, at least thirty people were convicted of satanic ritual child sex abuse; between 1991 and 2008, twenty-one of those people were exonerated.[49] Debbie Nathan, an award-winning investigative journalist who wrote extensively about the tsunami of satanic child abuse convictions, estimates that between 1984 and 1995, "at least 185 adults nationwide, about half of them women, were charged with ritualized sexual abuse. Of those, 113 were convicted, mainly on the word of young children."[50] It is hard to believe that jurors were convinced so frequently—and beyond a reasonable doubt—that these surreal and implausible allegations actually happened, but they were, and innocent people were convicted and sent to prison.

Part of the story in these satanic abuse cases is that children were subjected to aggressive and suggestive questioning that created and reinforced "memories" of fantastical and impossible events. The process of memory is complex. We'd like to believe our brains are like video cameras that record experiences and store them exactly as they happened for retrieval at will. In reality, memory is a process of construction and interpretation that begins the moment an event is perceived and continues well into the future. Memory is not stored intact in perpetuity. It can be contaminated, can fade with time, and can be otherwise altered by a wide range of factors. Memories also can be induced or falsely created. At the end of the day, what we think we remember is a product of exposure, time, and experience. It may not reflect exactly—or even at all—what actually happened.

Research demonstrates that memories of events that never happened can be planted in participants' minds through suggestion and other corroborative techniques.[51] After suggestive questioning, participants in research studies have "remembered" being lost in the mall, being bitten by animals, and riding in a hot air balloon, even though none of those events ever occurred in their own lives.[52] In one classic study, participants were shown a video of a car driving along a road. Participants were asked to estimate how fast the car was moving "when it passed the barn." One week later, one in six participants recalled seeing a barn—even though there had been no barn in the video.[53] In 1992 in Amsterdam, a plane crashed into an eleven-story apartment building and burst into flames. There was no video footage of the crash itself, but footage of the accident response, including images of the fiery wreck and the emergency responders, was broadcast throughout the news cycle within the first hour. Months after the plane crash, researchers surveyed numerous Amsterdam residents about the event. A majority claimed to have seen the plane hit the building and burst into flames, even providing detailed and vivid descriptions of the crash. Of course, since the crash had not been recorded by anyone, anywhere, it could not have been seen by these TV viewers.[54]

Children are particularly susceptible to suggestion. A detailed look at the Keller convictions discussed above provides an understanding of how false memories can come to prevail.[55] The investigation into the Kellers began with a statement by a disturbed three-year-old who was already in therapy for a variety of troubling behaviors, including trying to jump out of a moving car and repeatedly bruising herself by banging her body on the floor. One year earlier, during her parent's divorce proceeding, her mother had the child evaluated for child sexual abuse, for which no evidence was found. One day, on her way to a therapist appointment, the three-year-old told her mother that Dan Keller had pulled her pants down and spanked her and that he had "poo'd and pee'd" on her head. By the time she arrived at the therapist's office, she changed her story. But no matter. The therapist, whose licensing credentials were apparently questionable, "helped" the child "recall" that Dan Keller had actually sexually assaulted her with a pen and a belt.[56]

The child was then taken to a doctor for an examination. This doctor erroneously determined that the child's hymen had lacerations. The doctor later fully recanted his findings, admitting in a sworn statement that he had erred in using outdated medical techniques.[57] The next day, the child was interviewed by a social worker who worked at the sheriff's office. The social worker already believed that the child had been abused, and did not engage in an open, objective interview. Instead, she began with the conclusion that the child had been abused and set out to find evidence of that abuse. Proceeding under the cognitive bias known as premature cognitive commitment, the social worker pressed for abuse-consistent evidence, even when faced with the child's denials or implausible stories.

That is exactly what happened in the ensuing child interviews that eventually extended to three children in the case. The social worker engaged in highly inappropriate and suggestive questioning. For instance, while interviewing one of the children, she produced two anatomically correct dolls that she called Fran and Dan and manipulated them into various sexual positions. The child was rewarded with candy for "correct" answers. When the child wanted to leave, she was restrained. At one point, she asked the child what happened at the day care center. The child replied, "You tell me." The relentless questioning continued unabated, and the child's stories of ritual abuse, prompted by the interviewers, grew more and more fantastical.

In addition to intensive therapeutic questioning, a second child was also being interrogated by his parents and the police, who showed him satanic symbols and quizzed him at home. He initially denied that any abuse had occurred. Bombarded for eight months with suggestive questions and remarks by his parents and a therapist who believed that satanic abuse had occurred, the child finally declared he knew how to contact Satan and provided extensive and seemingly nonsensical tales of bizarre ritual abuse. The same child also believed his teddy bear was alive and could talk. Unlike the first child, who was unable to testify at trial, this boy testified to fantastical tales of the Kellers' abuse. He also implicated a wide variety of additional suspects, including law enforcement personnel. One man, Doug Perry, was interrogated for four and a half hours by Texas Rangers. Under this intense pressure, Perry confessed that he had participated in ritual abuse. He promptly recanted his confession, claiming it had been coerced by the Rangers. Eventually Perry pled guilty to crimes that had never happened and was sentenced to ten years' probation.[58]

Investigators expended extraordinary resources on the Keller case in an effort to prove the allegations of abuse. They poured over airport records to find evidence of an airplane that, without anyone noticing, landed in a residential area and transported children to and from Mexico for the purpose of being molested. They flew a helicopter over gravesites in search of evidence of alleged human sacrifice. Parents, believing there was an epidemic of satanic ritual abuse, took their three- and four-year-old children to cemeteries to find the spot where the satanic activities had taken place. They found nothing.

The prosecution's main evidence against the Kellers was the testimony of young children, manipulated by adults, who in turn were caught in a panic about satanic ritual abuse. There was no evidence of criminality—no photographs, no blood, no dismembered babies or mutilated animals, no DNA. As one judge scathingly wrote in the 2015 opinion that finally overturned the Kellers' conviction: "This was a witch hunt from the beginning."[59] A witch hunt, indeed, where innocent people were the prey, where common sense was checked at the door, and where incredible falsehoods snowballed into truths that destroyed the Kellers' lives.

Our entire legal system rests on the false belief that people can tell truths from lies. We believe law enforcement can detect false allegations, we believe prosecutors can vet accusations that are not supported by credible evidence, and we believe laypeople acting as jurors can figure out who is telling the truth and who is lying.

But the real-life stories in this chapter reveal just how bad we are at lie detection. In 100 percent of the no-crime wrongful conviction cases that started with a false accusation, the lie was believed. The police, investigator, prosecutor, judge, jury, and sometimes even the defense lawyer completely failed to detect that the complainant was lying. They failed to detect that no crime had occurred. They failed to detect that the accused defendant was telling the truth about his or her innocence. They failed, and because they failed, innocent people were wrongly convicted of completely fabricated crimes.

But it is not just civilian witnesses who tell unimaginable lies. The following chapter considers no-crime wrongful convictions based on an entirely different source of lies: corrupt police who fabricate crimes.

THREE

Police

CROSSING THE "THIN BLUE LINE"

IN ALASKA, NATIVE AMERICAN WASSILLIE GREGORY WAS CHARGED with resisting arrest and with disorderly conduct.[1] In the police report describing the incident, Officer Andrew Reid claimed that Gregory had been "clearly intoxicated" and that when Reid "kindly tried to assist Gregory into [his] cruiser for protective custody, [Gregory] pulled away and clawed at [Reid] with his hand." Without the advice of a lawyer, Gregory pled guilty to the misdemeanor charges against him and went home.

Typically, that would have ended the matter. Gregory, another poor defendant with a petty criminal record, would have been convicted of resisting arrest after pleading guilty, based solely on the officer's version of events. The case would never have been looked at again.

But Gregory got lucky. Two highly unusual events converged that helped exonerate him. First, a professor from the University of Arizona was conducting anthropological field work in the area and happened to see the entire incident. Outraged by what she saw unfold in front of her, she filed a complaint with the police, which prompted an internal investigation into the incident. Second, a store surveillance video captured the entire assault. It clearly showed Reid stopping Gregory for no apparent reason while Gregory was walking home from a store. Reid grabbed Gregory by his backpack and waistband, threw him about three feet into the air, and repeatedly slammed him to the ground before dousing him in pepper spray. Upon disclosure of the video and armed with the professor's complaint, Gregory, now aided by counsel, successfully moved to dismiss all the charges against him. Gregory had been convicted of a crime that never happened—resisting arrest—in order to cover up Reid's inexplicable wrongdoing.

ORGANIZATIONAL NORMS ENABLE POLICE MISCONDUCT

Organizational norms allow police misconduct to flourish. Officers see themselves as the "thin blue line" that separates societal order from disorder. Yet, they also perceive themselves as under attack on all fronts: unreasonable legal and constitutional restrictions on their behavior, the ungrateful public that they are tasked to protect, the biased and overly critical media that just don't get it, and the "criminals" themselves and other disrespectful citizens. The siege mentality fosters an us-versus-them perspective in which the police are pitted against virtually everyone else in a battle to keep the world safe.

Policing culture demands fierce loyalty among the police brotherhood.[2] One way loyalty manifests itself is in the "blue wall of silence," an unwritten code among police that bars officers from disclosing misconduct or untruths by fellow officers. The circling of the wagons among officers gives rise to a culture in which misconduct is difficult to identify and regulate. In 1992, after New York City police officer Michael Dowd and five other officers were arrested for drug trafficking and related gang activity, New York City mayor David Dinkins convened a commission to study police corruption and to make recommendations. The "City of New York Commission to Investigate Allegations of Police Corruption and the Anti-Corruption Procedures of the Police Department," informally known as the Mollen Commission (after its chair, Milton Mollen), carefully scrutinized the New York Police Department's (NYPD's) culture and practices.[3] In 1994, the Mollen Commission issued a scathing report, finding that the blue wall of silence enabled misconduct to flourish:

> because of a police culture that exalts loyalty over integrity; because of the silence of honest officers who fear the consequences of "ratting" on another cop no matter how grave the crime; because of willfully blind supervisors who fear the consequences of a corruption scandal more than corruption itself; because of the demise of the principle of accountability that makes all commanders responsible for fighting corruption in their commands; because of a hostility and alienation between the police and community ... which breeds an "Us versus Them" mentality; and because for years the New York City Police Department abandoned its responsibility to insure the integrity of its members.[4]

Although the Mollen Commission Report recommended a series of reform measures, the blue wall of silence remained very much intact. Officers who dared cross the "blue wall" risked retaliation in terms of job reassignments, loss of advancement opportunities, and sometimes, their lives.

In 1997, Abner Louima, a Haitian immigrant, was arrested outside a Brooklyn nightclub after a street brawl.[5] Police officer Justin Volpe arrested Louima for a number of misdemeanor offenses, including disorderly conduct and resisting arrest, that Volpe later admitted had no basis in fact.[6] What followed next was inexplicably violent and demeaning. Officers first beat Louima in the squad car on his way to the 70th Precinct station.[7] Then, in the precinct bathroom, Volpe used a broomstick to sodomize and brutalize Louima, causing severe colon and bladder injuries that required three surgeries to repair. Volpe also rammed the broomstick into Louima's mouth with such force that he broke a tooth. He bragged about the incident to other officers afterward. The attack was unprovoked, violent, and disgusting, and certainly fell well outside the realm of acceptable law enforcement behavior. Yet, of the roughly one hundred officers interviewed about the incident, only two dared to cooperate in the investigation. Those officers had to be placed in protective custody to shield them from violence and threats against their families for their perceived betrayal.[8]

Misconduct thrives within a culture that values police loyalty among officers above all else, including the law and the people they are tasked to serve. While it is true that most police officers do their jobs with honesty and integrity, within the policing world, there is an organizational impulse to protect those who do not. Misconduct flourishes when officers cross the line and abuse their authority, inventing crimes that never happened or engaging in criminal behavior, and police leadership and rank-and-file officers look the other way.[9]

The stories of particular incidents of police misconduct discussed in this chapter were selected not because they are egregious (though they are that) but to highlight the sweeping scope of misconduct that takes place every day in communities around the country. Whether in Alaska, Ohio, New York, or Maryland, examples of police misconduct that result in no-crime wrongful convictions can be found nearly everywhere.

Well, maybe not everywhere.

Most examples of police fabrication take place in poor communities and involve vulnerable and marginalized people, including racial and ethnic minorities and people with criminal records. In the latter case, corrupt police target and arrest the same old suspects, for the same old crimes, knowing that people with a criminal history are likely to be viewed with distrust and suspicion. Marginalized people make easy targets, and the police know it.

What motivates officers to fabricate crimes that did not happen? As explained below, the reasons are varied and overlapping. Officers may invent crimes in direct response to policing policies—such as operating under quotas—that implicitly encourage the abuse of authority to meet departmental arrest targets. Others invent crimes to cover up their own improper behavior, to obtain money or career advancement, or because they believe they are doing the right thing by getting the bad guys off the street, regardless of how it is done.

But the result is always the same. An innocent person is arrested, prosecuted, and convicted of a crime that did not occur, based solely on a police officer's word that it did.

Police Invent Crimes to Meet Departmental Quotas

Many police departments officially prohibit arrest quotas because they incentivize officers to manufacture crimes that do not exist or to stop and question people without legal cause. Although departments deny the existence of quotas, policing practices suggest otherwise.

Take the New York City police department.

Before 2010, the NYPD had no written policy prohibiting quotas in stop-and-frisks, arrests, and other enforcement activities. Officers in New York were often exhorted to go out and "get those numbers," typically by targeting poor minority communities.[10] One lieutenant, in comments laden with racial overtones, told his officer to make those arrests by "not working in Midtown Manhattan where people are walking around smiling and happy. You're working in Bed-Stuy [a largely poor community of color] where everyone's probably got a warrant."[11] The policy was to target poor communities of color, stop and arrest people first, and come up with a reason afterward—a clear inversion of constitutional law.

In 2010, the State of New York passed a law prohibiting quotas and any retaliation for officers who fail or refuse to meet quotas.[12] Yet, one year later, the NYPD implemented the "Quest for Excellence" evaluation program, which directed supervisors to set performance goals for proactive enforcement activities and suggested that officers "*whose numbers are too low* should be subjected to *increasingly serious discipline* if their low numbers persist."[13]

Sounds a lot like a quota system to me.

In 2012, Officer Craig Matthews challenged an arrest quota policy in his South Bronx precinct, claiming that the illegal policy was "causing unjustified stops, arrests, and summonses because police officers felt forced to abandon their discretion in order to meet their numbers."[14] When he complained, Matthews was retaliated against by "punitive assignments, denial of overtime and leave, separation from his career-long partner, humiliating treatment by supervisors, and negative performance evaluations."[15] Matthews sued the City of New York and was awarded a $280,000 settlement.[16]

In 2016, a group of twelve minority officers, called the NYPD 12, also sued the NYPD and the City of New York.[17] They too claimed that despite the 2010 statewide ban on quotas, the quota system persisted and unfairly targeted minority communities. The officers complained that they were forced to meet monthly quotas for arrests and summonses and that, when they objected, they were retaliated against with demotions, denial of overtime and vacation, and threats of firings.[18]

Although the NYPD 12 lawsuit is ongoing at the time of this writing, in 2017, New York City settled a different lawsuit for $75 *million* over allegations that it had issued hundreds of thousands of bogus misdemeanor summonses largely in minority communities to meet departmental quotas.[19] Sharif Stinson, an African American, was the lead plaintiff in this class action lawsuit. In 2010, when he was nineteen, Stinson was issued two summonses in the Bronx for trespass and for disorderly conduct. The trespass summons was based on his presence in his aunt's building, with her permission, and the disorderly conduct summons contained boilerplate alleging Stinson had used "obscene language and gestures, causing public alarm." Unlike many people charged with low-level misdemeanor trespass, however, Stinson did not plead guilty. Both of the charges were eventually dismissed as having no factual or legal basis. The class-action lawsuit explicitly alleged that police officers were told to issue summonses "regardless of whether any crime or violation" had occurred to meet minimum quota requirements. The city acknowledged that the policing policies disparately impacted people of color, particularly those who lived in poor communities, but denied the existence of quotas.[20]

Quotas—and the arrests of people for crimes that did not happen—have plagued police departments throughout the country. Los Angeles, in response to three separate lawsuits in 2011, 2013, and 2016, paid millions of dollars to settle lawsuits with officers who claimed they were illegally required to meet quotas.[21] In each lawsuit, the city insisted the numbers were not quotas but simply suggested targets.[22] In Dallas and Fort Worth, police departments were funded by a federal grant that required officers to make "four traffic contacts per hour."[23] In Atlanta, an officer complained that a written quota policy had been distributed throughout his department, while others alleged that officers who met their quotes were rewarded with tangible benefits.[24] In Miami Gardens, Florida, officers claimed they were told by superiors to "bring in the numbers" and were ordered to stop all black males between fifteen and thirty years old. One officer admitted to falsifying arrest reports to meet departmental quotas, even manufacturing criminal behavior for people who were "sitting in the county jail" when the alleged crime for which they were charged supposedly occurred.[25]

Quotas result in no-crime wrongful convictions because they motivate the police to arrest people for crimes that never happened and cause innocent people to plead guilty so they can go home. Despite denials from police departments, officers on the ground continue to claim that they are required to meet numerical arrest targets and that they are harassed and retaliated against by colleagues and police supervisors when they do not.[26]

Police Invent Crimes to Cover Up Their Own Police Brutality

The police are permitted to use force in making an arrest so long as that force is reasonable and proportionate to the threat they believe they are facing. Some officers, however, use force with impunity, even against citizens who did nothing wrong in the first place.

Take the crime of resisting arrest.

If an officer uses excessive force, they can justify their behavior by claiming the person was resisting arrest: "I had to strike him; he was resisting arrest." The amount of force used by an officer must be proportionate to the force allegedly presented to the officer by the suspect; a lethal threat posed by a suspect can be met with lethal force. In Baltimore, for example, corrupt police officers admitted to carrying BB guns in their cars to plant on unarmed suspects in the event of a police shooting so that they could later claim, if ever questioned, that they had been confronted with lethal force.[27]

Certain officers seem to bring resisting arrest charges far more often than others. In New York City, a 2014 study identified 51,502 cases involving charges of resisting arrest in the preceding five years. Of the officers who made arrests during that time, 5 percent were responsible for 40 percent of the resisting arrest cases; 15 percent of officers were responsible for nearly 75 percent of such cases.[28] Resisting arrest charges seem highly concentrated among a minority of officers. It may well be that these officers lie about resisting arrest to validate their own questionable activity. Or they may use overly aggressive tactics when confronting people in the first place, introducing volatility and an escalation toward violence in police-citizen encounters. In either scenario, bogus resisting arrest charges can be used to mask an officer's excessive or unwarranted use of force at the time of the arrest.

A few examples from around the country illustrate just how commonplace it is for the police to falsely claim a suspect was engaged in threatening behavior and resisting arrest in order to cover up the officer's own excessive use of force or wrongdoing. This happens in even relatively minor offenses, with great consequences for the innocent.

One evening in Ohio, Edward Williams and his wife were driving with their three children to obtain medical care for their asthmatic baby.[29] Williams, who is African American, was pulled over by Officer Donald Schismenos and his partner for having a burned-out license plate light and an expired temporary tag. According to Officer Schismenos's version of events, they ordered Williams out of the car and Williams, without provocation, got out and attacked the officers. Williams was arrested at the scene for assaulting the officers and resisting arrest. He refused to plead guilty, insisting he had done nothing wrong. He took the unusual step of contesting the charges. In the 1997 trial, officers testified under oath that Williams attacked them, while Williams swore that he never struck or assaulted the officers. At the trial's conclusion, the jury convicted Williams of resisting arrest and assault, and he was sentenced to probation and house arrest.

In the years after Williams's conviction, Schismenos continued to rack up citizen complaints of excessive force. After he was suspended for police brutality in 2004, it was discovered that Schismenos had been secretly recording his arrests and uploading the recordings onto the police department's computer database. Schismenos's arrest recordings took up nearly 30 percent of the department's computer capacity. Schismenos later admitted that that he started making the secret recordings after a supervisor had red flagged him for a high volume of citizen complaints about his improper use of force and racial profiling in traffic stops.[30] Amid those recordings was the Williams arrest tape. When the *Akron Beacon Journal* reported that the tape had been found, Williams filed a motion to review his case.

The video confirmed that Williams had not assaulted the officers. Instead, it shows the officers challenging Williams about whether his child was actually ill. They then ordered Williams out of the car and dragged him to the pavement, where they pepper-sprayed him and beat him with a baton. Schismenos can be heard boasting on the audio recording of the interaction: "You didn't know who you were messing with, did you?"[31] With the release of the video, in 2015, Williams's criminal conviction was vacated.[32] Williams, however, had been stigmatized for nearly two decades by a criminal record for an offense he did not commit. In accord with a settlement agreement with the city that resolved numerous allegations of brutality, Schismenos resigned from the force. He was never criminally charged with wrongdoing against Williams or any other civilian.

Like the Gregory case that begins this chapter, Williams's case was unusual, for three reasons. First, he fought the resisting arrest charges and demanded a jury trial. Even though he lost at trial, a record was made of the proceedings and of the sworn testimony of the officers, which made it easier to review the case in postconviction proceedings. Second, Schismenos made a real-time recording of the altercation, which helped establish Williams's innocence. Third, Williams persisted in his claims of innocence for years after his misdemeanor conviction was finalized, sought disclosure of the video in his case (once the recordings were found by happenstance), and then fought for his own exoneration. Most defendants, particularly in misdemeanor cases, lack the resolve or wherewithal to do as he did.

But Williams's case was typical in other respects. The officers lied in their charging documents, and they lied under oath at his trial. Police lying under oath is common enough in courtrooms around the country that it has its own name: "testilying" (an amalgamation of the words *testifying* and *lying*). They may lie in cases with a problematic search or arrest so that the case passes constitutional muster. They may lie to strengthen a weak evidentiary case. Or, as in the Williams case, they may lie to frame an innocent suspect. Although it was extraordinary that Williams took his misdemeanor case to trial, the trial and the outcome were not. The police officers testified and Williams testified, and the court credited the police version of events—even though it wasn't true. This happens all too frequently.

Raman Gill, a dear friend and outstanding criminal defense lawyer in Austin, Texas, told me a story that illustrates just how heavily the credibility scales are tipped toward officers and against defendants. When she was starting out as an assistant public defender in Dallas County in the late 1990s, she was assigned to represent a black man accused of resisting arrest after he was stopped by the police. Her client adamantly insisted he had offered no resistance. An impartial witness, someone who did not know Gill's client at all, happened to have seen the entire incident through the window of his home. This witness, also a black man, told Gill that it looked as though the officers (and there were multiple officers, all of whom were white) were using excessive force against her client. At trial, the officers claimed her client had resisted arrest. In contrast, the neutral witness told the all-white jury that he saw the police engaging in unprovoked police brutality. The jury nonetheless convicted her client of the resisting arrest charge, crediting the testimony of white police officers with incentives to cover up their own misconduct over the testimony of a neutral eyewitness who had no stake in the case at all. As relatively minor as the charges were, Gill says it was one of the most disheartening cases of her entire defense career.

I too saw firsthand the use of resisting arrest charges to cover up police brutality when I was a public defender in the South Bronx. When a client came through arraignment with a charge of resisting arrest, they would often have a black eye or a bruised cheek. When I asked what happened, the answer was often that they had been beaten by the police. When I asked why, my clients offered such explanations as the police said my client hadn't answered their questions fast enough, or my client had not been respectful enough. Sometimes they just shrugged their shoulders and said they had no explanation at all.

A final note is worth making here. As I explained earlier, the law allows police officers to use lethal force when they reasonably believe they are facing a lethal threat. Although not directly related to no-crime wrongful convictions,[33] in recent fatal police shootings of unarmed people, certain officers have offered inaccurate narratives claiming that the victims were armed or engaged in life-threating behavior (often disproved by civilian or surveillance video footage of the incident) in order to demonstrate that their lethal actions were reasonable under the law. After the fatal shooting of Stephon Clark in his grandmother's backyard by Sacramento police officers on March 18, 2018, both officers claimed that Clark was pointing a gun at them when they opened fire. In fact, Clark was unarmed; a cell phone was later found beneath his dead body. After a yearlong review, the prosecutor concluded that the officers had acted reasonably, and declined to pursue criminal charges.[34]

On rare occasions, however, officers have been held criminally responsible for their actions after they offered false explanations to justify their use of lethal force. Following the fatal police shooting in Chicago of seventeen-year-old Laquan McDonald, officers claimed McDonald had a knife and lunged at them; a police dash-cam video released months later showed McDonald walking away from the officers at the time of the shooting. Jason Van Dyke, the officer who fired the fatal shots, was convicted of second-degree murder and aggravated battery. The four officers who lied about what happened that night to cover up Van Dyke's wrongdoing were fired from the police force.[35]

Police Invent Crimes for Personal Financial Gain

Police officers are public servants, who earn relatively modest government salaries.[36] As some officers discover, there is good money to be made in inventing crimes that never happened, even if lives are destroyed in the process.

In Cook County, Illinois, Sergeant Ronald Watts and Officer Kallatt Mohammed routinely demanded payoffs from the largely African American residents of Chicago's now-shuttered Ida B. Wells public housing project.[37] People known to sell drugs in the buildings paid protection money to Watts and were thereby able to continue their work without interference. Innocent tenants also paid the bribes, a cruel additional financial burden for people without much cash to spare. Tenants who refused to pay the "protection tax" were abused and framed for fabricated drug charges. Leonard Gipson learned that lesson all too well.[38] Between 2003 and 2007, Sergeant Watts twice planted drugs on Gipson, who eventually pled guilty and served several years in prison. When he was later exonerated in 2017, Gipson explained that "if you weren't going to pay Watts, you were going to jail."[39]

Lionel White Sr. was another of Watts's victims. In April 2006, Watts and other officers banged on White's apartment door, demanding to see drugs and the money he had made from selling them. The officers ransacked his apartment but found nothing. They came back a few weeks later. One of the officers assaulted White and then arrested him for possession of heroin that White insisted had been planted by the officers. Yet, because White had prior felony convictions, he faced a potential sentence of life in prison without parole. When the prosecution offered him an on-the-spot, take-it-or-leave-it plea deal of five years' imprisonment, White took it. As he entered his guilty plea in June 2016, White told the judge under oath that Watts and the other officers were "in my house beating me . . . your Honor. This is wrong. I am pleading guilty because I'm scared. That's the honest to God truth, your honor."[40] The judge nonetheless accepted his plea. Shortly after his plea conviction, White filed a written complaint in which he claimed he had been framed by corrupt police. Within weeks of the filing, Watts arrested Lionel White Jr. for heroin possession. White Jr. also insisted the police had planted the drugs on him, in retaliation for his father's complaint, but agreed to plead guilty in exchange for a two-year probationary sentence. In 2016, both father and son were exonerated, having been found wrongly convicted of drug crimes that Watts and his cronies invented.

To date, at least sixty people have had their cases dismissed because of Watts-involved misconduct. One lawyer representing a group of recent exonerees estimates that more than five hundred Watts cases are questionable.[41] It is unlikely that all (or even most) of these convictions will ever be identified, or that the people convicted will ever be exonerated. These men and women will live their lives forever haunted by the brazen violence and criminality of the very people supposed to protect them.

Perhaps Watts felt emboldened to pursue his extortion scheme because many of the people who lived in the Ida B. Wells project already had criminal histories, some solely because of prior police overreach and misconduct in their community. People with criminal records are particularly vulnerable to arrest, making them easy prey for police looking to do wrong. Police misconduct that results in criminal arrests and convictions creates a circular loop in which poor people are targeted, arrested, and then plead guilty to get out (as discussed in more detail in chapter 8), which in turn makes them more vulnerable as targets for future arrests and prosecutions.

Against this backdrop, Watts likely assumed he could get away with extortion because the word of an officer would always be credited over a poor person of color with a criminal record. He was right. It was only when Watts was caught stealing money from a drug courier who turned out to be an FBI agent that Watts was prosecuted and convicted in *federal* court. He was sentenced to twenty-two months in federal prison based on the FBI sting operation.[42] To date, Watts has received no *state* criminal consequences for the long-term shakedown scheme that preyed upon the poor and vulnerable population of the Wells housing projects. He likely never will.

A separate Chicago unit, the Chicago Police Special Operations Section (SOS) was by itself responsible for a significant number of no crime convictions. The number of innocent people convicted of crimes invented by the SOS remains unknown. What is known is that the SOS made huge profits by robbing people during illegal searches and seizures and then fabricating the existence of crimes and criminals to cover up their actions.[43] The SOS targeted people suspected of drug dealing and having cash on hand, although its officers also targeted people who were entirely law abiding. In 2002, Gloria Salcedo, and her two daughters, Claudia (aged twenty-one) and Teresa (seventeen), were in their Southside Chicago apartment when members of the SOS entered their home looking for drugs.[44] Although no drugs were found, the three women were arrested for allegedly attacking the officers during the search. The women vehemently denied the charges and went to trial. In 2005, the women were convicted by a judge who credited the officers' testimony over their own, and were sentenced to probation. After the SOS's corruption was revealed in 2007, the Salcedos' convictions were vacated. They had been found guilty of crimes entirely fabricated by a gang of corrupt officers. Shortly afterward, in 2007, the Special Operations Section was disbanded.[45] Several officers were criminally charged in connection with their activities in the SOS, but the full scope of no-crime wrongful convictions and other damage caused by the SOS is unknown and perhaps unknowable.

Police fabrication of criminal behavior for personal financial gain extends well beyond Chicago. In 2013, narcotics officer Jeffrey Walker planted drugs in the car of a South Philadelphia man suspected of selling drugs and having a stash of drug money, and then broke into his home to steal $15,000.[46] This apparently was not unusual among the narcotics officers with whom Walker had worked. Acting as police, prosecutor, judge, and jury, the officers would decide that a person looked like a drug dealer who might have illegally obtained cash on hand. They would then steal money from them, along with any drugs found. They twisted justice even further by arresting their targets without probable cause on trumped-up charges to cover up their own wrongdoings.

Cops became robbers with badges.

Walker was eventually arrested for corruption and pled guilty. During sworn testimony against his fellow officers in a federal corruption trial, Walker admitted that he and his team had framed people and stolen over $1 million dollars from people they believed were selling drugs. In response, the Philadelphia district attorney's office dismissed cases against more than eight hundred suspects arrested by Walker and six other officers, and the city has paid over $2 million dollars to settle lawsuits.[47] Not all of these cases involved factually innocent people, but some did. The total number of people wrongly convicted in the Walker-involved cases based on police fabrications of crimes is unknown.

In Maryland, eight members of Baltimore's infamous Gun Trace Task Force made a small fortune from inventing crimes that never happened. Led by Sergeant Wayne Jenkins, the Gun Trace Task Force stole hundreds of thousands of dollars in cash and illegal drugs, and arranged for the drugs to be resold on the street.[48] They planted drugs and weapons on suspects. They lied in court papers and in courtrooms. They fabricated criminal charges against innocent people.

In 2010, for instance, members of the task force, dressed in black masks and street clothes and armed with weapons, ran up to an occupied car in which Umar Burley and his cousin were sitting.[49] Believing they were about to be robbed, Burley sped away and, in the process, crashed into another car and killed one of its occupants. The officers then planted a massive quantity of heroin in Burley's car. Burley was arrested for drugs and for manslaughter. Due to the seriousness of the charges, the judge refused to set bail for Burley, who sat in jail awaiting trial while insisting that the drugs were not his and that the police had planted them.

Burley faced a real dilemma. With the quantity of drugs the police claimed to have found in his car, and given his prior criminal record and the driving fatality, Burley knew that if he didn't plead guilty, he could be looking at upward of thirty years in prison if convicted after trial. Afraid that the jury would not believe him over the police, he pled guilty and was sentenced to fifteen years. While he was incarcerated, three grandchildren were born, his girlfriend died, and his father became ill. In 2017, it was uncovered that the officers in fact had planted the heroin in Burley's car and had staged the attempted gunpoint robbery. Burley's convictions were vacated and he was formally exonerated of any wrongdoing. Jenkins later admitted that he had planted the heroin in Burley's car to justify the fatal crash.[50]

Charged with making Baltimore safer, the members of the Gun Trace Task Force instead pillaged and plundered the city and its residents. The officers were charged with crimes that ranged from robbery to murder. They had planted drugs and weapons; stolen money, drugs, and jewelry; and beaten—and perhaps even murdered—innocent people. Sergeant Wayne Jenkins, the leader of the task force, pled guilty and was sentenced to twenty-five years to life in prison. But not before he and his team had fabricated crimes, brought about wrongful convictions, and ruined many lives in the process.

In what has come to be called the Rampart scandal, Los Angeles police officers affiliated with the Community Resources Against Street Hoodlums (CRASH) unit were arrested for rampant misconduct that resulted in the arrest and convictions of scores of innocent people.[51] According to Raphael Perez, a former CRASH officer who testified for the state as part of a cooperation agreement, the CRASH unit routinely engaged in a stunning range of illegal activity, including unauthorized killings, drug dealing, theft, and routine beatings of suspects. Perez also revealed the CRASH practice of planting evidence on suspects, lying in court, and knowingly obtaining coerced or fabricated statements. An investigation into the LAPD's Rampart Division CRASH unit resulted in the vacatur of more than 150 convictions, at least some of which involved people who were wrongly found guilty after being framed by the police for crimes that never happened.[52]

These no-crime wrongful convictions in Chicago, Philadelphia, Baltimore, and Los Angeles highlight the myriad ways that corrupt police seek personal gain by arresting people for crimes that never happened. But these examples, from four large cities where police departments erupted in scandal after widespread misconduct was uncovered, are only the tip of the iceberg. Because so many people wrongly arrested by corrupt police resolve their cases by plea bargain, most police misconduct is never exposed. How many innocent people throughout the country and throughout history have been convicted of crimes that never happened but were invented by financially motivated police corruption remains unknown.

Police Invent Crimes against Poor People of Color Because They Can

In an early-morning raid on July 23, 1999, Tom Coleman, a white undercover officer, arrested forty-six people in Tulia, Texas, for cocaine possession and sales.[53] The local police roused these men and women from their sleep and paraded them through the town in their pajamas. Local media were conveniently on hand to photograph the arrests, and promptly published the images for the local community to see.

Race played a major role in the case: forty of the forty-six arrested were African American, representing 10 percent of the adult black population in Tulia. Of the remaining six arrestees, three were Mexican and three were whites with close relationships to black individuals.[54] In describing the arrests, a headline in a local newspaper gleefully trumpeted, "Tulia's Streets Cleared of Garbage."[55]

Astonishingly, Coleman was the *sole* source of the evidence against the defendants. He worked alone, had no partner to corroborate his claims, used no surveillance equipment or wiretaps, kept incomplete and sketchy notes (sometimes written on his leg in ink that washed off in the shower), and had no supporting lab documentation to prove that the items he claimed to have seized had tested positive for cocaine. Yet Coleman was named "Texas Lawman of the Year" for his law enforcement efforts.[56]

The first Tulia defendants fought the charges and lost their cases after trial. In response, the defendants received draconian sentences, ranging from 20 to 361 years in prison.[57] In rapid succession, twenty-seven of the remaining Tulia defendants pled guilty to drug crimes that had never happened, terrified that they too would receive similar penalties if they contested the charges and went to trial.

Questions began to surface about Coleman's testimony. Tonya White was able to prove that she had been in another state conducting a bank transaction at the exact moment that Coleman claimed she sold him drugs. Billy Wafer produced timesheets proving he had been at work during the time Coleman claimed Wafer had sold him drugs. The Texas NAACP and other advocacy organizations began looking into the cases.

In September 2002, the Texas Court of Criminal Appeals ordered an evidentiary hearing. At the conclusion of the proceedings, Judge Ron Chapman described Coleman's testimony as "absolutely riddled with perjury" and added that Coleman was "the most devious, non-responsive law enforcement witness this court has witnessed in 25 years on the bench in Texas."[58] Chapman recommended that all the defendants convicted by Coleman's testimony receive a new trial. Shortly afterward, the charges were dismissed and then-governor Rick Perry pardoned thirty-five of the Tulia defendants. They had already collectively served more than seventy years in prison.

In 2005, Coleman was convicted of perjury. He was sentenced to probation.[59]

Tulia may be the best-known example of a drug sweep targeting a poor, black community for crimes that did not happen, but it is certainly not the only one. The South Central Texas Regional Narcotics Task Force engaged in racially motivated drug sweeps of African American communities in Hearne County. In one sweep on November 2, 2000, twenty-five men and two women were arrested for a drug-related conspiracy based on the word of an informant who was known to be mentally unstable. Among those arrested were Regina Kelly and Erma Faye Stewart.[60] Bail was set at $70,000, far too high for either woman to pay. Both were single mothers who waitressed to make ends meet. Neither had ever before been charged with a serious offense. Their assigned lawyers strongly encouraged the women to plead guilty.

But then the women's paths diverged. Three weeks after her arrest, Kelly's parents advocated to have her bail reduced to $10,000 and she posted bond to await her day in court. Stewart, however, remained in jail. Worried about her two small children, Stewart insisted she was innocent but decided to plead guilty in exchange for a sentence of ten years' probation. She was released immediately upon entering her guilty plea.

Stewart was one of seven defendants out of the twenty-seven people arrested who chose to plead guilty. Of the remaining defendants, some, like Kelly, were able to post bail; the others were held in pretrial detention at the local jail for *five months* while they waited for their cases to be called for trial.

Finally, in February 2001, after the first case was docketed, the prosecution admitted its case had crumbled. The charges against all of the defendants had been based on the word of an informant who had blatantly lied. There were no drugs and no drug conspiracy. The prosecution dismissed the charges against the arrestees who had not pled guilty.

The dismissals came too late for Stewart, whose short-term benefit of a prompt release after her guilty plea was eclipsed by the long-term consequences of being a convicted drug felon.[61] Because of her criminal record, Stewart was evicted from public housing and became homeless. Her children were placed in foster care. She is ineligible for food stamps. It is hard to find and maintain a job.

None of this should have happened. Stewart's entire life as she knew it came to an abrupt end because police wrongly presumed that all the members of the primarily black and poor community were criminals. She was caught up in a baseless drug sweep of her neighborhood on the word of an unreliable informant. Jailed pending trial because she was too poor to make bail, she spent a month with no clear end to her incarceration, worried sick about her children. Her assigned lawyer told her to plead guilty, and conveyed a plea offer that would allow her to return immediately to her children from a jail she should never have been put in. She took the plea and is now forever branded a felon, forever stigmatized, and forever burdened by the seemingly endless collateral consequences that flow from a criminal conviction.

I can't help but wonder what might have happened if the police had not been so ready to believe that the black residents of Hearne were all criminals. Stewart's life, for one, would surely be vastly different.

Police Invent Crimes in Pursuit of a Noble Cause

Misconduct that results in no-crime wrongful convictions can also result from a twisted perception of justice. Police believe that their "noble cause" is "a moral commitment to make the world a safer place."[62] It is only a small step down a slippery slope into "noble cause corruption."

Noble cause corruption is supported by a theory that justice should be meted out on the street and not in the courtroom. Some officers "see a cruel world in which good citizens are routinely victimized and a court system that is unresponsive, and believe they have few alternatives than to enact their own particular brand of extralegal justice."[63] Using this skewed moral compass, officers disregard constitutional mandates and legal standards because they believe they need to get the "bad guy" off the street—and keep him off the street—in any way they can. They believe it is appropriate to manufacture evidence against a suspect, because he or she is guilty anyway.[64] To meet the ends of justice, police may knowingly plant evidence or write a false report to "fluff up" a weak case against a suspect believed to be guilty.

Sometimes they are right about the guilt of an accused.

But, of course, sometimes they are wrong.

In the early 1990s, in the 39th District of Philadelphia, Betty "Mizzie" Patterson, a fifty-four-year-old grandmother and devout churchgoer, was convicted of selling crack cocaine from her home. Patterson spent over three years in a maximum security prison before it was proven that the drugs found in her bedroom had been planted by police officers. In later depositions, the officers explained that they had not intended to frame Patterson for selling drugs. Rather, they planted the drugs in her apartment to have an excuse to search her home for evidence against her three sons, who were suspects in a drug-related killing.[65] In the minds of the officers, the noble cause (searching for evidence against her sons) justified the means (planting evidence that resulted in Patterson's wrongful conviction and incarceration for a crime that never happened). Patterson, who went on to become a minister, was awarded $1 million from the city of Philadelphia. The officers were ultimately convicted of their own crimes, including robbery and corruption, and were sentenced to federal prison terms that ranged from ten months to thirteen years. More than one thousand cases were called into question, including the charges against Patterson's sons, as a result of the officers' misconduct.[66]

Officer Matthew Cornell worked at the Auburn Correctional Facility (ACF) in Auburn, New York, where he took the law into his own hands under the guise of a noble cause. In December 2016, a prosecutor revealed that Cornell had planted a weapon on an inmate who Cornell claimed was part of a prison gang so that the inmate would be transferred to a different prison.[67] This is a classic example of noble cause corruption, in which the ends (breaking up an alleged gang) justify the means (lying and planting evidence).

Cornell's admissions prompted an investigation into a series of cases in which the correctional officer had accused other incarcerated men of having weapons. Thomas Ozzborn, for example, was serving a five-year prison sentence for weapons and drug charges.[68] Several months before Ozzborn's scheduled release, Cornell claimed he found a metal shank in the prisoner's shoe. In January 2016, Ozzborn was arrested inside the prison for first-degree promoting prison contraband, a charge that carried a possible fifteen-year sentence. Ozzborn insisted he was innocent, but pled guilty because he feared that a jury would credit the word of an officer over that of a convicted felon. He was sentenced to an additional two to four years in prison, seven months of which were in solitary confinement. Cornell was the sole source of evidence against Ozzborn, whose conviction was ultimately vacated. The convictions of four other men, accused by Cornell under similar circumstances, were also vacated.[69]

Cornell was suspended from the ACF, but at the time of this writing no additional penalties have been imposed against him.

Police Cause False Confessions

Police interrogation techniques yield false confessions, which are a contributing factor in 5 percent of no-crime exonerations (see table 1, in the introduction). This differs from the previously discussed categories of police misconduct, but it too stems from an erroneous assumption by the police that an innocent person is in fact guilty. False confessions occur when the police, believing the suspect guilty, take extraordinarily coercive measures to induce the suspect to confess to their supposed wrongdoing. We have already seen multiple instances in this book when innocent people confessed to crimes that did not happen. Stephen and Jesse Boorn were subjected to questioning that caused them eventually to confess to the murder of their very much alive brother-in-law. Beverly Monroe, after months of questioning by the lead detective, was tricked into believing that maybe, just maybe, she had been with Burde at the time of his death. Medell Banks, an intellectually disabled man, admitted, after a relentless inquisition by investigating officers, to having killed a child who had never even been conceived.

Confession evidence is difficult for even an innocent defendant to overcome in a court of law. Studies on false confessions demonstrate that confession evidence has more of an impact on trial verdicts than other forms of evidence, and that jurors do not properly discount confessions, even when the suspect has retracted the confession or when the confession was made under police coercion.[70] As Saul Kassin, a leading scholar in the area of false confessions, explains: "False confession is not a phenomenon that is known to the average layperson as a matter of common sense."[71] This means that jurors are likely to wrongly credit confessions over virtually any other evidence—including DNA evidence pointing to the guilt of another person—in situations where the prosecution has offered a theory to explain away any contradictions between the two.[72]

False confessions often occur in cases involving serious crimes: arson murders, child sexual assault, and sexual assault. Police tend to lean harder on suspects in cases that they urgently want to solve and where they don't have a lot of other evidence. Nicole Harris, convicted of murdering her son, Jaquari, provides a classic example.[73]

In May 2005, Harris had recently graduated college with a psychology degree and had moved into an apartment on the Northwest Side of Chicago with her two young children, Jaquari, age four, and Diante, age five, and the boys' father. Jaquari was found dead in his bedroom with a bedsheet cord wrapped around his neck. Dianti said that Jaquari had been playing a game when he died. The police claimed to have received an anonymous tip that it was murder, and focused on Harris as the suspect.

Harris was arrested and the police refused to accept the grieving mother's protestations of innocence. Instead, they subjected Harris to at least four increasingly aggressive interrogations that culminated in a videotaped "confession." The first interrogation began around 9 PM on May 14, on the day of Jaquari's death. Questioned by two detectives, Harris vehemently denied any involvement and claimed that her son's death was an accident. The detectives left Harris alone in an interrogation room for hours. At 12:45 AM, two different detectives and one of the original interrogators began a second round of questioning. According to the interrogators, Harris then made a "spontaneous" confession that she had killed Jaquari by wrapping a telephone cord around his neck. Significantly, her statement was inconsistent with the actual facts of Jaquari's death, but perfectly matched the detective's mistaken theory that Harris strangled Jaquari with a phone cord found in Harris's apartment. An hour later, at approximately 1:45 AM, Harris recanted her "spontaneous" first statement and once again denied harming Jaquari. The interrogating detectives then suggested a polygraph examination, to which Harris readily consented. She was placed in a locked cell, with no bed on which to rest, for the remainder of the night.

Fifteen hours after her interrogation began, Harris took a polygraph examination. Harris says the examiner told her she had failed it, but in fact the examiner found the test results to be inconclusive. Harris was then questioned for a third time. This time, according to the officers, Harris confessed by admitting that she grabbed an elastic bed cord, put it once around Jaquari's neck, laid him on the top bunk, and left the room. This "confession," however, was inconsistent with the "crime scene" evidence. So, once again, the detectives began an interrogation in which they finally obtained a statement that aligned with the physical evidence. At approximately 1:06 AM on May 16, more than twenty-seven hours after being taken to the police station, Harris repeated on videotape the most recent version of her statement.

Harris's confession had the classic hallmarks of having been coerced.[74] The police interrogated Harris for twenty-seven hours, during which time the police deprived her of sleep, handcuffed her to a table in the interrogation room, threatened and called her a monster, lied to her about the outcome of the polygraph test, and denied her access to food, water, and the bathroom. That she finally confessed is perhaps less surprising than the fact that it took the twenty-three-year-old Harris, still in shock from the death of her child and in the absence of an attorney, more than twenty-seven hours to do so.[75]

In Harris's 2005 trial, the most powerful piece of evidence for the prosecution was the eighteen-minute videotaped confession. Of course, the jury did not see any of the previous twenty-six hours and forty-two minutes of relentless interrogation tactics. They saw only the finished, videotaped confession. In addition, the trial judge would not allow five-year old Dianti to testify for the defense, even though he had clearly told authorities on the day after Jaquari's death that he was in the room when he saw Jaquari wrap the elastic cord around his neck while playing a game. Dianti's testimony would have bolstered the medical examiner's initial findings that the death was a tragic accident. Instead, with the videotaped confession introduced as evidence and Dianti's testimony excluded from evidence, Harris was convicted of murder and sentenced to thirty years in prison.

Eight years later, a federal appellate court reversed Nicole Harris's conviction.[76] In its 2013 decision overturning the conviction, the U.S. Circuit Court of Appeals for the Seventh Circuit described Harris's highly problematic confession as "the most damning evidence" against her. The court also determined that excluding Dianti's testimony was a constitutional error that robbed Harris of "the most valuable piece of evidence" in her defense.[77] The prosecution declined to reprosecute the case and Harris was exonerated, having spent eight years in prison for a murder that never happened.

Corrupt police engage in flagrant misconduct by inventing crimes, arresting innocent people for them, and then doing whatever it takes to make the charges stick. They do this for a wide range of reasons: to meet quotas, to cover up their own wrongdoing, for personal greed, for career advancement, or because they believe the ends justify the means. Officers who do not engage in misconduct look the other way, ensuring that misconduct is permitted to flourish. Aggressive policing policies disparately target poor people and people of color.

Most no-crime wrongful convictions that result from police misconduct and aggressive policing policies may never be uncovered. Plea bargains insulate much of police misconduct. Yet, even when police behavior is challenged, courts and jurors almost always credit the word of an officer over the word of an average citizen, particularly if that citizen is poor, is a member of a racial or ethnic minority, or has a criminal record. When police manufacture crimes that never happened, innocent people find it nearly impossible to stop them.

Police officers are not the only government actors who contribute to no-crime wrongful convictions. The following chapter considers prosecutors who promise to "do justice" but who do the exact opposite and, in the process, cause innocent people to be convicted of crimes that the prosecution knew, or should have known, never happened.

FOUR

Prosecutors

WINNING, AT ALL COSTS

IN 1987, WILLIAM DOUGLAS CARTER was fifty-five years old, with a successful career and a promising future. He was president of his own engineering company, lived on an expansive farm in Loudon County, Virginia, and had finally seen the end of an acrimonious divorce from Carole Vandergrift Carter (Vandergrift).[1]

In the dark morning hours of July 31, 1987, Vandergrift was shot and wounded in her Virginia home by her own .38-caliber revolver. Later that day, Carter was arrested in Saratoga Springs, New York, for the shooting. He was indicted in Virginia on charges of malicious wounding and the use of a firearm during the commission of a felony.

The prosecutor in the case, William T. Burch, worked hard for Carter's conviction. During a four-day jury trial in March 1988, Burch put on a seemingly strong case. Vandergrift testified about the shooting and claimed that Carter had shot her in the head behind her right ear in the middle of the night. Burch also called a prosecution witness, Cathy Culver, to corroborate contested facts within the prosecution's case. For instance, one major issue at trial was that Carter had told police that Vandergrift shot herself with her own .38 revolver, a fact that the police claimed only the shooter would have known. Carter claimed that multiple people knew about the caliber of the gun and that they told him, but Culver testified that Vandergrift never said she was shot with her own .38 revolver.[2]

In his defense, Carter provided an alibi, explaining that he was in Saratoga, New York, on the night of the shooting and therefore could not have been the shooter. He also argued that Vandergrift was an emotionally unstable person who shot herself, either in a suicide attempt or in an attempt to frame Carter for the shooting because she wanted revenge for their breakup.

The jury convicted Carter and he was sentenced to fourteen years in prison. Four years into his prison term, on February 14, 1992, a court ordered Carter released due to prosecutorial misconduct: Burch had hidden important evidence from the defense and coached Culver to lie on the stand.[3]

It turns out that several months *before* the shooting, Vandergrift had interviewed former Loudoun County sheriff's investigator Douglas Poppa for a position as her bodyguard. Poppa now detailed a conversation that had taken place during the interview in which Vandergrift had rambled on about how much she hated her ex-husband: "I hate him so much . . . I would shoot myself even if I died if I could make it look like he did it so he would spend the rest of his life in jail, ruin the rest of his life."[4] Also during the interview, she showed Poppa her .38 revolver, the very gun Vandergrift later claimed Carter used in the shooting.

Poppa declined the bodyguard position. Several months later, after Poppa heard about the shooting on the evening news, he went to the head of the Criminal Investigation Division of the sheriff's office and told him what Vandergrift had said to him. Poppa was told to drop it: "The case is wrapped up and we got the guy in New York or Canada."[5]

Poppa nonetheless persisted. He went directly to Burch and told him about Vandergrift's statements. Burch, however, did not tell defense counsel about these statements, either before the trial or after Carter's conviction.

Time passed. Carter was still serving his time in prison while the case slowly wended its way through the normal appellate process. In fall 1991, Poppa happened to watch a movie in which a woman framed a police officer for murder. It reminded him of the Carter case, and he started to wonder why he had never been called to testify. Poppa contacted Carter's defense counsel and informed him about the statements and his efforts to share them with the police and prosecution. The defense filed a motion to vacate the conviction, and a new trial was ordered.

At the retrial, Poppa testified for the defense about his conversation with Vandergrift. Culver testified, as well, and admitted she had committed perjury during the first trial.[6] Culver also swore, in an affidavit and on the stand, that prosecutor Burch had coached her to lie during the first trial. In particular, Culver claimed she told Burch that Vandergrift had said she was shot with her own .38 and that Burch told Culver to deny that conversation on the stand. With the new testimony from Poppa and Culver, Carter was acquitted. He spent four years in prison and lost his company based on allegations of a crime that never happened.

The Virginia Bar Association investigated Burch and cleared him of any wrongdoing.[7]

Hiding evidence and presenting lies as truths under oath are among the two most egregious forms of prosecutorial misconduct that contribute to wrongful convictions in general, and to no-crime wrongful convictions in particular. Prosecutorial misconduct takes many forms, some more subtle and nuanced than what is described above. Whatever the form, prosecutors who fail to meet their duty to do justice cause innocent people to be convicted of crimes that never happened.

WHAT PROSECUTORS DO AND WHY
THEY ENGAGE IN MISCONDUCT

On the TV show *Law and Order,* the prosecutor starts each case with "The People v. [insert defendant's name here]." The People. Although most people think of the prosecution as standing up for victims of crimes, in truth, "the People" includes criminal defendants who are entitled to fair and just proceedings.[8] As the U.S. Supreme Court famously declared in *Berger v. United States* (1935), the prosecutor "is in a peculiar and very definite sense the servant of the law, the twofold aim of which is that guilt shall not escape nor innocence suffer."[9] They are "ministers of justice" who are required to be diligent in their pursuit of justice.[10] They can strike fair blows, but not foul ones, in a system that rests on the principal that it is "better that ten guilty persons escape than that one innocent suffer."[11]

Despite these lofty proclamations, prosecutorial misconduct is a frequent contributor to wrongful convictions. Prosecutors distort the criminal justice process by engaging in a host of unethical, questionable, and sometimes illegal behavior. In *Berger,* the Supreme Court reversed a defendant's conviction due to a laundry list of prosecutorial misconduct:

> misstating the facts in his cross-examination of witnesses; . . . putting into the mouths of such witnesses things which they had not said; . . . suggesting by his questions that statements had been made to him personally out of court, in respect of which no proof was offered; . . . pretending to understand that a witness had said something which he had not said and persistently cross-examining the witness upon that basis; . . . assuming prejudicial facts not in evidence; . . . bullying and arguing with witnesses; and, in general, . . . conducting himself in a thoroughly indecorous and improper manner.[12]

The *Berger* list, however, is only the tip of the misconduct iceberg. In case after case that resulted in a wrongful conviction, prosecutors knowingly relied on perjured testimony, presented faulty forensic science, falsified evidence, hid exculpatory evidence that they are constitutionally required to provide to the defense, tampered with evidence or court files, lied about deals offered to prosecution witnesses, threatened and coerced witnesses, exaggerated the strength of their case, and misstated the facts and law in arguments to the jury.[13]

What causes prosecutors to engage in misconduct in the first place? There is no single explanation. Rather, cognitive biases, electoral politics, the adversarial system itself, and a complete lack of internal oversight, combined with judicial rulings that render prosecutors immune from liability, create a system ripe for abuse.

Prosecutors are susceptible to the cognitive biases and institutional pressures discussed previously in the context of policing. They experience confirmation bias, in which they tend to favor evidence that confirms their theory of the case and disregard evidence that doesn't.[14] This selective information processing skews prosecutors toward evidence that is consistent with their theory of guilt, and causes them to minimize the importance of evidence that might challenge or contradict those beliefs. Combine that bias with belief perseverance, the tendency of people to adhere to beliefs even when new evidence entirely contradicts it, and we can begin to understand how cognitive biases cause prosecutors to zealously pursue cases that objectively do not withstand scrutiny.[15]

Of course, cognitive biases provide only one portal to understanding prosecutorial misconduct. Although prosecutors may be "ministers of justice," they are also competitors in an adversarial system where "wins" in the form of convictions are the metrics of success.[16] Prosecutor offices encourage this mindset. One office posts the "batting averages" of individual prosecutors.[17] In Colorado, prosecutors who obtained a 70 percent conviction rate (or higher) received a monetary bonus.[18] Peers boast to one another about their convictions and hold raucous celebrations when a jury renders a guilty verdict. I've always found something peculiar and inappropriate about this celebratory aspect of obtaining convictions: "We just sent someone to prison! Wha-hoo!" To me, a conviction of another human being, and their condemnation by the state to a term of prison or even death, is a somber and sobering moment, even when the defendant is factually guilty.

There are also institutional disincentives for putting merit over convictions. A prosecutor who expresses concern about the legitimacy of a case can find their careers in tatters. Christina Pumphrey had worked for nearly fifteen years as a state government attorney when, in early May 2018, she joined the 14th Judicial Circuit as a prosecutor in Florida.[19] Not long after, she heard rumors from public defenders that Jackson County deputy Zachary Wester could not be trusted. Intrigued, Pumphrey began carefully reviewing Wester's traffic stops and arrests. She pulled his body-camera videos and watched them. She read his reports. She compared the two and quickly realized something was not right—his reports did not match the video footage.

Pumphrey grew increasingly concerned about Wester's traffic stops. In one case captured on video, Wester claimed the female passenger was acting suspiciously, but the video showed her to be calm and cooperative. Wester could be seen "conducting" a drug field test in record time, after which he claimed that the woman possessed methamphetamine and arrested her in front of her children. In another case Pumphrey reviewed, Wester could be seen with what appeared to be drugs in his hand *before* he searched a car and claimed to find methamphetamines.

Pumphrey's decision to watch the body camera videos was atypical. Prosecutors had been routinely moving forward with cases without ever watching the accompanying videos. This may have reflected large caseloads or simple carelessness rather than maliciousness, but either way, prosecutors were making plea offers at arraignments, and defendants were accepting those offers, even though no one had actually evaluated the factual predicate on which the charges were based. No one, that is, until Pumphrey.

Pumphrey's investigation led to Wester's firing and the dismissal of nearly 120 cases involving Wester. It also, regrettably, led to her own resignation and the filing of a whistleblower suit in which she claimed supervisors had retaliated against her for "messing up investigations by dismissing cases." Pumphrey explained her resignation from a job she loved to a reporter from the *Tallahassee Democrat*: "I don't want to work in an environment that allows this to happen." She added, "I felt that instead of doing what I would call the right thing, there were steps to cover up the office's involvement. And not necessarily the office's malicious involvement, but the fact that the office hadn't been paying attention and let this happen."[20]

As Pumphrey learned, there can be a cost for doing the right thing.

Electoral politics also puts pressure on prosecutors to get convictions. District attorneys are elected in forty-five states.[21] District attorney elections are often pro forma; the racial justice organization Color of Change, which has taken up the call for reforming prosecutor elections, found that more than 70 percent of elected prosecutors in 2016 ran unopposed in a general election.[22] In a contested election, would-be district attorneys traditionally jockey to prove they are the candidate who is toughest on crime. Tough, of course, is defined by securing convictions and long sentences.

Mike Nifong, the interim chief district attorney in Durham, North Carolina, was up for election in 2006 when Chrystal Magnum, a black woman, claimed she had been raped by three white lacrosse players at a party hosted by the Duke University men's lacrosse team. Nifong immediately took to the media circuit, granting between fifty to seventy interviews in the first weeks after the allegations became public. In arguing that the rape was racially motivated, he publicly referred to the defendants as "hooligans."[23] Critics claimed Nifong pursued the charges so that he could curry favor with Durham's African American electorate. If that was indeed his plan, it worked. In 2006, Nifong was elected as Durham's new chief district attorney.

Nifong's newfound stardom was short-lived. In violation of his prosecutorial duty to do justice, Nifong had been playing fast and loose with the evidence in the case. He withheld exculpatory DNA results from the defense and lied to the trial court. Six months into the case, he claimed he still had not interviewed Magnum, who had changed her story multiple times to multiple people. As criticism of his handling of the case mounted, it was turned over to the state attorney general. By April 2007, the attorney general determined no rape had occurred and cleared the Duke lacrosse players of all charges. Nifong was eventually disbarred for his misconduct in the case and ordered to serve one day in jail for contempt of court.[24] And he lost his elected position as Durham district attorney.

Nifong's disbarment was highly unusual, and he is one of a select group of prosecutors to have *ever* served even one day in jail for his misconduct. A 2013 analysis conducted by the Center for Prosecutor Integrity found that less than 2 percent of prosecutors are ever sanctioned, in any form, for misconduct.[25] In its meta-analysis of nine studies that collectively examined prosecutorial misconduct at both the state and the national levels between 1963 and 2013, public sanctions were imposed in only 63 out of the 3,625 instances of misconduct identified. Many of these "sanctions" were minor, such as prosecutors being charged for the costs of the disciplinary hearings. The

Center for Prosecutor Integrity identified only fourteen instances where a prosecutor was suspended or disbarred from practice.[26] Nifong can now be added to the list.

Pervasive prosecutorial misconduct can be explained in part by a lack of accountability. In the first instance, prosecutorial misconduct rarely comes to light. It often happens behind closed doors and away from public scrutiny, in unethical initial charging decisions, in witness preparation, or in hiding exculpatory evidence. Plea convictions, which make up more than 95 percent of criminal case resolutions but are rarely challenged, further insulate prosecutors from review of their work.

Even when misconduct is revealed, however, the judiciary has crafted legal standards that make it hard to address. In other legal contexts, courts have devised "prophylactic rules" designed to deter misconduct, such as requiring the suppression of evidence in cases where the police violate search and seizure rules.[27] They have not done so in the context of prosecutorial misconduct. Although courts can (and sometimes do) reverse defendants' cases based on prosecutorial misconduct, courts do so only after they have applied a generous "harmless error" analysis. "Harmless error" allows courts to affirm defendants' convictions even when there was prosecutorial misconduct, so long as that misconduct did not impact the outcome of the case. Most instances of prosecutorial misconduct are found harmless. In 2003, the Center for Public Integrity analyzed 11,452 cases where charges of prosecutorial misconduct were raised by defendants on appeal. Appellate courts in more the 80 percent of the cases either ignored the misconduct claims outright or decided that misconduct had occurred but amounted to harmless error.[28]

Courts are clearly protective of prosecutors even when presented with compelling evidence of misconduct. In fact, they have granted absolute immunity to prosecutors for the wrongdoing they commit in their prosecutorial role.[29] The Supreme Court created the rule of absolute immunity out of concern that prosecutors would be deterred from zealously pursuing cases if they were always under threat of a civil lawsuit.[30] The result is that prosecutors cannot be held civilly liable for even egregious instances of misconduct, such as when they knowingly suborn perjury, tamper with witnesses, manufacture false evidence, or withhold evidence, resulting in the wrongful conviction of an innocent person.

Instead of civil lawsuits, the Supreme Court has suggested that prosecutorial misconduct can be addressed by state bar associations.[31] But the reliance on bar associations to sanction prosecutors has proven to be wishful thinking. In the first place, few prosecutors are ever referred to bar associations for review of unethical behavior. Perhaps this is because defense lawyers are often repeat players in the courtroom and do not want to risk retaliation by a prosecutor or one of their colleagues, and prosecutors are reluctant to report one of their own.

But even when referrals are made, bar associations rarely hold prosecutors accountable for their actions. A 2017 study in Massachusetts found that since 2010, only two prosecutors had been publicly disciplined by the Massachusetts state bar, while nine others were disciplined without the release of their names. Many of the Massachusetts prosecutors found by an appellate court to have engaged in misconduct suffered no ill consequences at all: "Three went on to become judges, one became Massachusetts attorney general, and others rose to top positions in district attorneys' offices and state legal-ethics bodies."[32] Two Massachusetts assistant attorneys generals, Anne Kaczemarek and Kris Foster, were found to have committed "fraud on the court" in failing to disclose evidence relating to a former state lab analyst who was addicted to drugs and lied about her lab results, resulting in the dismissal of more than eight thousand convictions.[33] Although the lab analyst served a few months in prison, the prosecutors were not charged with any crime. The two prosecutors and their supervisor, John Foster, who have since been employed at other government offices, have been recommended for possible discipline from the Massachusetts Bar Association.[34] Perhaps they will be among the rare group of prosecutors to receive sanctions for their fraudulent conduct.

THE INITIAL CHARGING DECISION

Prosecutorial misconduct can occur at the initial charging decision. Prosecutors may fail to check the factual basis for an arrest. They may also overcharge defendants to induce pleas, insulating evidentiary problems from judicial review and public scrutiny.

Rubber-Stamping Police Arrests

After the police make an arrest, they write an arrest report, a brief document written from the arresting officer's perspective of the events leading up to and during the arrest. The arrest report typically includes the arrest charges; details relating to the date, time, and location of the alleged offense; and additional information such as the names of potential witnesses, witness statements, and witness contact information.

Prosecutors are supposed to base their initial charging decisions on the arrest report, in-person meetings with the arresting officer, and any follow-up investigation. The intake prosecutor and the arresting officer quickly review the facts supporting the arrest. At that time, the prosecutor decides whether to pursue the case, what charges should be brought, and whether the case should be prosecuted as a felony or a misdemeanor. The prosecution may decide not to prosecute at all. If the police have determined that a crime was committed when in fact no crime occurred, the prosecution has a chance to catch that error before formal charges are filed. If the prosecutor looks with care and identifies inconsistencies or significant weaknesses in the police theory of the case, they can decline to prosecute and an innocent defendant in a no-crime conviction case can be spared the agony of being tried for and convicted of a crime that never happened.

It often doesn't work that way.

We will see in chapter 7 that thousands of people in New York were arrested and prosecuted for trespass. Many of these defendants were lawfully on the premises at the time of arrest (either because they lived there or because they were visiting someone who lived there) and were taken into custody as part of a policing initiative, when in fact they committed no crime at all. The prosecutors could have declined to pursue the many problematic trespass cases. They did so on occasion, but rarely. Far too many cases were permitted to proceed, based on pro forma language that appeared in the arrest reports and was repeated verbatim again and again in the prosecution's initial charging documents. The identical language of each charging document should have been a red flag that the crimes did not happen as reported. But it wasn't. For every case dismissed, there were thousands more permitted to proceed. In most of these cases, the prosecution served as a rubber stamp—rather than a check—on the police's authority to arrest.

It bears emphasizing that whatever charges the prosecution decide to bring, they have nearly unfettered discretion in making their decision as long as they have some seeming basis in the evidence as it appears at the time.[35] Prosecutors' charging decisions are not typically subject to direct judicial review. And what they charge a criminal defendant with—the charge's severity and the scope—has repercussions through the entirety of the case, from whether and how much bail will be set, to the plea offer and ultimate sentence.

Overcharging to Induce Pleas

One factor that influences initial charging decisions is the plea negotiation process itself. The more (and more serious) charges filed by the prosecution, the more bargaining leverage the prosecution has in subsequent plea negotiations. Why not pile on the charges first, and negotiate down later?

But here's the thing of it. At the earliest stages, only the prosecutor knows whether the evidence in their possession provides a factual basis for the charges they have brought and whether it will stand up to legal scrutiny. Importantly, in many jurisdictions, prosecutors do not have to turn over discovery materials before making an early plea offer, but they can make those offers contingent upon immediate acceptance by defendants. Defendants are required to make life-altering decisions in an evidentiary vacuum, without knowing the strength of the case against them. The process is opaque for defendants, with an informational imbalance that tips heavily toward the prosecution.

At one time, courts viewed pleas that were induced by the threat of severe sentences or by promises of leniency as constitutionally problematic. In 1968, the U.S. Supreme Court struck down a federal kidnapping statute as unconstitutional because it permitted a sentence of death only in cases where the defendant was convicted by a jury.[36] The court worried the statute would cause defendants to give up their right to trial and plead guilty solely to avoid a death sentence if convicted: "[T]he evil in the federal statute is not that it necessarily *coerces* guilty pleas and jury waivers but simply that it needlessly *encourages* them."[37]

Within a few short years, however, the membership of the Supreme Court changed and its concerns about prosecutorial plea practices seemingly evaporated. No longer troubled by laws and practices that encouraged pleas, the Court in *Bordenkircher v. Hayes* (1978) endorsed the prosecution's use of threats to seek more severe sentences after a jury trial, finding it to be the inevitable cost of doing business within a system that permits the use of negotiated pleas. The facts of the *Bordenkircher* case are worth reviewing, even though they do not involve a no-crime wrongful conviction. Paul Lewis Hayes had two prior felony convictions when he was arrested for one felony charge of uttering a forged check in the amount of $88.30.[38] The prosecution made Hayes a five-year plea offer, but also threatened to reindict him under Kentucky's Habitual Offender Crime Act, which carried a life sentence, if Hayes refused the plea. Hayes rejected the plea offer, and the prosecution made good on its threat, indicting Hayes as a habitual offender. Hayes went to trial, was convicted, and received a life sentence. The Supreme Court upheld Hayes's conviction and sentence, finding the prosecutor's threat of a more severe sentence—from only five years to a life sentence for refusing to enter a plea—was not unduly coercive and was well within the prosecutor's legitimate discretion.[39]

Medell Banks, whose case is discussed in chapter 1, was charged with killing a baby who had never even been conceived.[40] Banks was initially charged with capital murder. To avoid the death penalty, he pled guilty to manslaughter, all the while protesting his innocence. John Peel pled guilty to manslaughter for shaking his infant daughter to death to avoid a threatened life sentence.[41] Both men were later exonerated; neither alleged murder had happened.

Too many innocent defendants plead guilty simply to avoid the risks that come from more serious charges and their correspondingly serious punishments.

Prosecutors Offer Pleas in Cases They Can't Prove

Once the prosecution brings charges against a defendant and makes a plea offer, the defendant is then left to contemplate his options: plead or go to trial. It is a painful dance in which defendants have imperfect information. They are left to guess the strength of the prosecution's case, what the risks of trial are, what the potential penalties are after trial, and whether the plea offer is the best or most rational route to take in the case. As they make that evaluation, the prosecutor may add pressure by threatening to withdraw the plea offer if the defendant does not act quickly enough, or by threatening to add charges to the indictment or by promising to seek a maximum penalty if the defendant proceeds to trial.

Take the wrongful conviction of Devron Hodges after a plea of guilty to a robbery that the prosecution *knew* never happened.[42]

On May 10, 2012, Hodges was accused by Jonathan Conrad of robbery in Shiner, Texas. Conrad claimed that Hodges forced Conrad to turn over his credit card so that he could purchase cigarettes. The next day, Hodges was arrested for aggravated robbery and aggravated kidnapping. Hodges had a prior conviction for an unrelated robbery. With the advice of counsel (who was later disbarred himself after pleading guilty to an unrelated crime), Hodges pled guilty on January 10, 2013, to a reduced charge of robbery without a weapon, and was sentenced to ten years in prison.

By a fluke, a different prosecutor overheard something about a recorded statement in Hodges's case while prosecuting a different case in a different courtroom. With her assistance, a previously undisclosed, exculpatory version of events came to light. Six days *before* Hodges pled guilty, Conrad had recanted his accusation in a recorded statement taken by a state investigator and Assistant District Attorney (ADA) Michael Mark, the prosecutor assigned to Hodges's case. In that statement, Conrad freely admitted that he had falsely accused Hodges of a robbery that never happened in response to a dispute involving a small amount of marijuana.

Mark knew no crime had happened, and he also knew that without Conrad, he would never be able to meet his burden of proof. Yet, despite the existence in ADA Mark's file of two copies of Conrad's recantation, Mark did not turn over the statements to the defense or share them with the court. Instead, he sat silently while Hodges pled guilty and was sentenced to *ten years* in prison for a crime that the alleged victim admitted never happened.

Eventually, the recordings were uncovered, but it took two years and a new lawyer before Hodges was released from prison and exonerated. Mark could have prevented this entire injustice, but instead he knowingly allowed an innocent man to be convicted. Mark was later fired from the prosecutor's office for his misconduct. But he was not disbarred or disciplined. Instead, he went on to work as a defense lawyer and was eventually hired as an attorney for the Texas Department of Criminal Justice, which oversees Texas state prisons and jails.

Prosecutors' Plea Offers Hide Police Misconduct

When a defendant pleads guilty, no record is developed for the case. This means that potential issues, including official misconduct, are never explored. Guilty pleas often foreclose judicial and public scrutiny about important matters. No court ever decides whether the police properly searched a defendant or a location, whether probable cause existed, whether a confession was improperly coerced, whether eyewitness identifications were impermissibly prompted, whether the prosecution withheld material evidence it should have turned over to the defense, or whether there was an actual, factual basis that a crime occurred in the first instance. When the prosecution offers an extremely favorable plea to induce an innocent defendant to admit guilt, it insulates the case from judicial review and ensures that problematic practices are never brought to light.

Clinton Harris, for instance, pled guilty to being a convicted felon in possession of a firearm. The police claimed that they saw Harris wearing a gun in his waistband and that Harris admitted the gun was his. It was later revealed that Harris had been in a friend's apartment when the police burst in without permission and found a gun on the table. The police decided to pin the gun on Harris "because he was an ex-con."[43] Harris's innocence in this no-crime wrongful conviction case came to light as part of Officer Raphael Perez's sweeping testimony about misconduct in the Los Angeles Rampart policing scandal (discussed in chapter 3). But because Harris pled guilty, no court ever had the chance to evaluate the legality of the police entrance into the apartment or the validity of Harris's alleged confession.

What further compounds these problems is that prosecutors often require defendants to waive a panoply of rights as part of the plea agreement, including the right to appeal their conviction or specific legal rulings relating to official conduct. But appellate courts don't just correct errors; they also make new law. When prosecutors force defendants to waive their rights to appeal as a condition of a plea agreement, they strip appellate courts of not only their error-correction function but also their ability to create new legal precedent. Appeal waivers (and the waiver of various challenges) deprive appellate courts of the opportunity to craft legal decisions about the constitutionality or legality of procedural and substantive issues in any given case. The effect is to stunt legal jurisprudence and to bury in the shadows questionable police and prosecutorial conduct.

As has been shown time and again, our plea system does not just help the guilty resolve their cases with better sentencing outcomes. It also causes the innocent to plead guilty to crimes they did not commit. Scholars estimate that anywhere from 1.6 percent to 27 percent of people who plead guilty are actually innocent as a matter of fact.[44] The reasons for this are varied. At the low end of the crime spectrum, pleas are often the quickest way to go home and to avoid the hassle and associated expense of repeated trips to court. In the context of more serious cases, pleas enable defendants to avoid the risk of more severe sentences in the event of a conviction after trial.

PROSECUTOR MISCONDUCT AT TRIAL

Taking Advantage of One's Own Misconduct

In the infrequent event that a case goes to trial, prosecutors start with a stacked deck. They typically have more resources than defense attorneys, along with better access to police investigators, witnesses, and experts. Some prosecutors stack the deck even more by abusing their authority to manipulate prosecution outcomes.

Consider the case of Jerry Golding.

In June 1996, Golding was living with Jeri Baker, his then-fiancée, in Goochland, Virginia. On June 17, Baker called 911, threatening suicide. Golding spoke with the 911 dispatcher and assured her that there were no weapons in their home with which Baker might hurt herself or others. When a county sheriff arrived, Golding repeated his statement that there were no weapons in the house.

After Baker ran upstairs, Golding remembered that Baker had brought a gun into his home when they moved in together. Golding promptly warned the sheriff about the gun under Baker's side of the bed. The sheriff found the gun, calmed Baker down, and left the home, returning later that day with a warrant to search the home. The sheriff retrieved the gun, a box of .22 ammunition, and a small amount of marijuana. Because Golding had a prior felony conviction, he was prohibited from owning a gun. He was adamant that he did not own any weapons and that the gun belonged to Baker alone.

Although Baker also consistently claimed the gun was hers, Golding was charged in federal court with the illegal possession of a firearm, ammunition, and marijuana. Before the trial began, Golding and Baker married. Baker, now Jeri Golding, planned to testify at trial that the gun was hers. Shortly before trial, however, the prosecutor spoke with Golding's attorney. Mrs. Golding was advised to retain her own counsel, and ultimately did not testify. Golding was convicted.

Mrs. Golding claimed that the prosecutor threatened her with prosecution if she testified against her husband. The prosecutor, in a written proffer to the court, claimed she had simply expressed surprise that Mrs. Golding might testify, because she "potentially is going to be admitting to a crime."[45] The district court accepted the prosecution's proffer and did not conduct a hearing.

The issue went to the circuit court on appeal. In a surprise development, in oral argument, the prosecutor admitted to the court that she had in fact threatened to prosecute Mrs. Golding if she were to testify. The court found this to be highly improper; prosecutors are not allowed to threaten witnesses to keep them from testifying for the defense.

The court was also deeply troubled by the prosecutor's conduct at trial. As the prosecution fully knew, Mrs. Golding wanted to testify but had been deterred from taking the stand by the prosecutor's threat against her. The prosecution also knew that Mrs. Golding, had she testified, would have provided critical testimony that the gun was entirely hers. Indeed, Mr. Golding's entire defense was that the gun was not his but rather was owned by Mrs. Golding.

In its closing argument during the trial, the prosecution seized on the absence it had created, claiming that Mrs. Golding's failure to testify was proof that Mr. Golding was lying. Here are the excerpts from the trial as described by the circuit court:[46]

> If his story were true, wouldn't the best evidence that this stuff belonged to this lady be for her to come in and tell you all that it was.

The district court overruled Golding's objection to this line of argument. Bolstered by that ruling, the prosecutor became even more expansive:

> She didn't ever come up here and testify, and we don't know why.
>
> What wife in the world wouldn't just come right on in and tell you the truth, if that was the truth, to prevent her husband from going to prison? You can infer from the fact that she didn't come in, why not? Why wouldn't she come in if it were the truth? It would be that simple. You can infer that it is not the truth.
>
> And if his story were true, I think that any wife in the world would come in and tell the truth.
>
> If that is true, there is nothing wrong with her possessing a weapon and ammunition, and she is the one who possessed them, why didn't she just walk right up here and tell you?

The circuit court reversed Golding's conviction due to prosecutorial misconduct. It ruled that it was entirely improper for the prosecutor to threaten a defense witness to keep her from testifying, and even more improper to benefit from that threat by arguing that her absence meant something that it didn't.[47]

Prosecutors also behave improperly when they encourage or induce a witness to lie or exaggerate under oath in court. For instance, the prosecution often relies on police witnesses to prove its case. Police have been known to commit perjury in court.[48] But police lying on the stand is only half the story; their lies gain credence because the prosecution presents them as truth.[49] Prosecutors also deliberately elicit expert testimony that is wildly exaggerated or unsupported, and they present unreliable and highly suspect informant testimony.[50]

Prosecutors have an ethical obligation as officers of the court not to suborn perjury.[51] When prosecutors present lies as truths, no-crime wrongful convictions often occur.

HIDING EVIDENCE THAT PROSECUTORS ARE CONSTITUTIONALLY REQUIRED TO TURN OVER TO THE DEFENSE

In *Brady v. Maryland* (1963), the U.S. Supreme Court ruled that prosecutors before trial *must* disclose evidence that is favorable to the defense.[52] Favorable evidence falls into two main categories. The first is evidence that tends to establish a defendant's innocence, such as recantations by the victim, forensic lab reports that test negative for illegal drugs, or recordings that show the police planting evidence. The second is impeachment evidence, or evidence that contradicts or raises questions about the accuracy and reliability of the prosecution's evidence. Examples include evidence relating to the credibility of a witness, prior inconsistent statements, or a witness's motive to lie.

Prosecutors ignore the *Brady* rule far too often. As former Ninth Circuit judge Alex Kozinski bitterly complained: "[T]here is an epidemic of *Brady* violations in the land."[53]

The *Brady* rule causes so many problems, in part because the prosecutors themselves decide what material is favorable to the defense and what they need to turn over. Sit with that for a minute. We have an adversarial system that pits the prosecutor against the defendant in a courtroom battle where justice is the theoretical objective but where the measure of a prosecutor's success is their number of convictions. Then we tell the prosecutor that they have to turn over to the other side all the evidence that hurts their case.

That's like asking the wolf to guard the chickens in the coop.

Take Clinton Turner, an African American man who was wrongly convicted of a robbery that never happened, and was sentenced to ten to twenty years in prison.[54] In 1987, William Clarke, a white man, claimed Turner robbed him at 5 AM outside a topless bar—an accusation that Turner denied. Turner claimed that Clarke was lying in retaliation for a bad drug deal. As the case drew closer to trial, the defense counsel asked for the criminal records of any witness the prosecution planned to call. This is classic *Brady* material in that a witness's criminal record raises questions about their credibility. The prosecution ignored the request.

At Turner's trial in 1988, Clarke testified that Turner robbed him. Before trial, Clarke had told two different versions of events to two different officers; at trial on the stand, he offered a third one. The prosecutor asked Clarke, under oath, whether he had a criminal record, whether he used alcohol or drugs, and whether he had known Turner prior to the alleged robbery. Clarke denied it all.[55]

Taking the stand in his own defense, Turner testified that he had not robbed Clarke. He explained that he knew Clarke from the neighborhood and that he sometimes sold him drugs. During Turner's cross-examination, the prosecutor interrogated Turner in detail about his criminal record. Then, in his closing argument, the prosecutor encouraged the jury to believe Clarke, in part because he allegedly did not have a criminal record, and to disbelieve Turner, who did.

The jury convicted Turner and a judge sentenced him to ten to twenty years in prison.

Not long after Turner was convicted, Clarke ran into Turner's wife. Clarke admitted to her that Turner's version of the story was correct, that Clarke had been using drugs at the time, that Clarke himself had a lengthy criminal record, and that he had testified and lied under oath only because the prosecution made him.[56] In 1993, Turner filed his first postconviction appeal and presented the new evidence. It took numerous court proceedings, but eventually a federal court reversed Turner's conviction based on the prosecution's failure to turn over *Brady* material and for its use of perjured testimony. As the court noted:

> The ADA's [assistant district attorney's] knowledge that the defense was [that] the alleged victim had made up the robbery in retaliation for a bad drug deal, all pointed to the need to check Mr. Clarke's record before offering him as a witness, and indeed offering him as a witness *without a record*. Other than the police officers, who testified only as to what Mr. Clarke told them, Mr. Clarke was the only witness to the alleged crime.... [The ADA never] sought the requested impeachment evidence from any police officer or investigator, or ran a routine check for the presence of a criminal record.[57]

In other words, the prosecution, with a simple click of a computer mouse, could have obtained Clarke's criminal record and turned it over to the defense. Instead, the prosecution engaged in strategic and willful ignorance, even though it knew that Clarke's credibility was central to proving that a crime had taken place and that Turner was the culprit. To make matters worse, the prosecution went on to bolster Clarke's trial testimony with the argument that Clarke had no criminal record, when in fact he did, and then compounded this error by urging the jury to credit his testimony *because* of Clarke's allegedly unblemished past.

Turner was incarcerated in 1987, was released on parole after ten years in prison in 1997, and was finally exonerated in 2005. The prosecution fought tooth and nail to preserve Turner's conviction every step of the way, costing Turner years of his life for a crime that never happened.

Brady violations happen all too frequently. Cameron Todd Willingham, discussed in chapter 1, was executed in 2004 for the arson murder of his children. Not only did the prosecution rely on shoddy and outdated forensic evidence, but it also failed to tell the defense that its star witness was a jail-house snitch who had received a sweetheart deal in exchange for his testimony: classic *Brady* material that should have been, but was not, turned over to the defense in a case where the defendant's life hung in the balance.

Wolves and chickens.

But believe it or not, courts do not simply consider whether the prosecution failed to turn over favorable evidence. Rather, courts ask whether the evidence was material and whether the failure to disclose it would have impacted the outcome of the case. As Judge Kozinski lamented, "The materiality bar [is] impossibly high . . . invit[ing] prosecutors to avert their gaze from exculpatory evidence, secure in the belief that, if it turns up after the defendant has been convicted, judges will dismiss the *Brady* violation as immaterial."[58]

No wonder there is an "epidemic" of *Brady* violations. Prosecutors have little to fear when hiding exculpatory evidence. Courts rarely reverse convictions for *Brady* violations. And prosecutors themselves are almost never held accountable for their wrongdoing.

To make matters worse, defendants have difficultly bringing *Brady* challenges because *Brady* violations are hard to discover. Most never come to light. Finding out that the prosecution possessed exculpatory evidence but did not turn it over is often a matter of pure luck or happenstance. How can a defendant learn that the prosecution hid evidence the defendant never knew about in the first place? They often can't.

Further complicating the *Brady* analysis are guilty pleas, which make it even more difficult to detect that *Brady* material was not turned over. When defendants plead guilty, the case is typically closed. If favorable evidence existed that was not turned over to the defense before the plea was entered, the defendant likely never finds out about it. Instead, the *Brady* material remains tucked away in a prosecution file while defendants serve their sentences, woefully unaware of evidence that could have established their innocence.

PROSECUTORS MAKE IMPROPER ARGUMENTS

We have already seen prosecutors who induce false testimony and then rely on it in their closing argument (Carter and Turner); and prosecutors who threaten a witness to keep them from testifying and then argue an improper conclusion from that witness's absence (Golding). But prosecutors also have been known to step way out of line in their closing arguments. The closing argument is an opportunity for each side to urge the jury to rule in its favor based on the evidence offered at trial. It can be passionate and persuasive, but neither party is permitted to inflame the emotions of the jury by making inappropriate arguments. Prosecutors, for instance, may not appeal to a jury's biases and prejudices, because it could taint the jury's fact-finding process.

In 2000, Leigh Stubbs and Tammy Vance were wrongly convicted of aggravated assault involving a third woman, Kim Williams, in a case explored in more detail in chapter 6. At trial in Lincoln County, Mississippi, the prosecutor made arguments designed to inflame the passions of the jury and prejudice them against the defendants, without any factual or evidentiary basis for doing so. Specifically, the prosecutor suggested without evidence that Stubbs and Vance were a lesbian couple, an argument likely designed to provoke the prejudices of the Mississippi jury. Mississippi's socially conservative state legislature had banned gay marriage just four years earlier, in 1996,[59] and retained criminalization of same-sex sexual activity (until those laws were struck down in 2003 by the U.S. Supreme Court).[60] The state had also amended its constitution to define marriage as the union between a man and a woman (also struck down by the U.S. Supreme Court).[61]

The prosecutor's argument went something like this. First, a forensic odontologist who had been discredited in multiple jurisdictions testified that the so-called victim had bite marks on her body. The prosecutor then asked the odontologist whether it would be especially likely to find bite marks in an assault perpetrated by a gay person. The expert replied that "it wouldn't be unusual." When the prosecutor pressed this issue, the expert claimed that bite marks would "almost" be expected in cases involving people who are gay.[62] He provided no scientific or evidentiary basis for this conclusion.

Later in the trial, the prosecution again pursued this inflammatory line of questioning. The prosecutor asked a different witness whether he would expect, in a lesbian rape situation (which was not alleged here), to find biting. The witness answered affirmatively, adding that "homosexual crimes are very sadistic. They do what we call overkill . . . they're more gory, the more repulsive crimes I've ever seen were homosexual to homosexual." The prosecution in closing argument told the jury: "[W]hen you look at all the evidence, you'll realize that while it's a circumstantial evidence case, these two women who were living together were lovers—whether because of the drugs or the alcohol or their lifestyle—viciously attacked Williams and tried to cover it up."[63]

In short order, Stubbs and Vance were convicted, and each was sentenced to forty-four years in prison. Their convictions were ultimately reversed after it was revealed the prosecution failed to turn over exculpatory evidence in violation of its *Brady* obligations. Although defense lawyers raised the prosecutor's improper arguments on appeal, the appellate court in its written opinion ignored the prosecutor's highly improper line of questioning and arguments in summation.

PROSECUTION COMPLEX

Finally, prosecutors sometimes dig in their heels to maintain a defendant's conviction, even when presented with compelling evidence that the defendant is innocent and that no crime happened in the first place. Mark Godsey, in his book *Blind Injustice,* talks about the "fervent denial" of logical, smart, hardworking prosecutors who admit in theory that innocent people are sometimes convicted, while vehemently denying that an innocent person was ever convicted on their watch. They will invent alternate theories to explain away inconsistent evidence. Recall Gerald and Dewey Davis from chapter 1, who were wrongly convicted of raping a family friend in a crime that never happened. When postconviction DNA testing exonerated them, the prosecutor retried Gerald Davis under a newly concocted theory that he had raped her but had not ejaculated.[64] The prosecution's attempt to offer new and implausible theories for exculpatory DNA evidence is so common that it has its own name: "the unindicted coejaculator."[65] Legal scholar Daniel Medwed suggests that prosecutors' deep-seated denial is a coping mechanism to "avoid facing the unfaceable": that they could ever be responsible for the conviction of an innocent person.[66] But these "innocence deniers" cause tremendous harm to the wrongly convicted. Innocent people remain in prison, sometimes for years, while prosecutors fiercely and reflexively fight to defend the indefensible.[67]

Sometimes, even in the face of overwhelming evidence of innocence, prosecutors refuse to dismiss the case outright and instead insist that the defendant plead guilty to *something* in order to be immediately released. Ha'im Al Matin Sharif (who changed his name from Charles Robins while he was in prison) was convicted in 1988 of murdering and torturing his girlfriend's eleven-month-old daughter. After nearly thirty years on Nevada's death row, medical evidence proved that Britany had died of a medical condition, not abuse. Sharif's conviction was vacated in 2016, and a new hearing ordered. Even though a different medical expert hired by *the prosecution* agreed that the baby had died from a disease, the prosecution would not agree to dismiss the murder charges. Instead, the it offered a plea to second-degree murder, which enabled Sharif to be immediately released. He took the deal.[68] He is now freed from prison, but not from a criminal conviction for a murder that never happened.

Here too, psychological theory helps explain the prosecution's refusal to consider innocence after a conviction is obtained. Cognitive dissonance suggests that people naturally seek consistency or alignment between their beliefs and their behaviors. When there is an inconsistency between the two, dissonance results. To return to a natural state of consistency, people have three choices: change their beliefs, change their behaviors, or change how they view their behavior by rationalizing or justifying it.

Prosecutors see themselves as the good guys who don't put innocent people in jail. When they find out they may have made an error, it is too painful for some to face. It creates too much cognitive dissonance. As one former federal prosecutor explained: "Prosecutors think they're doing the Lord's work, and that they wear the white hat.... I thought everything I did was right. So even if you got out of line, you could tell yourself that you didn't do it on purpose, or that it was for the greater good."[69] Rationalizations are a powerful way to reconcile internal dissonance.

On some level, I understand the prosecution's need for certainty and internal consistency. Once a prosecutor is assigned to a case that may go to trial, they work to develop a theory consistent with the accused's guilt beyond a reasonable doubt. They spend time, sometimes years, working with the police and other forensic experts, talking with witnesses, maybe rounding up informants, parsing the evidence, presenting the evidence to the grand jury, responding to defense motions and almost always prevailing, preparing witnesses, and then, if the case goes to trial, writing and presenting opening and closing arguments that tie their theory of the case to the evidence in a compelling narrative. All the while, the prosecutor is convinced the defendant is guilty. They've consciously or subconsciously shrugged off or reconciled any inconsistencies, any doubts, any problems in the case. Guilty, guilty, guilty. So when they get a conviction, they feel good. Satisfied. The "bad guy" is off the street. They move on to the next case.

And then BAM.

The wrong person, you say? Nah, not a chance.

But we should also pause and consider the fact that most cases do not go to trial. They are resolved by plea bargain. Even in the assembly-line criminal justice docket, prosecutors assume they are just doing their jobs, punishing lawbreakers who would not be in the courthouse if they hadn't done something wrong. It would take too much time and too much effort for prosecutors to view each defendant as a complex individual with emotions, a family, and a narrative far more expansive than a criminal complaint could ever capture. It is far easier to look through the file and make a plea offer. Maybe negotiate a little. And then move on to the next case. It's a question of efficiency, not of individuals, and certainly not of justice.

Therein lies part of the problem as well. Good guys versus bad guys. It's a false dichotomy, a two-dimensional cartoon rather than a multidimensional, full-blown portrayal of actual people. Constructs like these minimize the humanity of the people being prosecuted. Criminal defendants become a parade of disposable people who are somehow less than human and not worthy of careful, sometimes agonizing consideration of the possibility that somewhere along the line something went terribly wrong.

Dehumanization has occurred throughout history to justify acts of unspeakable horror. In the Rwandan genocide, Hutus murdered nearly 1 million Tutsis who were referred to as "cockroaches" that needed to be stamped out, or as "tall trees" that needed to be felled. During World War II, Nazis called Jews parasites and animals and portrayed them as horned-rimmed devils. As history has shown, it is far more palatable to stamp out a cockroach, or eliminate a parasite, than it is to kill a human being.

Genocide is, of course, an extreme comparison. But the same process of dehumanization can be seen at work on a daily basis in the criminal justice system. If defendants are the "bad guys," the "criminals," the "evil-doers," if they get what they deserve or what they were asking for, then it is easier to discard "them" in the landfill of our prison system. The "Central Park 5," accused and later wrongly convicted of raping and brutalizing a jogger in Central Park, were not five frightened teenagers, entitled to due process and a fair criminal proceeding. The five young men were called a "wolf pack," a bunch of "animals," who deserved severe punishment for their crimes.[70] People who have been reduced to the "other" stop being individuals who matter. It is far easier to ignore or reject evidence that the accused is innocent if we conceive of them as less than fully human.

There is also the issue of prosecutorial mentality. Being part of a group where everyone is acting the same way in the context of a bureaucracy legitimizes behavior that is not actually acceptable. The individual's moral code and compass are subsumed in the larger group ethos. Prosecutors, and the offices in which they work, are not exempt from this phenomenon. When winning is the end all, be all, it may make sense that prosecutors don't turn over evidence that they should, or that they say nothing in the face of lying witnesses or incompetent lawyers, or that they stand by and let people plead guilty to crimes that never happened.

In one relatively simple study in 1952, psychologist Sam Asch created an experiment where student subjects were told in a group setting that they were taking a vision test and were asked to view a series of lines and select the one that best matched the "comparison line." It was an obvious choice. Seven confederates who were "in" on the experiment agreed in advance to choose a line that did not match the comparison line. They did so, out loud, in front of the subject. Three out of four times (75%), the subjects of the experiment conformed to the group's clearly incorrect suggestion and agreed that the clearly wrong line was a match. In a control group without confederates, subjects picked the wrong line less than 1% of the time—the choice was just that clear.[71] When the subjects were later asked about their responses, many admitted they conformed to the group choice because they wanted to fit in. Some, however, chose the wrong line because they genuinely believed the group must have known something they did not.

Given the influence of the group, is it really so surprising that prosecutors do things to maintain convictions that, objectively, they shouldn't?

IMMUNITY

The final reason prosecutors engage in misconduct is that they can. Prosecutors are almost never punished for their wrongful actions, not by criminal prosecutions, formal reprimands, admonishments by name in published court opinions, or even the loss of their jobs. There seems to be little downside to bad or unethical behavior.

Consider one of the rare cases where a prosecutor was criminally prosecuted and sent to jail for misconduct.[72] Ken Anderson prosecuted Michael Morton for the murder of Morton's wife. Anderson deliberately hid important evidence from the defense and the court, then watched as Morton spent the next twenty-five years in prison for a murder he did not commit. After Morton was exonerated by DNA evidence, Anderson was prosecuted for his misconduct and sentenced to ten days in jail, five hundred hours of community service, and a loss of his license to practice law. He was released after five days for "good behavior."

More often than not, though, nothing happens to the prosecutors.

Perhaps this will soon change. California recently passed a law that would hold prosecutors criminally liable for failing to disclose evidence.[73] No other state to date has followed suit, and no prosecutor has yet to be charged under the California law, but it at least suggests that perhaps prosecutorial misconduct is to be taken seriously.

It's just too bad that some prosecutors are the last to realize it.

Prosecutorial contributions to no-crime wrongful convictions are significant, problematic, and avoidable. But, as is discussed in the following chapter, defense lawyers—perhaps the most important protection an innocent defendant has against injustice— also often fail to do the minimum required under the law.

FIVE

Defense Lawyers

DROWNING IN CASES

AS BRIEFLY MENTIONED IN CHAPTER 4, Charles Robins, now Ha'im Al Matin Sharif, was convicted and sentenced to death based on charges that he had murdered his girlfriend's eleven-month-old daughter, Britany.[1] The aggravating factor that elevated Britany's death to a capital murder case was the allegation that Robins tortured Britany by breaking her leg. Robins insisted he was innocent.

At trial, the prosecution's case rested largely on forensic evidence provided by a local medical examiner who testified in detail that Britany had been physically abused and murdered. In addition, Britany's mother and other relatives testified that Robins had abused Britany. During the defense case, Robins's defense lawyer presented no forensic evidence about the timing or cause of Britany's leg fracture. In closing arguments, Robins's defense lawyer idly wondered aloud about what could have caused Britany's broken leg, but offered no alternative theory that would have aided his client.

A jury convicted Robins of capital murder and sentenced him to death.

That was in 1988.

Robins repeatedly appealed his conviction, which state appellate courts repeatedly affirmed. Having exhausted his state appeals, Robins sought relief in federal court. In 2012, nearly twenty-five years after his conviction, the federal public defender for the District of Arizona stepped in to handle Robins's petition. The new lawyers took an entirely fresh look at the evidence. For the first time in the history of Robins's case, the new lawyers arranged for a forensic investigation into Britany's death. In short order, medical experts determined that Britany had not been murdered, but rather had died from Barlow's disease (infantile scurvy).

This was not a difficult diagnosis to reach. Indeed, had trial counsel in 1988 simply consulted a competent radiologist to examine Britany's X-rays, the diagnosis of scurvy would have been obvious and readily obtained. Scurvy provided a compelling, cohesive, and corroborative diagnosis that explained Britany's skin discoloration, bruising, and leg fracture. In short, it provided a defense that would have corroborated Robins's innocence.

The new appellate lawyers doggedly continued their investigation. Britany's mother and brother, who testified against Robins at the trial, both now admitted that they had lied and that they never saw Robins abuse Britany. They also claimed that the Las Vegas Police Department and prosecutors had threatened them with imprisonment for Britany's death and also the loss of custody over her remaining children unless they testified against Robins.

Presented with an entirely different, empirically based noncriminal explanation for Britany's death, the federal court held the proceedings in abeyance so that Robins could present the new evidence to the state courts. But the state trial courts refused to even hear the claims, citing procedural barriers. Finally, on September 22, 2016, the Nevada Supreme Court ordered an evidentiary hearing on Robins's innocence claims and on the claims of police and prosecutorial misconduct.[2]

A doctor hired by the *prosecutor's* office to review the case found that Britany had suffered from scurvy.[3] Despite the compelling evidence of innocence, the prosecution would not agree to dismiss the charges, insisting that Robins was guilty of the crime of murder.[4] But the prosecution offered Robins a guilty plea to second-degree murder with a sentence of time served. Rather than remain in prison for any additional time, Robins made the painful decision to plead guilty and was immediately released.[5]

Robins spent more than twenty-eight years on Nevada's death row for a murder that his trial lawyer, with minimal effort, could have shown was a death caused by disease, not homicide. But because his lawyer did not investigate the case at all, Robins was convicted of capital murder and sent to death row, where he languished under severe deprivation and the threat of execution for three decades.

DEFENSE LAWYERS MATTER

Defense lawyers are supposed to be the great equalizer in the criminal justice arena. In theory (and certainly in the movies), defense lawyers are masters of the courtroom universe. They are legal scholars who keep abreast of ever-developing criminal law standards. They closely sift evidence to confirm that every criminal charge has a factual basis. They are forensic experts, challenging arcane and sometimes unreliable forensic evidence. They carefully counsel their clients, negotiate with the prosecutor, pursue viable defenses, and fiercely advocate for the best possible outcomes. They are persuasive, authoritative, and single-minded in pursuit of their client's best interests. They are all that stands between innocent people and prison.

A competent, committed defense lawyer is often the last, best, and only hope an innocent defendant has. But the ideal defense lawyer is hard to find. This chapter considers the less-than-ideal representation that some criminal defendants receive, and the many ways incompetent lawyering results in, or at least contributes to, no-crime wrongful convictions. While bad defense lawyering can be found throughout the criminal justice system, it plays a pivotal role in no-crime wrongful convictions. In many cases, a better lawyer would have discovered at the outset that no crime had occurred at all.

LOOKING BACKWARD: HISTORY, CRIMINAL JUSTICE, AND BAD LAWYERING

At the turn of the twentieth century in the Deep South, justice for African Americans was often found at the end of a lynching rope. White people routinely accused African American men of "offenses" that violated no criminal code but challenged southern racial norms. Think here of Emmett Till, lynched for supposedly whistling at a white woman, or Jeff Brown, lynched for accidently bumping into a white woman as he ran to catch his train.[6]

White people made baseless accusations against African Americans and promptly formed lynch mobs that decreed guilt and meted out punishment; the accused would be found the next morning, swinging lifeless from a makeshift gallows, another victim of justice by lynching. Between 1877 and 1950, 4,084 people, mostly black men, were victims of racial terror lynchings throughout the South. A lynching occurred in the South on average once a week, every week, for seventy-three years. Several hundred additional lynchings were recorded in other states throughout the country in the same period.[7]

But as the public appetite for lynchings slowly declined, a new system of "justice" for African Americans emerged. Courts convened sham trials in which African Americans were accused of crimes, subjected to hastily called criminal proceedings, and quickly condemned by all-white juries who pronounced guilty verdicts and (where available) imposed death sentences, which were followed by rapid executions.[8] These "legal lynchings" paid lip service to justice, but were actually designed to perpetuate and reinforce racial inequities. White lawyers assigned to represent the accused were willing and necessary participants in this farce.

In the infamous Scottsboro cases in 1931, two white women accused nine African American teenagers of raping them as they rode a train in Alabama. Eight of the nine faced the death penalty in response to the allegations. On the morning of the trial, the court appointed two lawyers to represent all nine defendants. The first lawyer was an alcoholic from Tennessee who was so intoxicated in the courtroom that he could "barely ... walk straight."[9] When that lawyer protested that he was entirely unprepared and had no knowledge of Alabama criminal law and procedures, the court appointed a local lawyer to help. In his seventies, he had not tried a case in thirty years. The lawyer from Tennessee was given a mere half hour to meet with his clients before the trial began.[10]

With no investigation, no motions or legal filings of any kind, and no interviews with witnesses—and with their clients' lives hanging in the balance—the defense lawyers made no demand for more time to prepare. Instead, they legitimated the sham trial by providing representation in name only. They made no opening or closing statements, engaged in a lackadaisical and ineffective cross-examination, and did not prepare their clients to take the stand (many of whom implicated the others in desperate and ill-conceived attempts to avoid the death penalty).[11] All nine defendants were quickly convicted, and eight were sentenced to death (the ninth, who was only thirteen years old, was sentenced to life in prison). Decades later, it was revealed that the rape never happened. The state pardoned the men, most of whom were by then deceased.[12]

In the meantime, the Scottsboro case yielded one positive outcome for the legal community. In *Powell v. Alabama* (1932), the U.S. Supreme Court ruled in eloquent and soaring language that the Scottsboro defendants had been denied their right to counsel in violation of the Due Process Clause of the U.S. Constitution:

> The right to be heard would be, in many cases, of little avail if it did not comprehend the right to be heard by counsel.... Left without the aid of counsel, [a defendant] may be put on trial without a proper charge.... He requires

the guiding hand of counsel at every step in the proceedings against him. Without it, though he be not guilty, he faces the danger of conviction because he does not know how to establish his innocence.[13]

Nearly thirty years later, in 1963, the Supreme Court decided *Gideon v. Wainwright.* That case involved Clarence Gideon, a down-and-out drifter with a petty-criminal record who was accused of burglarizing a pool hall. When Gideon had been arrested before, he'd promptly pled guilty, but this time he insisted he was innocent and asked for a lawyer to represent him at trial. The Florida court denied his request, and Gideon attempted to represent himself. Not surprisingly, he was convicted. His handwritten appeal to the U.S. Supreme Court expressing his dismay that he had been denied a lawyer got the attention of a law clerk. The rest, as they say, is (legal) history.

In *Gideon,* the Supreme Court ruled that all defendants, even those too poor to pay for counsel, were entitled to a lawyer under the Sixth Amendment to the Constitution.[14] *Gideon* was a major triumph in that it went much further than *Powell* in ensuring the poor would be provided with counsel. In the wake of *Gideon,* "counsel for all" was trumpeted across the land.

But despite the Court's best intentions, *Gideon*'s impact was limited at the outset for two major reasons. First, it failed to address issues of cost, making the right to counsel an unfunded mandate that states would soon chafe against. Second, it failed to set a minimum standard for the quality of representation required by the Constitution. The criminal justice system has been struggling ever since to comply with *Gideon,* leaving innocent defendants caught in the crosshairs.

YOU GET WHAT YOU PAY FOR: INADEQUATE FUNDING AND EXCESSIVE CASELOADS

Roughly four out of five defendants are too poor to hire a lawyer.[15] *Gideon* required only that poor defendants be provided with a lawyer, but offered no prescription as to how that mandate be fulfilled. The result is an inconsistent patchwork of indigent defense models that exist in three primary forms.[16] First, public defender officers focus solely on indigent defense and are funded either by the state or the county in which the services are provided. Second, assigned-counsel models allocate cases to private attorneys, who are paid either by the case or by the hour at a (typically low) wage. In 2012, for instance,

Wisconsin paid just $40 per hour to appointed lawyers providing indigent defense; in Florida, appointed lawyers received a flat fee of $2,500, even in cases where a defendant faced a life sentence.[17] Jurisdictions often employ a hybrid of these two models, so that private attorneys are assigned cases where the public defender has a "conflict," as when there are multiple codefendants. Thirdly, the contract counsel model awards attorneys a contract, typically to the lowest bidder, to handle a certain number of cases per year. In each model, you get what you pay for. For many indigent defendants, the representation is severely lacking.

Indigent defense funding varies tremendously from state to state, and even across counties in the same state. More than twenty states, including New Jersey and Florida, pay the entire cost of statewide indigent defense services, while Utah and Pennsylvania provide no state funding and require counties to cover all the costs of indigent defense services.[18] Whatever the model, funding for indigent defense remains woefully inadequate.

Severe underfunding creates a caseload crisis where too few lawyers handle far too many cases. In Nashville, Tennessee, for instance, each public defender was assigned 1,000 misdemeanor cases on average in 2012, giving them less than one hour to spend on each case.[19] In 2013 in Washington State, two part-time attorneys each handled approximately 1,000 cases—again leading to them spend less than an hour on each case.[20] In 2009, Louisiana public defenders handled the equivalent of 19,000 misdemeanor cases annually, which gave them *seven minutes* per case.[21] And that's just an average, which means some lawyers spent even less than seven minutes with their clients on some misdemeanors.

Felony cases fared equally poorly. In Louisiana, a single public defender randomly selected by the *New York Times* had a caseload on a given day of 194 felonies. The *Times* calculated that the Louisiana lawyer would need almost 10,000 hours (the equivalent of five work-years) to provide truly competent representation to his existing clients. Alarmingly, the *Times* analysis *excluded* the one death penalty case on the lawyer's roster and any new cases that he or she would surely be assigned as the year progressed.[22] In New Mexico, the number of felony cases almost doubled in 2016, while the number of public defenders dropped by one-third due to funding cuts.[23] In the same year, New Mexico public defenders were averaging more than 200 felony cases per attorney. When the chief defender directed his attorneys to stop accepting new cases, a court held the chief defender in contempt and ordered him to resume taking cases.[24] In Florida, one attorney handled 971 cases in a single year, of which nearly 80 percent were felonies.[25] In Texas, "a number of attorneys were paid for 500 to 1,400 court-appointed cases in FY 2014. Moreover, for some, this was just a portion of their total caseload. At least 14 individuals representing more than 600 indigent defendants claimed those clients comprised just 40 to 70 percent of their total cases."[26] Also in Texas, the defense spent an average of two hours investigating serious felony cases—nowhere near what would truly be needed in even a moderately complex case.[27]

Excessive caseloads like those described above mean that poor defendants receive essentially no representation at all. It is simply impossible for a lawyer in seven minutes—or even in two hours—to meet a client, discuss the charges, learn the client's perspective on the case, interview potential witnesses, investigate any defenses, explore possible mitigating factors, file motions, negotiate a plea and sentence when appropriate, and properly advise the client about the consequences of going to trial or taking a plea. If the client claims innocence, the lawyer is supposed to challenge the state to prove its case. But even deciding whether to take a case to trial based on actual innocence takes more time than most defenders have to spend.

Excessive caseloads provide a framework in which indigent defenders learn the harsh reality of what it really means to represent the poor: whispered hallway conversations with clients they meet for the first and often only time; a lack of time to forge connection and trust between attorney and client; rushed plea agreements; and the reality that tomorrow you will wake up and do it again. This is how indigent defense is done, and zealous lawyers who try to do more may find themselves explicitly admonished by the judge that this "is not how we do things here."

Jonathan A. Rapping, McArthur Genius Award recipient, law professor, and founder of Gideon's Promise, an organization devoted to training new public defenders in the South, explains the problem this way: "When poor people are provided lawyers who do not care about them, who are unwilling to advocate for them, or who prioritize the interests of others above their clients', they cannot receive the "guiding hand of counsel" our Constitution guarantees."[28] Although it is certainly true that defense lawyers for the poor are woefully underfunded and work under crushing caseloads, they are often complicit in providing bad representation. Rapping argues that lawyers who lackadaisically "play along, to get along" have bought into a lawyering culture that assumes "their clients are guilty; their clients cannot be trusted; independent investigation and meaningful attorney-client communication are a waste of time; their role is to help judges process cases quickly; this goal is most often served by convincing their clients to accept guilty pleas; and cases, when they must be tried, should be tried quickly."[29] When defense lawyers perceive their jobs as helping the system to function better instead of providing zealous advocacy for individual clients, bad lawyering results.

Criminal defendants languish in the worst of all possible worlds, where form trumps function and the pursuit of justice is lost in the exchange. They appear from the outside to have a lawyer as mandated by the Constitution, but they receive no actual legal assistance. Instead, they are hastily processed through the court system, accompanied by harried and overwhelmed attorneys who engage in meet-and-greet advocacy, essentially accepting the police report at face value, and typically insisting that a quick plea is the best way to resolve a case. Appointed counsel never have a chance to evaluate the evidence or their clients' protestations of innocence, or to consider whether a crime was even committed in the first place. Thoughtful and critical examination of the state's case is rare and, when it occurs, fleeting; there is simply no time. In such a representational void, no-crime convictions are unavoidable.

Today's criminal justice system has been compared to an assembly line in which a seemingly endless stream of faceless, interchangeable defendants made up of poor people, mostly of color, are charged, prosecuted, convicted after a guilty plea, and sentenced, one after the other.[30] But assembly lines are designed to move goods, not people—especially not people whose lives, liberty, and future prospects hang in the balance.

The case of "Mary" can perhaps be called a near-miss no-crime wrongful conviction. A pregnant eighteen-year-old with no criminal record, Mary missed the bus on her way to a scheduled appointment with her obstetrician.[31] She accepted a ride from an acquaintance who was driving a stolen car. The police pulled the car over and arrested the driver and Mary, even though Mary had committed no crime because she had no knowledge that the car was stolen. Initially released on minimal bond and told to find her own lawyer, Mary returned to court multiple times without having secured representation. She was eventually assigned a public defender, who knew nothing about Mary or her case. After a quick in-court conversation with Mary, the newly appointed public defender stood by while the court increased Mary's bail to $20,000, an amount she could not afford. Mary—now nine months pregnant—was hauled off to jail because she could not make bail. She gave birth while incarcerated, without her family by her side as she had planned, and the baby was given directly to Mary's mother. Mary was returned to jail while she awaited legal assistance on her case.

Weeks passed, and the public defender assigned to her case suddenly realized that he was already representing the driver, which meant the office had a conflict of interest and could no longer represent Mary. Her case was reassigned to a third-year clinical law student from Loyola Law School. Within *hours* of meeting Mary, the clinical law student was able to secure Mary's release from jail. The student then worked with the prosecution, which eventually dismissed the case against Mary because there was no evidence that Mary knew, or could have known, that the car had been stolen.

The initial public defender in Mary's case was likely underresourced, overwhelmed, inexperienced, or simply resigned when he was assigned to Mary's case. But when a law student zealously advocated for Mary, the tide immediately turned. In the middle was Mary, too poor to hire her own lawyer, and therefore stuck with whatever representation her appointed lawyer provided. Although she finally got lucky with the appointment made by the Loyola Law School Clinic, luck is a relative term. Mary first had to suffer the shame and trauma of giving birth in prison, unable to nurse or even hold her newborn child until she was finally released. All for a crime that she did not commit.

It is easy to imagine a different outcome for Mary's case had she remained with the assigned public defender, who did no investigation or advocacy. Despite the absence of a criminal record, Mary likely would have pled guilty to some crime—a crime she never committed—simply to return home to her new baby. She would have entered a misdemeanor plea or maybe even a felony plea, but either way, she would likely have wound up with a criminal record, with all of the attendant consequences. She may even have been sentenced to time in prison or lost her parental rights. It seems likely that Mary would have suffered a worse fate had she been forced to remain with the lawyer initially assigned to her case.

INEFFECTIVE LAWYERING: A LOW BAR FOR COMPETENT REPRESENTATION

The 1963 *Gideon* decision clearly contemplated strong representation for all defendants, regardless of their ability to pay for a lawyer. But by the time the Supreme Court in 1984 was asked to clarify the meaning of effective counsel, the Court's composition had dramatically changed. In *Strickland v. Washington*, the Supreme Court defined *effectiveness*, setting an extremely high hurdle for defendants, who bear the burden of proof on appeal, to demonstrate that counsel was constitutionally ineffective.[32] First, a defendant must prove that counsel was deficient. Second, the defendant must prove that, "but for" counsel's deficient performance, the outcome in the case would have been different. One federal district court judge described the *Strickland* competency bar this way:

> The Constitution does not guarantee that a defendant will have a perfect lawyer. It does not guarantee that he will have a good lawyer. It does not even guarantee that he will *not* have a "really bad one." . . . [T]he Supreme Court has gone out of its way to make clear that, in order to obtain a new trial on ineffective-assistance grounds, the petitioner must do more than show that he had a bad lawyer—even a really bad one.[33]

In other words, even "really bad lawyering" is constitutionally acceptable unless a defendant can prove that the outcome of their case would have been different with a different lawyer or without the claimed legal error. In an article describing the "national crisis" of indigent defense, law professors Mary Sue Backus and Paul Marcus complain that "courts have relied upon *Strickland* to refuse to find ineffective assistance of counsel even where the defense attorney was silent during the entire trial, shared delusions about his involvement in a murder conspiracy with the jury, or was arrested on the way to the courthouse for driving with a .27 blood-alcohol content." To find effectiveness, courts claim the outcome of the case would not have been different even if the lawyer had been awake, sane, or sober.[34]

In the cases discussed below, innocent defendants convicted, and eventually exonerated, of crimes that never happened were able to prove, at some point in the usually long and protracted legal battle over innocence, that they had received ineffective assistance of counsel. But these cases are exceptional: we know that courts routinely find the very worst examples of lawyering to be legally "effective."

Failure to Know the Law

Lawyers can be ineffective in not knowing or understanding the laws under which they are operating. When lawyers make legal mistakes, their innocent clients suffer.

In 2005, Israel Grant was accused of robbing two people at gunpoint in a Circle K parking lot. Grant, from the moment of his arrest, insisted that he was innocent.[35] He provided a compelling alibi, with time-stamped evidence, that he had been applying for a job shortly before the alleged robbery and had been in a pawn shop shortly afterward, and therefore could not have been in the Circle K parking lot at the time of the incident. Grant was tried for two counts of robbery with a dangerous weapon and one count of being a felon in possession of a dangerous weapon. Grant had a prior felony conviction, which made it illegal for him to carry a gun.

At trial, his lawyer made a series of egregious legal errors. One of them involved the way the lawyer handled Grant's prior criminal record. To meet its burden of proof for the felon-in-possession charge, the prosecution was required to prove that Grant had a prior felony conviction. Most lawyers would have "stipulated" (or agreed on the record) that Grant had a prior conviction—because he did. Had the lawyer agreed, the jury would have learned that Grant had a prior felony, but not which type of prior felony.

But, for no apparent reason, his lawyer refused to stipulate to Grant's prior conviction. As a result, the prosecution was allowed to introduce evidence not only that Grant had a prior felony conviction but that he had a prior *robbery* conviction. The damage was done. Known as propensity evidence, which is usually *not* admitted in court because it is so prejudicial, evidence of a prior robbery in a robbery case could cause the jury to assume that if Grant committed a robbery before, he must have committed a robbery again. That assumption is not permitted under the law, because prosecutors bear the burden of proving that a defendant is guilty in a particular case based on actual evidence that he or she committed a crime. The danger of propensity evidence is that it can lead the jury to conclude a defendant is guilty, even in the absence of other evidence, based solely on the defendant's prior behavior. Because of the harm such information can cause, good defense lawyers typically fight tooth and nail to prevent it from being heard by the jury.

Further compounding this error, the lawyer did not ask the judge to instruct the jury that it could consider the evidence of Grant's prior robbery conviction only for purposes of being a felon, and that they were specifically prohibited from making the propensity inference of "once a robber, always a robber." This left the jury to imagine Grant as a chronic robber who must be guilty of the charges.

Tainted by evidence they never should have heard, the jury disregarded Grant's alibi and found him guilty on all counts. Before the judge imposed his sentence, Grant again protested his innocence. He was sentenced to 222 to 286 months in prison. The appellate courts rejected his claims of ineffective assistance of counsel.

But then, in 2014, one of the so-called victims recanted her testimony and admitted there had been no robbery. Soon thereafter, the case was referred to the North Carolina Innocence Inquiry Commission. In a 2017 hearing, the second so-called victim also recanted his testimony, explaining that no robbery had occurred and that he had invented the story to avoid having to repay Grant for money he owed him from a drug deal.

In 2019, a three-judge panel determined there was clear and convincing evidence of Grant's innocence, and he was exonerated of all robbery charges.[36] He served nearly a decade in prison for a crime that never occurred. Given the strength of his alibi and the witnesses' ever-changing stories, one can only wonder to what degree defense counsel's legal errors affected the case's outcome.

In 2006, Herbert Landry was convicted in Utah of arson based largely on expert testimony that relied on discredited fire science and on evidence of "alerts" signaled by Oscar, a certified fire accelerant detection dog.[37] Although Landry's trial lawyer had never worked on an arson case before, she did not consult with her own arson expert to determine the cause and origins of the fire. A defense fire expert would have helped dismantle the prosecution's case, which was based heavily on questionable fire science. Instead, she met only with the *prosecution's* lead arson investigator and uncritically accepted his fire analysis as correct.

Landry's trial lawyer also neglected to object to the admissibility of the Oscar's dog alerts, which were offered to prove the existence of accelerants on Landry's shoes. Oscar's canine detection of accelerants was never validated by laboratory testing. Yet, counsel did not challenge the admissibility of testimony about Oscar's alerts. Had she conducted even basic legal research, she would have found a Utah Supreme Court decision that specifically prohibited canine evidence unless it is corroborated by lab results. Oscar's alerts should never have been admitted as evidence. Because Landry's lawyer did not investigate the validity of the state's expert witnesses by securing one of her own, and failed to do even minimal legal research, she missed a clear defense path that could have turned the tide against the jury's finding of arson. Instead, counsel's incompetence led to Landry's conviction for an arson that never happened.

Failure to Investigate the Facts

Sometimes the defense lawyer fails to conduct a basic factual investigation that would lay bare the inaccuracy of the charges. The following cases illustrate just how damaging an unmotivated lawyer can be.

Darian Contee was arrested in Lubbock, Texas, on February 18, 2006.[38] The police entered his motel room after allegedly receiving a complaint about the smell of marijuana. They searched the motel room and found a handgun. Contee was arrested and, on the advice of counsel, in December 2007, pled guilty to the unlawful possession of a firearm by a felon. He was sentenced to three years in prison. In 2010, the police retrieved the weapon from a storage room because they suspected it had been used in a murder. The crime technician discovered that the "hand gun" was actually an air pistol. But Contee's defense lawyer had never bothered to confirm that the police had recovered an actual gun; and instead he had advised Contee to plead guilty based solely on the allegations in the arrest report. Upon learning the "gun" was not actually a gun, and with the cooperation of the district attorney's office, Contee was released from prison and his conviction vacated. His conviction for a crime that didn't occur could have been avoided had counsel properly investigated the allegations.

Or consider what happened to Nick Rhoades. Rhoades was charged with transmission of HIV under the Iowa criminal statute that banned "the intentional exposure of the body of one person to a bodily fluid of another person in a manner that could result in" the transmission of HIV to a person who did not know the defendant's HIV status.[39] The basis for the criminal charge was that Rhoades had "consensual unprotected oral and protected anal sex" with Adam Plendl, who did not know that Rhoades was HIV positive. Upon learning that Rhoades was HIV positive, Plendl went to the hospital to receive precautionary treatment; he did not contract HIV.

Rhoades hired a lawyer who advised him to plead guilty. He was sentenced to *twenty-five years* in prison with the added requirement that he register as a sex offender upon his release. His case and sentence prompted national outrage, and he was soon resentenced to a five-year term of probation.

The Iowa Supreme Court later reversed Rhoades's conviction in its entirety, citing his counsel's ineffectiveness. As the court noted, had Rhoades's lawyer investigated the case properly, he would have learned three details that were critical to his client's defense. First, Rhoades was taking retroviral medications that rendered his viral load "undetectable," making it nearly medically impossible for him to transmit the HIV disease. Second, Rhoades had used a condom during anal intercourse and therefore did not "intentionally expose" anyone to the HIV disease; indeed, he arguably tried to protect Plendl from exposure to the disease. Third, although the men had unprotected oral sex, the chance of transmission from that act was exceedingly minimal. As the Iowa

Supreme Court observed, whether a crime was committed was pure speculation: "At the time of the plea, Rhoades's viral count was nondetectable, and there is a question of whether it was medically true a person with a nondetectable viral load could transmit HIV through contact with the person's blood, semen or vaginal fluid or whether transmission was merely theoretical."[40]

In other words, Rhoades's lawyer—a lawyer whom he hired—apparently conducted no research or investigation into his client's medical status or the law. Instead, counsel advised Rhoades to plead guilty to a crime that from a medical, practical, and legal standpoint had not happened, without ever challenging the factual basis of the charge in the first place.

Although his conviction was reversed, the fallout for Rhoades from his conviction continues to this day. Because of his initial guilty plea, he was denied compensation for his wrongful conviction,[41] and his name continues to surface erroneously in background employment checks as a registered sex offender.

While on the subject of sex offender registrations, I should mention that no-crime wrongful convictions for failing to register also can result from bad lawyering. Every state and the federal government have laws requiring people convicted of sex offenses to register with authorities.[42] Registration requirements vary considerably depending on the nature of the offense (which falls into designated tiers) and the jurisdiction. Many sex offender registries include mandatory community notification requirements and provide public access to the offender's name and address. As a result, registered sex offenders are often the target of public hostility, harassment, and even violence. Depending on the state and the crime of conviction, there may be additional registration restrictions as to where an offender can live or work in relation to a broad list of public places, including schools, public parks, places of worship, and even sports stadiums. Registration requirements make it difficult, if not impossible, for people convicted as sex offenders to find and maintain housing and employment or to engage in community life. In states with lifelong registration requirements, persons convicted of a sex crime are under perpetual surveillance for the rest of their lives. Some states have added sensationalist requirements to show that they are truly "protecting" the community. In Missouri, for instance, registered sex offenders are prohibited from engaging in Halloween-related activities involving children, and must be in their homes on Halloween evening, with the exterior lights off, unless they are required to be at work.[43]

Sex offender registries have become so onerous, overly broad, and complex for people to comply with that in 2019 the Michigan attorney general took a public position *supporting* challenges to the Michigan sex offender registry.[44] In an amicus brief to the Michigan Supreme Court, the attorney general argued that Michigan's sex offender registration and notification requirements are additional punishments that violate the ex post facto clause of the Michigan constitution because they are so burdensome and fail to distinguish between dangerous offenders and those who are not a threat to the community. State supreme courts in Alaska, California, Indiana, Kentucky, Maine, Maryland, Ohio, Oklahoma, and Pennsylvania have also concluded that existing registries are unconstitutional punishment because they are onerous, too complex, and overinclusive.[45]

The life of someone listed on a sex offender registry is fraught and difficult, as it is for that person's family. But the failure to register when one is required to do so is itself a crime that can be punishable by imprisonment.

In 1978, nineteen-year-old Longino Acero pled guilty to lewd contact with an adult woman, a misdemeanor charge that did not require registration.[46] A California clerk erred in recording his crime as child molestation, which did require registration. Between 1994 and 2004, Acero was arrested *three* times for his failure to register as a sex offender. In each instance, Acero told his public defenders that he was not required to register as a sex offender. No attorney bothered to pull the original case file to see what he was talking about; instead, they each advised him to plead guilty. Acero was sentenced three times, based on his guilty pleas, to three different terms of incarceration for failing to register as a sex offender. He was also publicly listed as someone who had been convicted of child molestation in the California sex offender registry. A flier with his name and photo was distributed by the police throughout his neighborhood and at his daughter's elementary school, identifying him as a high-risk sex offender. When he moved, the police distributed the flyers again. In 2003, he was arrested for jaywalking and again for failing to register—crimes to which he pled guilty—and was jailed. When he was identified by name in the local newspaper as a high-risk offender, word reached the local jail. As he explained to a local newspaper reporter, Acero was isolated, harassed, and scorned while serving his time: "Nobody wants to be around a 'Chester' (the slang for 'child molester'). . . . It was a label I was carrying around for years and years."[47]

In 2005, Acero received a letter from the San Jose Police Department confirming that its clerk had made a clerical error relating to his original misdemeanor conviction and that he was not—and had never been—required to register as a sex offender. Acero hired a new lawyer, who actually took the time to pull the original case file. It corroborated what Acero had been saying all along. Because Acero had never been required to register, he could not have committed the crime of failing to register. His plea convictions for failing to register were finally vacated in 2006, ending a decade-long saga of humiliation and incarceration for crimes that never happened. Acero had been the victim of a clerical error—and three different lawyers who failed to do their jobs.

Pleasing Judges over Advocating for Individual Clients

Another major challenge to quality representation is the independence of defense lawyers vis-à-vis judges. Rapping explains that many long-standing chief public defenders resist adopting more effective and zealous representation practices, in part because they worry about how judges would react if lawyers started filing routine motions; they do not want their lawyers to "cause trouble."[48] Sirens should blare when chief defenders are worried more about their lawyers upsetting judges by filing necessary motions than about providing quality representation to their indigent clients. When a defense lawyer "avoids trouble" to please a judge, indigent defendants pay dearly.

The lack of independence between defense lawyers and judges is revealed in many ways. When a judge pressures a defense lawyer to quickly resolve one case, for example, defense counsel might yield in that case to avoid a reprisal in another. If a lawyer pushes too hard for one client and thereby irritates or exasperates a judge or prosecutor, it could redound to the detriment of other clients in unrelated cases. Repeat defenders may choose their battles carefully, obtaining a more lenient sentence in one case but perhaps conceding ground in another.[49] They go along to get along, often at the expense of the very people they are assigned to represent.

In jurisdictions where judges oversee the appointment of cases to individual lawyers, those lawyers have an even greater incentive not to "cause trouble." Judges may appoint cases to lawyers who move the judge's docket along rather than to those who slow down the justice machinery with "excessive" (albeit zealous and necessary) advocacy.[50] In return, appointed lawyers have financial incentives to resolve cases in ways that please the assigning judges so that the lawyers receive future appointments.

Consider Harris County in Texas, home to the city of Houston. A 2016 state audit found that elected judges routinely appoint their favorite attorneys to cases, even when it means that those attorneys will have caseloads that well exceed the recommended levels. One lawyer explained, "Attorneys are generally selected for their efficiency with moving the court's docket. . . . This rarely translates to quality representation."[51] In 2009, judges were skewered in the local press for appointing the majority of cases to a handful of attorneys who undertook little preparation or investigation.[52] In response, in 2011, a public defender office was created. But judges continue to maintain discretion over whom they appoint, including lawyers who directly contribute to the judges' reelection campaigns. These same judges often (and explicitly) refuse to assign cases to the public defender office.[53]

It is in this context that we should recall the hundreds of no-crime conviction cases that came out of Harris County, Texas (see chapter 3), where defendant after defendant pled guilty to felony drug possession charges, on the advice of counsel, based solely on field test results later proven false by lab results. Where were the defense lawyers in these cases? Given the ways in which cases were assigned and the sheer volume of drug cases, perhaps it is not surprising that defense lawyers did not insist on lab test results before pleading their clients guilty. Here is another example of lawyers conducting business as usual at the expense of justice.

CONTEMPT AND DERISION LEAD TO NO-CRIME WRONGFUL CONVICTIONS

Defense lawyers are supposed to provide a robust and meaningful defense to their clients regardless of guilt or innocence. Some defense lawyers seem to forget that obligation. They dismiss their clients as "guilty" or unworthy, and don't worry too much about providing zealous advocacy.

Cameron Todd Willingham (whose case chapter 2 discusses) was sentenced to death and later executed in Texas for the arson murder of his children based on bad forensic science. Willingham was represented at trial by a court-appointed lawyer named David Martin. Martin, a former state trooper, contacted just one fire expert, who he claimed agreed with the prosecution's fire experts. Martin apparently conducted his own "fire experiment" in his backyard and concluded that Willingham was guilty.[54] At trial, rather than calling a forensic expert to refute the fire science claims at the heart of the prosecution's case, Martin called the *babysitter* to testify that she couldn't imagine Willingham would ever harm his children.[55]

The lack of zealous advocacy was particularly stunning in a death penalty case, given that fire scientists across the nation who later reviewed Willingham's case universally agreed that the original arson investigation was flawed and that the conclusions reached were flat-out wrong. And experts at the time of Willingham's trial could have reached that conclusion, since new guidelines published one year later had been percolating through the ranks for some time.

But rather than serve as an ongoing advocate for Willingham, Martin took to the popular press to share his personal belief in Willingham's guilt.[56] Martin dismissed an extensive investigative report by the *Chicago Tribune,* including the opinions of four fire science experts who found that the fire was accidental and that Willingham was innocent.[57] When the Innocence Project also hired experts to review the case and released a forty-eight-page report detailing why the fire could not have been arson, Martin dismissed its conclusions: "The Innocence Project is an absolute farce. It's a bunch of hype, in my opinion."[58] He was so strident in maintaining his belief in Willingham's guilt that CNN's Anderson Cooper told him he sounded more like a "sheriff than a defense lawyer."[59]

Yet Martin was the lawyer assigned to Willingham. When you are poor, you get what you get. Willingham got a lawyer who was so convinced of his client's guilt that he didn't bother to be an advocate. Martin's lack of loyalty was a stunning betrayal of Willingham, a seemingly innocent man whom Martin was assigned to represent but whom he instead helped send to his grave for a crime that most experts agree was not a crime at all.

Ineffective Lawyers Distracted by Their Own Misconduct

Timothy Britt, a high school dropout who tested in the bottom 1 percent in reading, was charged with sexually assaulting a relative's ten-year-old step-daughter based on the girl's accusation.[60] At trial, the girl initially testified Britt had not touched her at all. After her father gestured to her in the court-room, however, the girl repeated her accusations against Britt. No physical or forensic evidence was offered at trial, but the prosecution introduced Britt's signed confession. In his defense, Britt testified and denied the allegations. He also denied confessing to the crime, asserting that the police had given him papers that he signed without reading, believing he would be allowed to go home.

In 2013, Britt was convicted and sentenced to twenty-five to thirty years in prison.

New appellate counsel then filed an eighty-eight-page motion seeking to vacate Britt's conviction.[61] The motion provided evidence that the girl had admitted to a friend that she lied and that Britt did not molest her, as well as evidence of prosecutorial misconduct. But at the heart of the motion was the failure of Britt's lawyer to provide competent representation. The attorney conducted no investigation, and therefore did not discover that the girl had previously made false allegations of sexual abuse, had a juvenile criminal record, and had been involuntarily committed to a hospital for violent behavior; that a doctor had said the girl did not know right from wrong; or that there were numerous and unsubstantiated reports of abuse involving the girl and her family, documented in thousands of pages by the North Carolina Division of Social Services. Counsel also did not interview any members of the girl's family who could have informed him that her parents had lengthy histories of drug abuse, that they often threatened or brought false criminal charges and lawsuits to manipulate others, and that the girl had a reputation for lying. The lawyer was on notice that something was very wrong because one of the girl's family members had in fact outlined to him the girl's medical and psychological history and had urged him to request access to her records.

But counsel was otherwise occupied. At the time he should have been developing Britt's defense, he was defending himself in an ongoing investigation by the North Carolina Bar Association. In 2015, the attorney was disbarred for his dishonest and unethical conduct in an unrelated matter.

In response to appellate counsel's motion, the trial judge, with the consent of the district attorney, agreed that Britt had been denied the effective assistance of counsel and vacated Britt's conviction. But not before Britt spent multiple years in prison and was labeled a child molester for a crime that his lawyer could have shown never happened, if only he had done his job.

Guilty Pleas and Official Misconduct: What's a Lawyer to Do?

It is not just ineffectiveness, laziness, or incompetence that prevents defendants from having true advocates. Structural realities aside from excessive caseloads also prevent defense lawyers from protecting the innocent. Because the system is stacked so heavily against defendants, it is often in the best penal and practical interests of even innocent clients to plead guilty, even to crimes that never happened.

Innocent people plead guilty because the alternative is often much worse. Innocent individuals may plead guilty to avoid prolonged pretrial incarceration because they know they cannot make bail, or because they lack child care or cannot miss work, or simply because they do not believe their word will be credited over that of the police. And because of these realities, defense lawyers often find themselves negotiating plea bargains for innocent clients. After all, defense lawyers are supposed to counsel their clients on the options and the likely outcome of their cases.

Consider the defendants in Tulia, Texas, discussed in chapter 3. In 1999, roughly 10 percent of the African American population was arrested for drug crimes on the say-so of Tom Coleman, a lone undercover officer. The first Tulia defendants went to trial and were convicted on Coleman's testimony; they received stunningly long prison sentences. In response, defense lawyers for the remaining defendants began advising their innocent clients to plead guilty to avoid the severe punishments that would come if they were convicted after a trial. Everyone in the case was culpable: prosecutors met with defense lawyers and brokered those plea deals, judges accepted those plea deals, and the defendants—almost all black and poor—with counsel by their side pled guilty. As a result, innocent people were convicted and sent to prison for crimes that everyone knew (or should have known) did not happen.

One may wonder in shock how it is that our system is so broken that judges, prosecutors, defense lawyers, and even defendants tolerate the idea that innocent people should plead guilty to crimes they did not commit because the alternative is worse. But that is exactly what happens every day in courtrooms around the country, and there is not much any individual defense lawyer can do about it.

A final structural factor that prevents defense lawyers from protecting defendants against no-crime wrongful convictions is official misconduct. Even the very best defense lawyers—the most diligent, the most persistent, the smartest, the got-your-back kind of lawyers who work round the clock— are completely hamstrung when the police and prosecutors intentionally lie about evidence or hide favorable evidence, or when forensic scientists patently falsify their findings. Defense lawyers are not Marvel superheroes; they cannot penetrate the equivalent of steel walls constructed from official falsities. They cannot challenge what they do not know about, cannot access, and cannot discover even with diligent effort. Many have fought the good fight and lost. The tools in even the most seasoned defense lawyer's toolbox can't fix the problems caused by official misconduct.

Defense lawyers are supposed to serve as a firewall against wrongful convictions. But there are many obstacles that prevent that ideal from becoming a reality. Inadequate public funding creates excessive caseloads and fosters a culture that focuses on the efficient processing of cases, rather than the zealous advocacy to which defendants are entitled. It is no wonder that charges for crimes that never happened are rarely unearthed; lawyers simply have no time even to consider whether a factual predicate exists for the accusations against their clients before they have to move on to the next case. When lawyers accept the prosecution's version of events at face value and fail to conduct even basic investigations, the entire adversarial system crumbles. When lawyers do not understand existing law or fail to keep up with legal developments, the advice and advocacy they provide to their clients are often misguided or wrong. In these scenarios, prosecutors are not forced to prove a defendant's guilt because defense lawyers do not require them to do so.

To make matters worse, most instances of ineffective lawyering are never uncovered. When an innocent defendant is convicted by a guilty plea, any ineffectiveness on the part of counsel is rarely considered and almost never recognized. But even when the issue is litigated after a full-blown trial, appellate courts usually decide that counsel was not constitutionally ineffective.

Criminal defense lawyers are essential to protecting the rights of the accused—both the factually innocent and the factually guilty—in the criminal justice system. When lawyers fail to do their jobs well, when they neglect to talk with their clients or to file motions in order to avoid "causing trouble" with judges, or when they view themselves as cogs in the system instead of advocates for the individual accused, the integrity of our system crumbles. No-crime wrongful convictions are a tragic but foreseeable outcome of bad lawyering. Only a committed lawyer, with sufficient time and resources, who listens to their client, investigates the case, and knows the relevant law can challenge the very idea that a crime occurred when it did not.

SIX

Judges

TILTING THE SCALES OF JUSTICE

IN 2004, RAYMOND TUCKER WAIVED his right to a jury and instead chose to let a judge decide his fate through a bench trial. In a bench trial, the judge is the decider of the facts as well as the law, and determines whether the prosecution has proved the defendant's guilt beyond a reasonable doubt.[1] At Tucker's bench trial, the prosecution called just one witness, Nicholas Sutliff.[2] Sutliff testified that he was mowing his lawn on August 18, 2003, when he saw a person whom he believed was Raymond Tucker jump over the fence from his backyard into the Tucker family's yard next door. The fence was twenty to twenty-five feet away from the back door of Sutliff's home. Sutliff had not seen Tucker for a long time, because Tucker had moved away years before. Sutliff and Tucker had a "history," and Sutliff had been "looking for [Tucker]" because there had been break-ins recently in the neighborhood. In fact, Sutliff warned police that Tucker had been paroled not long ago and that they should be looking for him; he further explained that he had been "tracking" Tucker using the Michigan Department of Corrections Offender Tracking Information System.

After he allegedly saw Tucker, Sutliff went into his home through his unlocked back door, which he claimed was slightly ajar. Sutliff also claimed that the top two dresser drawers were open. Initially, he did not notice that anything was missing. He then went to the Tucker family home to see if anyone there had seen Tucker. They had not. When he returned, Sutliff claimed that two rings he had placed on top of his dresser were missing. His watch, which he had also left atop the dresser, was still there, as were additional items and clutter.

At the conclusion of the bench trial, the judge ruled that the prosecution had offered evidence that Tucker had, beyond a reasonable doubt, committed the crime of home invasion, a second-degree felony:

Now, obviously there is not what you might call direct evidence about him being there, but ... I'm persuaded that the prosecution has proven their case beyond a reasonable doubt there, that the address was entered without permission and that it was done with the intent to commit larceny, and more importantly that the witness has identified [Tucker] as the person that entered the dwelling and I am persuaded beyond a reasonable doubt that he identifies this person as the person and not because of some prior history or some kind of vendetta, but that he is the person that he saw.[3]

The trial judge then sentenced Tucker to seven to fifteen years in prison.

On direct appeal, both state appellate courts affirmed his conviction without opinion. When Tucker filed a petition for a writ of habeas corpus in federal court, the U.S. district court ruled that his conviction should be reversed because it was not supported by the evidence.[4]

The prosecution then appealed the district court's ruling to the U.S. Sixth Circuit Court of Appeals. There, a panel of three judges reviewed the case. Two judges had no trouble upholding Tucker's conviction, finding it was supported by the evidence.[5] But one judge vehemently disagreed with his brethren and wrote a blistering dissent, the likes of which is rare to see.[6] I quote the dissenting opinion at length below because it makes a compelling case that Tucker had been convicted of a crime that simply did not occur, while judge after judge let it happen:

It is frightening that, in a case this devoid of facts, the prosecutor could have ever prosecuted Tucker in the first place. No reasonable jury (or judge), by any stretch of the imagination, could come to the conclusion that Tucker committed home invasion beyond a reasonable doubt.[7]

There was no evidence showing that Tucker damaged Sutliff's property to gain entrance into his house, there were no fingerprints placing Tucker in the Sutliff's home, there was no one who claims they saw Tucker in the Sutliff's home, there was no one who claims they saw Tucker exiting the Sutliff's home, the rings Sutliff claims Tucker stole were never found, and there was no evidence found on Tucker's person or in his possession that could link him to Sutliff's home.[8]

No rational trier of fact could find, beyond a reasonable doubt, from such evidence that Tucker entered Sutliff's home and stole rings therein. To infer that Tucker took the rings Sutliff allegedly owned solely based on the averred proximity of Tucker to Sutliff's house is to infer a fact from an inference. The state trial judge inferred from Tucker's presence in Sutliff's backyard that he entered Sutliff's home, and then from that inference, inferred that Tucker stole Sutliff's rings. In fact, there never was any proof that the rings existed in the first place.[9]

I am saddened, outraged, and in fact embarrassed for our judicial system that this case has reached this point. That this Court could affirm a state trial judge's conviction and sentence of seven to fifteen years in prison without a semblance of evidence of wrongdoing is a pathetic and dismal reflection of our judicial system. The trial judge, the state courts that affirmed his conviction, and indeed this Court have ruined Tucker's life (and likely that of his family as well). This case is so devoid of evidence that Tucker should never have been prosecuted, much less convicted.[10]

Unfortunately for Tucker, the dissenting opinion does not rule the day. Tucker remained in prison to complete his sentence, based on the thinnest of evidence that a crime even occurred in the first place.

Judges, up and down the legal system, decided Tucker's fate.

Judges often get a pass in the academic literature in discussions about causes of wrongful convictions. I don't think that pass is warranted. For every single wrongful conviction, a trial judge sat through the pretrial proceedings, decided motions, made evidentiary rulings, accepted a plea or the jury's verdict (or served as the finder of fact and law in a bench trial), entered the conviction, and pronounced the sentence. At any given moment, the trial judge had the power to question the factual sufficiency and quality of the evidence. In every no-crime case resulting in a wrongful conviction, the trial judge did not exercise that power. The same is true of appellate judges. For every no-crime wrongful conviction that a defendant appealed, a panel of appellate judges reviewed the record and decided to allow the conviction to stand or, on rare occasions, reversed and vacated the conviction with an order for a new trial or additional proceedings, usually after years of litigation and countless court filings.

At every stage of the criminal process, judges have the power to prevent or correct no-crime wrongful convictions. They often fail to do so.

THE ROLE OF THE TRIAL JUDGE

The adversarial system of American criminal justice rests on the premise that the truth will emerge through a clash of zealous advocates on the courtroom battlefield: the innocent will be acquitted and the guilty will be convicted. Presiding over the battle is the trial judge, tasked with safeguarding a defendant's constitutional rights which ensure that evidentiary and procedural rules are followed and that lawyers act in an ethical and responsible manner.

Trial judges' responsibilities are numerous. They are neutral umpires among adversaries, gatekeepers of evidence, and managers of pretrial litigation. They set their courtroom calendars, run their dockets, and call the cases. In some jurisdictions, they select and appoint attorneys to a case—no small power in what may be a saturated legal community where access to case appointments may determine a lawyer's livelihood. They resolve pretrial motions including, for example, defense requests to review the sufficiency of the grand jury proceedings, to suppress evidence such as eyewitness testimony or confessions, and to appoint an expert witness. If there is a hearing, judges make factual and legal determinations. If there is a trial, they oversee jury selection. They make evidentiary rulings such as whether a witness is qualified to testify as an expert and whether forensic and other physical and documentary evidence should be admitted. They rule on objections and issue instructions to the jury. Upon motion by the defense, they decide whether the prosecution presented legally sufficient evidence to support a conviction. If defendants, like Tucker, want to proceed to trial but waive their right to a jury, the judge conducts a bench trial, deciding the facts and applying the law in the case, and determines whether the prosecution met its burden of proof beyond a reasonable doubt. In many jurisdictions, if a defendant is convicted in a noncapital case, the judge determines the sentence.[11] Judges also accept plea bargains (or, in rare instances, reject them), after confirming that defendants are aware of the rights being waived and that there is an adequate factual basis for the plea, and then enter convictions and impose sentences.

In theory, trial judges perform these roles with fairness, impartiality and judiciousness. But the theoretical world of judges and judging is, regrettably, often light years away from what judges actually do, each and every day, in courtrooms around the country. First and foremost, judges are human beings, with their own biases and fallibilities. When they fail to do their jobs properly, they contribute to wrongful convictions generally and to no-crime wrongful convictions specifically. This chapter begins by examining judges who are anything but fair, focused, or impartial.[12] It then explores judges who fail to correctly and accurately perform the task of judging.

Bigotry in the Courtroom

Today's judges know that explicit bigotry is unacceptable. The American Bar Association rules for trial judges clearly state: "It is the responsibility of the trial judge to attempt to eliminate, both in chambers and in the courtroom, bias or prejudice due to race, sex, religion, national origin, disability, age, or sexual orientation."[13] But judges bring to the bench a whole host of biases that unconsciously—and sometimes quite consciously—impact their decision making beyond the facts of the case.

Research demonstrates that judges have unconscious biases that they bring to the bench. Legal scholar Jeffrey Rachlinski and colleagues conducted a study of the influence of unconscious racial biases on judges using the Implicit Association Test (IAT).[14] The IAT is a research tool developed by Harvard University psychologists that allows people to measure their unconscious biases. Millions of people have taken the IAT, which is available online for public use.[15] Participants are asked to associate words and faces; once their responses are put through a computer-based sorting program, their unconscious biases are revealed.

The Cornell study involved 133 trial judges from three different jurisdictions.[16] Researchers administered the IAT to the judges, and then gave them two hypothetical vignettes where the defendant's race was not made explicit but was subliminally primed, and another hypothetical vignette in which the defendant's race was made explicit. The judges were then asked to apply relevant law to these three fact patterns and render a decision.

The study found that judges have implicit racial biases and that those biases influence their judging. In cases where the judges were subliminally primed, white judges exhibited significantly high levels of implicit racial bias, with 87.1 percent of white judges and 44.2 percent of black judges showing white preference. When white judges, however, were given a fact pattern with race explicitly referenced (e.g., a black defendant assaulting a white victim or vice versa), they appeared equally willing to convict black and white defendants. The researchers hypothesized that when the white judges were alerted to the potential for race bias, they consciously compensated because they did not want to appear to have any racial preference.[17] The study demonstrated that judges' unconscious racial biases affected outcomes in hypothetical criminal cases, even though the race of the defendant should not have been a factor.

Civil rights attorney Bryan Stevenson is one of my personal heroes. Stevenson is the founder of the Equal Justice Initiative, a MacArthur Genius Award recipient, a death penalty lawyer who has successfully argued multiple cases before the U.S. Supreme Court, a law professor at New York University School of Law, and the author of the award-winning book *Just Mercy*.[18] He has testified before Congress, been a keynote speaker around the world, appeared on *60 Minutes,* was interviewed by Oprah, and has been featured in movies, magazines, and newspaper articles. He is also African American.

Stevenson talks about judges' implicit biases that he personally observes in his own work. He told the following story to Terry Gross on *Fresh Air* because it shows just how racially biased judges continue to be:

> I was in a courtroom in the Midwest not too long ago getting ready for a hearing. It was my first time there, and I had my suit on. I was sitting at defense counsel's table. I wanted to be early and the judge walked out followed by the prosecutor. And when the judge saw me sitting at the counsel table, he looked at me and he said, Hey, hey, hey, you get out of here. I don't want any defendant sitting in my courtroom until their lawyers get here. You go back out there in the hallway and wait for your lawyer.
>
> And I stood up and I said, Oh, I'm sorry your honor. My name is Bryan Stevenson. I'm actually the lawyer representing the client today. And the judge started laughing and the prosecutor started laughing and I made myself laugh, too, because I didn't want to disadvantage my client. And then my client came in. He was a young white kid who I was representing. And we did the hearing. And I went to my car after that, and I was really just tired. You know, you get so burdened down. It's exhausting confronting these presumptions. And I was worried about being in front of a judge that was prepared to presume my dangerousness, my status—even though I was in a suit—just because of my race.[19]

The judge who presided over that courtroom had formulated the unconscious belief that all black men in his courtroom were criminal defendants. He didn't even entertain the possibility that the black man in his courtroom was a lawyer. When the judge saw Bryan Stevenson—*Bryan Stevenson*—the judge assumed he was the criminal defendant. That's just what the judge believed.

That belief matters. It matters when judges act on unconscious racial biases in a criminal justice system that continues to disproportionately target and disfavor people of color.[20] When judges presume that the people in their courtroom must be guilty of *something* because of their race or ethnicity, they fall prey to implicit biases and make assumptions about guilt that are not supported by evidence. When judges minimize the humanity of the individual people before them, they become inured to the impact their decisions have and make careless or poorly conceived judicial rulings.

Aside from unconscious and implicit biases, some judges still put overt bigotry on full display in their courtroom dealings. Mississippi police pulled California truck driver Jagjeet Singh over in Pike County, Mississippi, for driving with a flat tire and ordered him to go to the nearest weigh station.[21] Singh, a devout Sikh, dressed according to the tenets of his religion. He wore a dastaar, which looks much like a turban, and a kirpan, a small, sheathed ceremonial dagger. Traffic officers wrongly contended that the kirpan was illegal and ordered Singh to remove it. Singh objected on religious grounds. Referring to him as a "terrorist," the officers arrested him for "failure to obey a lawful command." To be clear, there is no law that requires people to remove lawful religious symbols, which include a kirpan. Singh appeared in court, posted bail, and promised to return to Mississippi from California for his court date.

On the scheduled date, as promised, Singh traveled from California to court. While he sat waiting for his case to be called, Singh's lawyer went around the back of the courtroom to Judge Aubrey Rimes's chambers to request that the case be called as early in the day as possible to accommodate the other cases on the lawyer's schedule. This was a relatively common request as lawyers frequently have to attend numerous proceedings in any given day. Judge Rimes, however, informed the lawyer: "[Singh's] not going to be heard in my court until he takes that rag off his head." Stunned, the lawyer went to the courtroom to speak with Singh, who was at that very moment being escorted out of the courtroom by deputies. Singh and his lawyer were forced to wait the entire day for the judge to finish his calendar before they were permitted to reenter the courtroom. No doubt in an effort to avoid returning to court, Singh pled guilty to disobeying a lawful order and agreed to pay a fine.

The ACLU filed a complaint.[22] After the incident became public, the U.S. Department of Justice opened an investigation, resulting in the creation of new anti-harassment and nondiscrimination policies in Pike County. Judge Rimes, however, was not disciplined for his bigoted actions; at the time of this writing, he remains on the Pike County bench.[23]

Judge Rimes's display of bigotry is not unique. In 2018, Judge Peter Evans retired abruptly from the bench in Belle Glade, Florida, after he was caught referring to a black attorney as a "gorilla" in the West County Courthouse.[24] In that same year, Miami-Dade County circuit judge Stephen Milan described an African American defendant as a "moolie" and another African

American man's supporters as "thugs." Once the story broke, Milan too suddenly retired.[25]

Charleston, South Carolina, chief magistrate James B. Gosnell Jr.—the judge who presided over Dylann Roof's trial in 2017 for the racially motivated shootings of nine African Americans in Charleston, Virginia—had himself been publicly reprimanded for telling an African American man who appeared in his courtroom in 2003, "There are four kinds of people in this world—black people, white people, red-necks and n——s."[26] Gosnell shocked many at the 2015 bond hearing for Roof, when he reminded the packed courtroom full of African American mourners that, in addition to the nine shooting victims and their families, "there are victims on this young man's side of the family."[27]

In cases involving defendants of color, unconscious and overt racial biases may cause judges to set higher bail, rule against defendants more frequently than they should, allow prosecutors to violate the law by excluding black people from juries, lackadaisically review evidence while failing to ensure that the charges against the defendant have some basis in fact, accept guilty pleas with only cursory inquiries, fail to enforce legal and ethical standards, and mete out harsh sentences without regard for the facts or law.[28] When judges reduce people to one or another racial monolith who do not merit careful, individualized, thoughtful judging, the entire system stops functioning as it should. It is within that system that no-crime wrongful convictions—and perhaps all wrongful convictions—occur.

Judges Distracted by Addictions, Elections, or Greed

If biases have no place on the bench, neither do personal drug and alcohol addictions. It is the height of hypocrisy for judges to come to work drunk or high and then send people to prison for being drunk or high.

It also makes for bad judging.

Consider here the wrongful conviction of Raynella Dossett Leath for the murder of her husband, whose death was actually a suicide, after two trials presided over by the same drug-addicted judge.

Leath was a nurse in Texas. In 2003, her husband, David Leath, who had been diagnosed with dementia, was found dead of a gunshot wound. In her 911 call, Leath screamed into the phone that David had shot himself.[29] More than three years after his death, Leath was charged in 2006 with murdering David and then trying to make it look like a suicide.

Leath was tried *three* times for David's murder. The first trial, in 2009, was assigned to Judge Richard Baumgartner, and ended in a hung jury. Judge Baumgartner also presided over the second trial, in January 2010. This time, Leath was convicted of murder and sentenced to life imprisonment.[30] Leath filed a motion for a new trial in February 2010, and supplemented that motion in March and again in October. In her motion, Leath raised a host of legal claims and argued that she had newly discovered medical and scientific evidence that proved her innocence. In January 2011, Judge Baumgartner denied her motion. It was his last legal ruling from the bench; he resigned a few days later after learning he was the subject of an inquiry by the Tennessee Bureau of Investigation for drug-related misconduct.

Unbeknownst to Leath, Baumgartner had been in the full throes of opioid addiction throughout her trial. According to the appellate court, Baumgartner had been transformed from a "sound legal mind" in the period before 2008 to a "drug-induced judicial tyrant" who was completely "unhinged" during Leath's trial and while he was considering Leath's motion for a new trial.[31] During the trial, Baumgartner was taking twenty to thirty opiate pills a day. He adjourned court early and arrived late, and was in such a "fugue" state that he could not follow proper procedures. While on the bench during the Leath trial, he would lay his head down on the bench and appear to be sleeping. Meredith Driskell, Baumgartner's former court officer and a deputy sheriff, would repeatedly slam the courtroom door *during the trial* in an effort to wake him. Jurors approached Driskell to ask if Baumgartner was having problems. When he was awake, Judge Baumgartner could not remember details or his own rulings from one moment to the next. Inexplicably, he told the jury in the second trial that there had been a first trial, a highly improper comment, and then later acted surprised that the jury knew of the first trial.[32] His speech was slurred. He denigrated witnesses and interrupted the defense counsel's cross-examination of witnesses in an effort to move the proceedings along so he could get his next opioid fix.[33]

After Leath's conviction was reversed on appeal, she was tried for a third and final time in front of a new judge.[34] Leath presented compelling evidence of David's dementia diagnosis and mental deterioration, of his death as a suicide, and of her own alibi.[35] The newly assigned judge, after carefully listening to all the evidence presented by both the prosecution and the defense, took the highly unusual step of issuing a directed verdict in favor of Leath (that is, before the case was handed to the jury).[36]

Of course, Judge Baumgartner is not the only judge to have served on the bench while dealing with substance abuse.[37] While there are no definitive data about rates of addiction among judges, we do know that most judges come from the ranks of lawyers, and that an estimated 20 percent of lawyers have substance abuse problems and related issues.[38] When judges are impaired on the bench, they cannot properly perform their judicial functions. Perhaps Leath's first wrongful conviction for a murder that she claimed all along was a suicide could have been avoided with an alert and focused judge on the bench.

Electoral politics can also distract and improperly influence judges. Thirty-nine states use elections to choose at least some of their judges. Many candidates' judicial campaigns tout their "tough on crime" credentials. In one North Carolina judicial election, a judge was attacked for siding "with child predators" after having made a favorable defense ruling regarding the use of a monitoring bracelet.[39] Judicial electoral politics may result in decision making designed to curry favor with an electorate clamoring for convictions and lengthy sentences, rather than based on what the evidence requires.

Still other judges are distracted by greed, and they sell themselves—and justice—to the highest bidder. In 2007, Pennsylvania was rocked by the "Kids for Cash" scandal after it was discovered that two county judges had received more than $2.6 million from for-profit juvenile detention companies in return for steering as many juveniles as possible to their detention facilities. More than half of the children who appeared before these two judges had no legal representation and were not advised of their rights. Many had done no wrong under the law.[40] Fourteen-year-old Hillary Transue was adjudicated a delinquent and sentenced to three months in a juvenile detention facility because she posted a MySpace page mocking her school's assistant principle.[41] Twelve-year-old Justin Bodnar was found delinquent for making terroristic threats and was also shipped off to a juvenile detention center. His "offense"? Cursing in front of a classmate's mother at the bus stop. As these cases illustrate, many of the children sentenced to detention had committed no act of delinquency. Yet corrupt Pennsylvania judges packed juvenile detention centers to fill their wallets, punishing *thousands* of children for juvenile offenses that never happened.

Judges Who Are Antagonistic to the Defense Function

Judges are supposed to serve as the neutral arbiter between adversaries. Yet they sometimes engage in partisanship that favors the prosecution because they are antagonistic to the defense function. Many judges are former prosecutors; in the federal judiciary, the ratio of former prosecutors to former criminal defense attorneys is four to one.[42] As a result, they may continue to align themselves with the prosecutorial function.

Others judges simply view public defenders as a waste of court resources. Consider this anecdote that legal scholar Norman Lefstein tells in describing the hostility of judges to defense lawyers who try and do their jobs well:

> A part-time defender advised the Indiana Public Defender Commission that the trial judge in his county was refusing to assign cases to him. When interviewed, the judge readily explained that he regarded the defense attorney as a problem because his frequent visits to his jailed clients led to complaints from other defendants whose court-appointed lawyers visited them much less frequently. The judge also stated that this same defense lawyer filed too many motions, and as a result, prosecutors were less willing to plea bargain the cases of his clients. Finally, the judge noted that the defense lawyer's reimbursement claims were higher than those submitted by other defenders, which meant that his representation was costing the county too much money.[43]

In other words, the judge limited the number of cases he assigned this Indiana defense lawyer to punish him for providing good representation to clients. Worse, the judge saw nothing wrong with doing so. I've heard this frustration expressed by defense lawyers around the country who did "too good" of a job, and lost court appointments because of it.

Other judges express their disapproval of the defense function by abusing their power to hold lawyers in contempt of court. In New Orleans, judges held public defenders in contempt for reasons that are mind-boggling: for not being in a particular courtroom at a particular time, even if they notified court personnel of a schedule conflict in advance; for refusing to participate in a hearing for a client whom the lawyer had never met; for asking a question the judge deemed irrelevant; and for refusing to start a murder trial on a Monday after the prosecutor provided discovery only on the previous Friday.[44]

When judges liberally use their contempt power against defense lawyers, it sends a message of contempt to all defense lawyers. This can damage the attorney-client relationship, signal to jurors that the defense is not worthy of belief, and otherwise undermine the fairness and functionality of the adversarial system. It can also discourage defense lawyers from fully advocating for their clients; lawyers who fear punishment for doing their jobs may well decide it is not worth the risk. When demoralized or intimidated defense lawyers provide lackluster representation, the risk of no-crime wrongful convictions increases.

JUDGES WHO MISJUDGE THE LAW

Beyond the biases and distractions they bring to the courtroom, judges also contribute to no-crime wrongful convictions by failing to properly apply the law. Judges are tasked with ensuring that evidence is reliable and accurate before it is admitted at trial, but some allow evidence into court that is highly questionable and has no basis in reality or law. They look away when faced with bad lawyering or prosecutorial misconduct. They impose shocking sentences on defendants who exercise their right to trial. In the context of guilty pleas, they fail to properly probe the factual basis for the admission of guilt.

Judges Admit Unreliable Evidence in Court

With regard to forensic evidence, trial judges act as gatekeepers in deciding which evidence to allow in court. But not all forensic evidence is created equal. Contrary to the *CSI* television shows, not all "forensic science" is reliable and accurate—or even based in science. This includes most comparative-pattern forensics, such as fingerprint identification, shoe print analysis, bite mark analysis, bullet-matching analysis, hair-matching analysis, and voice identification. In 2009, the National Academy of Sciences issued a landmark report condemning the pervasive use of junk forensic evidence in criminal cases: "With the exception of nuclear DNA analysis . . . no forensic method has been rigorously shown to have the capacity to consistently, and with a high degree of certainty, demonstrate a connection between evidence and a specific individual or source."[45] Even DNA evidence—the forensic gold standard—is not foolproof. DNA evidence can be contaminated, degraded, improperly transferred, or improperly interpreted—all of which can result in the erroneous conviction of an innocent person.

The judge should not allow any irrelevant or unreliable evidence to be presented in court, because it might mislead or confuse the jury. The standard used by judges to evaluate the admissibility of evidence depends on the jurisdiction. In a minority of states, judges apply the *Frye* test, which asks whether there is "general acceptance" of the proffered testimony in the field from which it comes.[46] Most states, however, use the *Daubert* test, which requires judges to evaluate the methods and principles on which the evidence is based.[47] Under *Daubert,* courts should admit only science supported by appropriate validation and empirical testing. The *Daubert* standard encourages peer review and publication, examination of error rates, maintenance of standards, and general acceptance by the scientific community.

Daubert sets a high standard for the admission of forensic evidence. Yet, as a 2015 *New York Times* editorial lamented: "[C]ourts have only made the problem worse by purporting to be scientifically literate, and allowing in all kinds of evidence that would not make it within shouting distance of a peer-reviewed journal. Of the 329 exonerations based on DNA testing since 1989, more than one-quarter involved convictions based on 'pattern' evidence— like hair samples, ballistics, tire tracks, and bite marks—testified to by so-called experts."[48]

Innocent people, such as Leigh Stubbs and Tammy Vance (whose cases are mentioned in chapter 4), know firsthand what happens when a judge allows an unreliable expert to present bad forensic science at trial.[49] Stubbs and Vance met in a Mississippi drug rehabilitation center.[50] In March 2000, the two women, along with a third acquaintance, Kim Williams, were released from the rehab center. The three women drove to the home of Williams's boyfriend, who had a vial of OxyContin, prescribed by a doctor for an injury.

Williams and Vance relapsed immediately, taking the boyfriend's OxyContin and drinking alcohol. Stubbs remained sober. The three women left the boyfriend's home and checked into a Comfort Inn in Brookhaven, Mississippi, where they fell asleep. The next morning, Stubbs and Vance realized Williams was having trouble breathing, and they called an ambulance for assistance. Williams had overdosed. She recovered but claimed to have no memory of what, if anything, had happened the previous night.

Enter Michael West. Throughout the 1990s, Michael West, a dentist from Mississippi, was one of the nation's most prolific forensic odontologists (a fancy title for someone who claims to be able to match bite marks on a victim or an object to a criminal suspect).[51] West invented a method of bite mark analysis that he called the "West Phenomenon" and that, he insisted, only he could perform.[52]

West was at the heart of a firestorm about bite mark testimony. Although he considered himself a "genius" and once claimed under oath in court that his own error rate was merely "something less than [that of] my savior, Jesus Christ," West came under fire as a "quack" starting in the mid-1990s.

Nonetheless, even though he had been widely discredited in Mississippi and elsewhere, a few days after Williams was admitted to the hospital on that March 2000 evening, the prosecutor asked West to examine Williams's injuries.

The rest of the story is beyond bizarre.

West first claimed that Williams had bite marks on her body that no other reviewing medical professional—or anyone else for that matter—had seen. By the time West obtained dental impressions from Stubbs and Vance, however, Williams's alleged bite wounds had healed. West did not see this as a forensic obstacle. Instead, he analyzed the dental impressions and compared them to his own *photographs* of Williams's so-called bite wounds. Not surprisingly, he claimed to find a match between Stubbs and the alleged bite mark.

But West's abilities seemed to have no end.

The Comfort Inn had a security camera in the parking lot. The prosecutor sent the low-quality video recording from the security camera to the FBI. The FBI found nothing incriminating in the grainy video footage. The prosecution, however, did not release the video or the FBI findings to the defense as required under *Brady*. Instead, it gave the video to West, who, unlike the FBI, claimed to have enhanced the video and to have identified images that, he claimed, showed Stubbs and Vance injuring Williams. While his conclusions were impressive, they were also impossible. Video enhancement from a grainy recording of a dimly lit parking lot is the stuff of television shows, but not the stuff of real forensic science—certainly not back in the year 2000.

But the trial judge allowed all of West's "evidence" into the courtroom. The judge allowed West to testify that Williams had been bitten and that the bite marks matched the defendants' dentition. The judge further allowed West, *the dentist,* to testify about his enhanced video techniques— techniques so sophisticated that even the FBI didn't have them—to prove that Stubbs and Vance had harmed Williams. Rather than serve as an evidentiary gatekeeper, the trial judge threw the courtroom gates wide open and allowed in a parade of unreliable evidence.

This was not the only evidentiary error in the case. As discussed in chapter 4, the judge also admitted inflammatory testimony at trial that should have been excluded as irrelevant, speculative, and prejudicial. He allowed West and another prosecution witness to insinuate—without evidence—that Stubbs and Vance were lesbians, and then to testify, without any evidentiary support, that bite marks in an assault involving gay people "wouldn't be uncommon" and that they would "almost" be expected.

Stubbs and Vance were convicted in 2001. The judge sentenced each of them to forty-four years in prison.

After eleven years in prison, an appellate court overturned their convictions. The reversal rested solely on the prosecution's failure under *Brady* to turn over exculpatory evidence in the form of the FBI's report about the video.[53] The appellate court, however, did not decide whether the trial court erred in allowing West to testify or about the quality of the bite mark evidence or the inflammatory evidence that the judge had permitted at trial.

I'm going to say what the appellate court did not. The judge should never have qualified West as an expert in the first place. He should not have allowed West to testify about questionable bite mark comparisons. He should not have allowed West to testify about his findings from an allegedly enhanced surveillance video that even the FBI could not improve. He should not have allowed the prosecutor to make innuendos about the sexual orientation of Vance or Stubbs, or to introduce unproven expert testimony about the so-called violent tendencies of people who are gay. But the judge allowed that, and more, and as a result, the women collectively lost more than two decades of their lives.

No-crime wrongful convictions are plagued by unreliable forensic evidence, provided by unqualified and unreliable experts. Table 1 in the introduction shows that 29 percent of no-crime wrongful cases in the NRE database involved bad forensic science. Yet judges across the country continue to admit discredited science—such as bite mark comparisons and blood splatter analysis—into courtrooms as evidence against defendants.[54]

Judges Ignore or Acquiesce to Horrendous Lawyering and Prosecutorial Misconduct

This book has already recounted horror stories about defendants whose lawyers failed to provide even minimal representation for their clients. Where were the judges who retained responsibility "for the proper functioning of our legal system?"[55] Judges who witness bad lawyering—sleeping or drunk lawyers, lawyers who are unaware of the law or the facts, lawyers who did no investigation, lawyers who call the wrong witnesses or make the wrong arguments—are supposed to take measures to ensure that a defendant is actually receiving effective assistance of counsel. Most of the time they choose to do nothing.

Judges have a front row seat. But they act as if they can't see the show.

Similarly, judges rarely call out prosecutorial misconduct. They routinely ignore the prosecution's improper questioning of witnesses, inflammatory closing arguments, and blatant *Brady* violations.

On the rare occasion that they do take action, they may be reprimanded for it. Consider what happened in one courtroom in the Bronx, where Criminal Court judge John Wilson forcefully intervened in the face of a *Brady* violation that nearly resulted in a no-crime wrongful conviction. Segundo Marquez was held at Rikers Island for more than eight months while awaiting trial for a sexual assault. At the very end of the two-week trial and after the defense made its closing argument to the jury, the prosecutor revealed for the first time that it possessed evidence that supported Marquez's innocence. Apparently, the alleged victim had initially told the police that the purported sexual encounter was consensual and not an assault. In other words, as conceded by the alleged victim, no crime had occurred. This statement had been in the file since the defendant was arrested and throughout the investigation of the case, the pretrial proceedings, and the trial. When a supervisor finally disclosed the information to the judge, the case was promptly dismissed and the defendant was released.[56] The prosecutor claimed no malice, explaining that the error occurred because multiple lawyers had handled the case.[57]

Judge Wilson was livid. He castigated the Bronx assistant district attorney Megan Teesdale: "To my mind, this is an utter and complete disgrace—not just for you, but for your office in general." Wilson continued: "The excuse you offer, passing the file back and forth, no one looking and no one knowing what anything is, saddens me on one level and makes me sick on another." Wilson then barred the prosecutor from his courtroom, an infrequently invoked rebuke that judges can use to hold prosecutors accountable for misconduct.

Shortly after this incident, however, Judge Wilson found himself the subject of an investigation for ordering Teesdale from his courtroom.[58] The New York State Commission on Judicial Misconduct asked Judge Wilson to justify his courtroom remarks to the prosecutor. The *judge*—not the prosecutor—was investigated for misconduct. The outcome of this judicial inquiry was never made public, nor does it appear that Teesdale was ever disciplined, at least not in public, by her office or the bar association for her failure to meet the *Brady* mandate.

It is not surprising that judges so rarely call out prosecutorial misconduct when they see it.[59]

JUDICIAL ACCEPTANCE OF PLEAS TO CRIMES
THAT NEVER HAPPENED

In the plea process, the prosecutor and defense attorney actively engage in plea negotiations, while the trial judge takes a passive role. The American Bar Association (ABA) Standards of Criminal Justice and Rule 11 of the Federal Rules of Criminal Procedure, as well as many state court systems, require judges to refrain from participating in the plea process until an agreement is reached.[60] The idea is to encourage judges to remain impartial and to avoid any coercion that could come from judicial intervention in the plea process.

But judges are not without any power with regard to pleas. They have an obligation to ensure that the plea is voluntary, knowing, and intelligent, and that it serves the public interest and would otherwise further the administration of justice. Judges are required to ensure that there is a factual basis for the plea. If any of these conditions are not met, judges can reject the plea. Yet, as shown throughout this book, judges accept pleas from innocent people without an established factual basis, such as in drug cases without lab tests, or where people proclaim their innocence but nonetheless plead guilty. In fact, they seem most likely to reject plea offers they consider too lenient given the particular crime and the particular defendant rather than because they are concerned about a dearth of evidence.[61]

Because judges are not part of the negotiation process, they fly blind when performing their task of ensuring a factual basis for the plea conviction. They have no real sense of the alleged crime or the strengths or weaknesses of the prosecution's case or of the defendant as an individual. The easiest route for a judge to take is to defer to the prosecution and defense, accept the negotiated plea agreement, and not deliberate much about whether it is just or appropriate to do so. Further, judges know that most plea convictions are not subjected to appellate review, especially in plea cases involving a waiver of the right to appeal. It is a quick and easy way to move weak or problematic cases through the system while avoiding appellate scrutiny.

Judges accept pleas from the factually innocent for various reasons. Plea bargains promote efficiency, reduce excessive caseloads, and prevent a crushing backlog of cases. This is a real and pressing concern. A 1982 study found that a reduction of just 10 percent in the number of defendants who plead guilty would require more than twice the number of judges and related judicial resources than existed at the time.[62] And that study was conducted *before* the tough-on-crime policies of the 1980s and 1990s flooded the criminal justice system and left judges staggering under heavier caseloads. Judges continue to experience increased caseloads without a corresponding increase in the number of members on the bench. The number of judges in federal court, for instance, increased by 4 percent from 1993 to 2013, while caseloads in that same period increased by 28 percent.[63]

Then there are the controversial *Alford* pleas, in which defendants plead guilty while maintaining their factual innocence. In *Alford v. North Carolina* (1970), the U.S. Supreme Court recognized that sometimes it is in a defendant's best interests to plead guilty, regardless of their protestations of innocence. Judges are supposed to find a "strong factual basis" before accepting an *Alford* plea. But examples abound from across the country where judges have accepted *Alford* pleas given a record completely devoid of evidence.[64] Failing to hold the prosecution to its evidentiary burden while accepting a guilty plea from a defendant who is proclaiming their innocence seems problematic, to say the least.

To make matters worse, some judges do everything they can to entice defendants to plead. Senior Judge Leonard Zito has run the Northampton County Criminal Docket in eastern Pennsylvania since 2010. Home to about 300,000 people in the waning steel town of Bethlehem, Judge Zito has done his work with great efficiency.[65] Even though the state of Pennsylvania expressly prohibits judicial participation in plea bargaining,[66] Judge Zito has created a court culture that encourages defendants to plead guilty at arraignment. His "meet 'em and plead 'em" vision of justice has proved incredibly successful from a case management perspective: more than 80 percent of cases in Northampton County are resolved at arraignment.[67] As a point of comparison, in New York City, home to one of the nation's largest and most congested criminal dockets, roughly 57 percent of misdemeanor cases are resolved at arraignment.[68]

But efficiency has its price. While defendants may receive attractive plea deals at arraignment, this is the accused's first appearance in court. At that early stage of the proceedings, they have not seen the evidence against them, and their lawyers have not had an opportunity to investigate their cases, file motions, or explore possible defenses. When Northampton lawyers pushed back on the expedited timeline, Judge Zito allegedly retaliated. One defense lawyer took the extraordinary step of asking the judge to recuse himself from a case, alleging that Zito routinely strong-armed defendants into pleading guilty even when they were not ready to do so.[69]

Examples of Zito's alleged tactics abound. The judge forced Brian Turner, a defendant who refused to plead guilty, to represent himself at trial without first informing him of his right to counsel or asking him whether he was willing to proceed to trial without a lawyer. At a bench trial, Zito found Turner guilty. The conviction was overturned when a higher court determined that Zito had deprived Turner of his constitutional right to an attorney.[70]

Or take Jessica D. Trump (no known relationship to the presidential family). She was arrested in Northampton County for a drunk-driving offense but insisted she was innocent. When she said she wanted her day in court, Judge Zito confiscated her driver's license in the courtroom. *At arraignment.* Apparently, Zito routinely confiscated defendants' driver's licenses as a condition of bail in cases not resolved by plea at arraignment—no small consequence in an area that requires people to drive to get around. When asked about the policy, the judge made clear his opinion about the accused: "Should we just scrap the whole thing, buy them a case of beer, and let them go out and drive?"[71]

Trump, however, argued that she was not driving the car, which was stopped on the side of the road with its hazard lights flashing. She wanted a trial, even after Judge Zito confiscated her license. At the proceedings before Judge Michael J. Koury, a colleague of Zito's in the small courthouse community, she told her story to a jury and called other witnesses to testify on her behalf, all of whom agreed she was not driving the car. Instead, they said that the actual driver, Brad Wilcox, had just gotten out of the car to unlock the back door of his home. Even the arresting officer conceded on the stand that he could not be sure that she had been driving. A jury of twelve people acquitted her of second-offense drunk driving. Minutes later, Judge Koury volunteered to resolve, rather than dismiss, a lesser included general impairment DUI charge, a petty offense for which defendants are not entitled to a jury. Unlike the jury, Judge Koury did not credit Trump's testimony and instead found her guilty.[72] This extraordinary action sent a clear message to anyone paying attention about the dangers of going to trial in Northampton.

Judges Threaten Heavy Penalties after Trial, Causing Innocent Defendants to Improperly Plead Guilty

As the following chapter further details, innocent defendants plead guilty to crimes they did not commit and that did not happen. They do so for a variety of reasons, including the threat of the "trial penalty," defined by the National Association of Criminal Defense Lawyers as the "discrepancy between the sentence the prosecutor is willing to offer in exchange for a guilty plea and the sentence that would be imposed after trial."[73] Sometimes, innocent defendants are offered lenient sentences in exchange for pleading guilty; they reject those offers at great risk, because the outcome after a trial conviction is often dire.

While prosecutors are the ones primarily in control of plea negotiations and agreements, judges often decide the sentence after trial and do so harshly. In some cases, judges may have no choice but to impose a mandatory minimum sentence after trial. But sometimes judges impose severe sentences to punish defendants for asserting their constitutional right to proceed to trial. The resulting trial penalty is often exponentially more severe than the plea offer and sends a clear warning about what happens to defendants who dare to demand their day in court.

Consider the trial penalty in the Tulia cases discussed in chapters 3 and 5. When the first defendants took their cases to trial, they received absurdly long sentences. In the worst example, William Cash Love, a twenty-five-year-old white father of a biracial child, was sentenced to *361 years* in prison after he took his case to trial. After hearing about the lengthy trial sentences, the remaining Tulia defendants lined up quickly to take pleas.

In all the coverage of Tulia, judges were rarely mentioned. Yet judges blithely accepted guilty plea after guilty plea from Tulia defendants who had been intimidated by the trial penalties into admitting guilt to crimes that never happened. Did the judges truly believe that those pleas, made solely to avoid draconian sentences if the defendants exercised their right to trial and lost, were knowing and voluntary, as required by the Constitution?[74]

Even those Tulia defendants who took a plea deal did not fully escape the extraordinarily harsh sentencing regime. At least three of the defendants who pled guilty received sentence as long as eighteen years in prison.[75] Judges are supposed to impose sentences that are not only lawful but also fair and proportionate. The Tulia judges seemed to have checked those principles at the courthouse door, perhaps assuming no one would be the wiser.

Courts Apply Appellate Legal Standards That Don't Help the Innocent

Appellate judging is dramatically different from trial judging in that the purpose and function of appellate courts are different. Whereas a trial is a search for truth in which the defendant is presumed innocent until proven guilty, an appeal is a check to ensure the defendant was convicted after a fair process. On appeal, where defendants are now presumed guilty, the defense—not the prosecution—bears the burden of proving the conviction is invalid. Innocence claims can get lost in the appellate process because appellate courts do not make factual determinations on direct appeal. Indeed, appellate courts apply extremely deferential standards of review when considering the merits of defendants' claims of error.

Harmless Error

One of the reasons that criminal defendants rarely prevail on appeal is that courts rely on "harmless error" in reviewing appellate claims. Applying the harmless error doctrine can be quite complex, and the standards of review that appellate courts apply vary depending on the nature of the claim. But, as discussed briefly in chapter 5, the harmless error doctrine enables courts to find that even if a legal error occurred at trial, the conviction can be upheld because the error was not material, substantial, or prejudicial to the defendant. In other words, courts can find the existence of an error, but dismiss it as harmless.

Harmless error requires judges to look in hindsight and predict what might have been; that is, "Would the result have been different but for the error?" This speculative process is made all the more difficult because judges fall prey to "hindsight bias."[76] Briefly stated, hindsight bias makes past events seem inevitable and clearly predictable after they have actually unfolded.

Psychologist Daniel Kahneman won a Nobel Prize in 2002 for his work in behavioral economics. In his award-winning book *Thinking, Fast and Slow,* Kahneman describes the phenomenon of hindsight bias by looking at sport teams. Let's say there are two football teams that appear evenly matched. In a game between the two, one team prevails over the other by a wide margin. That team was, we conclude, clearly stronger than the other. In retrospect, the victory of the winning team often seems to have been inevitable. Winning teams, Kahneman writes, appear in hindsight to have been much stronger than losing ones.[77]

Kahneman's insight about hindsight bias applies equally to appellate judges. The very fact that a defendant was convicted influences appellate judges' assessment of what might otherwise have been.[78] Judicial awareness of the result (i.e., that a defendant was found guilty) creates a bias that makes a defendant's conviction seem inevitable despite whatever error may have occurred leading up to it. This hindsight bias causes judges to minimize errors as harmless: they think the conviction would have happened even in the absence of the error.

Legal scholar Brandon Garrett conducted a groundbreaking study of the first two hundred DNA-based exonerations.[79] More than 90 percent of these cases involved rape and murder. In each of those cases, DNA evidence conclusively established that the defendants were factually innocent of the crimes for which they had been convicted. But *before* the DNA results were available, courts throughout the appellate process misjudged the likelihood that a defendant was innocent. In 50 percent of the cases in Garrett's study, courts that denied a defendant's claims of error referenced the likely guilt of the accused, and in 10 percent of cases, courts cited the *overwhelming evidence* of guilt in their harmless error evaluation.[80] As DNA would later prove, the appellate courts were entirely wrong.

As with the actual-crime wrongful convictions referenced in Garrett's study, harmless error analysis can also fail the innocent in cases where no crime was committed. Take, for instance, the case of Gregory Agnew.[81] Agnew was charged in Illinois with armed robbery after an altercation at a gas station where he allegedly hit a man with a garden hoe and then took one dollar. After a jury trial in Illinois in 1988, Agnew was convicted of robbery and was sentenced to thirty years in prison. (Before reading further, please pause for one moment to process the fact that a judge sentenced a man to thirty years in prison for allegedly stealing a dollar and for causing eight stitches. A serious incident, perhaps, but people who commit far more serious offenses are routinely sentenced to far less than thirty years in prison.)

Before the trial, Agnew had planned to testify. He would admit that there was an altercation but that the so-called victim had been the aggressor and that his use of force was not a crime because it was legally justified and permissible under the circumstances. In an effort to prove its case, the prosecution initially called three witnesses, including the so-called victim, who told conflicting and changing stories. Later, the prosecutor announced that it was also going to call the courtroom bailiff to testify, Deputy Fred House. Throughout the trial, Deputy House had been attending to the jury, providing them with lunch, escorting them to and from the courtroom and to the bathroom, and engaging in idle chitchat. Despite his active influence with the jury, the prosecution wanted Deputy House to testify as a rebuttal witness if Agnew raised a claim of self-defense. According to the prosecution, the deputy would testify that Agnew, four months earlier and on the date of his arrest, confessed to stealing the dollar.

Agnew's lawyer immediately moved for a mistrial. This makes sense. A bailiff often forms a special bond with the jury, whose members would therefore tend to trust his or her testimony because they had previously trusted the bailiff with their safety and well-being. It would have been easy enough for the trial judge to grant a mistrial and begin again. The trial court instead denied the defense motion.

Agnew testified on his own behalf, and the prosecution called the deputy to the stand, who testified that he had met Agnew on the day he was arrested and that Agnew told the deputy he was at the jail "over a dollar. Fucked up. This is over one dollar. Someone should beat my ass and let me go home." In closing arguments, the prosecution characterized Agnew's statement as an admission of guilt and mentioned it no fewer than six times.

It took the jury just thirty-one minutes to find Agnew guilty.

On appeal, Agnew argued that the trial court should have granted a mistrial and that it erred in allowing Deputy House to testify about this so-called confession. The state intermediate appellate court found that the deputy's dual role in the courtroom as a bailiff and a witness was harmless. The Illinois Supreme Court twice refused to review his case on direct appeal, finding no issue worthy of appellate review. Agnew then filed a petition for habeas corpus in federal district court, arguing among other issues that it was error to have allowed the deputy to testify. The district court dismissed this claim, again finding harmless error.

Finally, thirteen years later, in 2001, the Seventh Circuit U.S. Court of Appeals reversed Agnew's conviction. The court determined that the trial judge's decision to allow the deputy to testify was not harmless after all. Deputy House was the only witness to testify about the alleged confession, and his testimony was uncorroborated by any other witness, many of whom told inconsistent stories. Further, the court found, the deputy had formed a relationship with the jury, and his testimony was likely to influence their view of the case. As the court ruled: "[B]ecause the bailiff's contacts with the jury were of a continuous and intimate nature typical of the bailiff/jury relationship and because Deputy House's testimony constituted substantive evidence of Agnew's guilt, the trial court should have granted a mistrial to avoid the extreme prejudice inherent in these circumstances."[82]

Agnew was tried again in 2001. The prosecution witnesses had recanted their testimony long before, and this time there was no improper testimony from a bailiff. Agnew was acquitted. He had spent thirteen years in prison for a crime that never happened. It took him another sixteen years—until 2017—before the state of Illinois officially recognized his innocence and provided compensation for his wrongful conviction.[83]

Appellate court after appellate court relied upon the harmless error doctrine to uphold Agnew's conviction. How many other innocent defendants languish in prison because of damning errors that appellate courts wrongly label harmless?

Various iterations of harmless error analysis are used to sustain innocent defendants' convictions. Consider the appellate standard articulated in *Strickland v. Washington* (1984) for evaluating whether a defendant was denied his right to the effective assistance of counsel. *Strickland* requires a defendant to prove not only that counsel was deficient but that the deficient performance prejudiced the defendant.[84] The *Strickland* prejudice standard has been cynically called the "warm body" test. In all but the most egregious of cases, any defense counsel who can fog a mirror held under their nose is deemed effective.[85]

The same is true of appellate standards in the context of *Brady* violations. A defendant's conviction on appeal is rarely overturned unless the defendant can show that the prosecution failed to turn over evidence that was *material* to the defendant's case. But despite the prevalence of *Brady* violations, defendants almost never obtain relief because the appellate standard of review for *Brady* violations is "impossibly high."[86] In other words, appellate courts promote a culture in which prosecutors flout their constitutional obligations, secure in the knowledge that they will never be held accountable by a reviewing court. It is within this *Brady* vacuum, where exculpatory evidence is hidden from the defense, that no-crime wrongful convictions occur.

The black-robed men and women who sit in judgment on people in the criminal justice system contribute to no-crime wrongful convictions in ways that could be greatly curtailed. On a personal level, judges could become more aware of their own biases and work harder to ensure fairness and impartiality in their courtrooms. They could eschew electoral politics and focus on meting out justice for each individual who comes through their courtroom doors. They could serve as a check against bad lawyering. They could require that prosecutors and their witnesses meet evidentiary and constitutional standards, and prevent them for making improper arguments to the jury. They could carefully screen forensic evidence, and limit admission only to reliable science. They could ensure that defendants plead guilty only to crimes that have a factual footing.

But they don't. And because trial judges don't do what they should, innocent people are convicted of crimes that never happened. They then wind up in an appellate process that sometimes feels like Alice in Wonderland, where judges deem harmful errors to be harmless and prioritize finality over factual innocence.

SEVEN

Misdemeanors

NOT MINOR MATTERS

I WORKED AS A PUBLIC defender in the late 1990s, in a busy office of a bustling courthouse in the South Bronx once made famous by Tom Wolfe in *Bonfire of the Vanities*. The building was dusty and packed with people from all walks of life: defendants, their families (including children), lawyers, prosecutors, court officers, correctional staff, security personnel, police officers, investigators, stenographers, witnesses, jurors, grand jurors, inmates, judges, defense attorneys carrying multiple files from courtroom to courtroom in search of their clients, prosecutors, and anyone else who might be needed in court on any particular day. It sometimes felt like ordered chaos—and sometimes just chaos—but I loved my job and worked hard, albeit not always successfully, to reach outcomes that were in my clients' best interests.

The way I received new cases was through arraignments. There, in the holding cells tucked behind the arraignment court, I would meet my new clients for the first time. After being arrested and booked, they had spent hours (sometimes overnight) behind bars waiting for their first court appearance.[1] They would appear dazed and uncomfortable as they urgently tried to explain to me what had happened, a process made all the more difficult when English was not their first language. These semiprivate conversations would take place amid a cacophony of clanging cell doors, officers talking and shouting orders, and outbursts from other defendants who, like some of my own clients, may have been high, experiencing withdrawal, or suffering from severe mental illnesses. I would nonetheless try to get as much information as I could from them about their case and the basis for their arrest, about their family and their employment history, and about anything else that could be useful in those brief few minutes before their cases were called before the judge.

One common misdemeanor charge my clients faced was trespass. Trespass involves one person entering or staying on another person's property without legal authority or permission to do so. In New York, trespass can be a noncriminal violation, a misdemeanor, or in rare cases, a felony.[2] In virtually every case, the misdemeanor trespass allegations in my client's criminal complaints contained the same boilerplate. The police would claim they saw my client in a building, that they asked my client whether they lived there, and that my client said they did not know anyone in the building. Based on this alleged conversation, the police would arrest the suspect, conduct an invasive search of their person as part of the arrest, and bring them to the precinct for further processing.

At arraignment—the very first time my client would appear before a judge—the prosecution would likely offer a plea. For a first offender, the plea offer might be a reduction from the misdemeanor trespass to a noncriminal violation with time served. Or the prosecution might offer only the misdemeanor trespass conviction, but with time served. If my client had a criminal record or a history of trespass charges, the prosecution might seek added conditions, such as a monetary fine, community service, or even a short jail sentence.

I would ask my clients, usually and ideally before the arraignment, what they wanted to do. I would explain that trespass occurs only when a person enters or remains *unlawfully* in a building, and that it was not a crime to enter and exit your own apartment building or to visit a friend or family member in their apartment building. For those who had permission to be on the premises, I would tell them that they did nothing wrong and that they should not plead guilty to a crime that never happened. I would promise my clients that if they were willing to fight the charges, I would make a motion to dismiss the case because it had no basis in fact. I would promise to have a hearing on the issue. Or even go to trial. If they would come back to court, I would do my best to prove the charges had no legal basis.

My innocent clients, who were poor and almost always black or brown, invariably took the arraignment plea offer. They didn't want the very real hassle and inconvenience of having to deal with the criminal court logistics—endless security lines, bag searches, and courtroom delays—even to fight a case that should never have been brought. They could not afford to miss more work. They had no one to watch their children or help their elderly relatives. It was a rare case when my client was willing to litigate a trespass charge to the bitter end. For the few who agreed to return, I filed motions to dismiss their cases. We often, though not always, prevailed. In other cases, my clients started out willing to challenge the charges but eventually decided to plead because the fight was too burdensome.

I left the Bronx public defender's office well before a series of lawsuits were filed, discussed later in this chapter, that challenged the NYPD's aggressive pursuit of trespass cases and the NYPD's stop-and-frisk practices in general. But they highlight a much larger problem that exists in urban policing today: the routine and indifferent arrest and processing of massive numbers of poor people of color into and out of our criminal justice system for low-level misdemeanor offenses, many of which never happened in the first place, under the guise of fighting crime.

MISDEMEANOR PROCESSING IN THE CRIMINAL JUSTICE SYSTEM (THE BIG PICTURE)

Misdemeanor crimes are crimes that can be punished by up to one year in jail. Minor drug possession, driving while intoxicated, petty theft, prostitution, fare jumping, graffiti, trespassing, loitering, certain assaults, and disorderly conduct are all examples of misdemeanor crimes. By one estimate, 13.2 million misdemeanor cases are filed *every year,* yielding millions and millions of misdemeanor convictions annually.[3]

How many of these cases involve innocent people who were charged with crimes that did not happen? No one knows the answer to that question. In truth, data about misdemeanor wrongful convictions are scarce. Innocent people who plead guilty in misdemeanor cases are rarely later identified and almost never exonerated for their crimes. In fact, even though misdemeanor cases make up the bulk of crimes in the criminal justice system, they represent less than 4 percent of all known exonerations in the NRE database.[4] The dearth of information in this area reflects practical limits to data collection, and not the actual absence of wrongful convictions in misdemeanor cases. As this chapter shows, it appears that innocent people are convicted of misdemeanor crimes that never happened far more often than anyone realizes.

The Misdemeanor Process Itself Encourages No-Crime Wrongful Convictions

Once the police decide that a person has committed a misdemeanor, they have a choice: they can do nothing or issue a warning and send the person on their way; they can issue a summons, which directs the person to go to court to resolve the charges; or they can make an arrest. The initial police decision about whether to place a person under arrest has consequences for the individual and for the entire trajectory of the case.

An arrest itself is a traumatic affair. In 2006, the National Association for the Advancement of Colored People (NAACP) in Maryland sued the Baltimore City Police for what it described as their practice of illegally and unconstitutionally arresting young men—many of whom are African American—without any basis for doing so.[5] The NAACP's legal complaint vividly describes the humiliating and all too typical experience of two young men who were arrested for the low-level misdemeanor offense of loitering in an area where they were permitted to be.

Evan Howard and Tyrone Braxton were talking on the sidewalk outside of Howard's home at around 8:30 PM on Friday, April 15, 2005.[6] The police arrived in an unmarked car, and soon after arrested Howard and Braxton for loitering. The police used plastic handcuffs to bind the young men's hands tightly behind their backs. Howard and Braxton were taken to the Maryland Central Booking and Intake Center (CBIC), where they waited for roughly an hour to be booked. They were screened with a metal detector for weapons that they did not have. At approximately 11:00 PM, the police engaged in a humiliating public strip search in which Howard, Braxton, and two other detainees were "placed in a holding cell, ordered to remove all of their clothing down to their underpants, face the wall, pull their underpants down to expose their buttocks, and submit to a visual body cavity search."[7] No contraband was found.

After the strip search, Howard and Braxton were taken to a "small, filthy, and overcrowded cell, where they stayed with about ten other detainees through the night. The cell had no bathroom and was so overcrowded that both Howard and Braxton were forced to sit in uncomfortable positions on filthy floors for long periods of time." The next morning, Saturday, April 16, Howard and Braxton were moved to a slightly larger cell with fifteen other detainees. This cell was also "filthy and unsanitary," and again Howard and Braxton were forced to sit in uncomfortable positions on filthy floors for extended periods. The meals provided to them three times a day consisted of "two slices of bread covering shiny and slimy meat."[8]

Thirty-six hours after his arrest, Braxton was released from the CBIC. Howard was finally released on Monday, April 18, at 4:00 A.M., after being held at the intake center for fifty-four hours. Neither Howard nor Braxton was ever formally prosecuted for the crime of loitering—presumably because the alleged loitering had never happened. But they had been forced to endure mistreatment and degradation during their arrest for a low-level crime that had not occurred.

As the above account illustrates, the experience of being arrested is not a trivial matter. And it is only the beginning. Defendants can be held for hours or even days from the first moment of their arrest to their first court appearance, a process that varies in length depending on the jurisdiction and the volume of cases. Even this relatively brief initial detention can prove catastrophic for the misdemeanor defendant. Children may have been left unattended or with an unwilling neighbor. Child protective services may have been contacted, triggering a lengthy and costly legal process in family court. Sick or elderly family members may have been left without care. Jobs may be jeopardized or lost, as employers may be less than understanding about a late or missed workday caused by an arrest. Even in those rare instances when people do not have a pressing need to return home, hours or days spent in a holding cell waiting for a case to be initially processed can prove emotionally and physically debilitating.

In the Bronx where I worked, any person arrested and placed in a holding cell to be arraigned in court was assigned a lawyer. This is not the case for every misdemeanor defendant in every jurisdiction. In *Gideon v. Wainwright* (1963), the Supreme Court ruled that all defendants charged with a felony must be provided with counsel if they are too poor to hire their own. This right was extended in *Argersinger v. Hamlin* (1972) to misdemeanor defendants who face the possibility of a jail sentences.[9] But the Court did not say the Constitution requires the appointment of counsel to all poor misdemeanor defendants in all circumstances. Although many states have enacted their own statutes requiring counsel for indigent defendants who face possible imprisonment, it is still not unusual for poor misdemeanor defendants to find themselves in court without representation. This circumstance is fertile ground for wrongful convictions, as defendants who are unfamiliar with and intimidated by the law and court procedures may not try to argue their claims of innocence.

Even the presence of a lawyer, however, is not fool-proof protection against wrongful convictions for misdemeanor crimes that never happened.

First, there is the problem of misdemeanor bail. For many people charged with misdemeanors who do not resolve their case with a guilty plea at arraignment, the court can release them on their recognizance and provide them with a date to return to court. The court, however, has the power to set bail, which a defendant can pay by cash or bond. In theory, bail is the court's way of ensuring that a defendant will return to court. The thinking is that if a defendant has a stake in the proceedings in the form of the cash or collateral they posted for bail, they will be more likely to appear in court when ordered to do so. The problem, of course, is that poor people can ill-afford to pay even modest bail amounts. Prior to bail reform measures implemented in 2019, the average bail set in New York City in a misdemeanor case was $1,000.[10] This was well beyond an indigent defendant's reach. A defendant who cannot make bail, even in a nonviolent misdemeanor case, will sit in jail while waiting for their day in court—a wait that could take months due to calendar issues and case backlogs.

Nearly all misdemeanants plead guilty, including the innocent arrested by the police for crimes created from whole cloth. For innocent people who cannot make bail but are offered a short term of imprisonment in exchange for a plea, the decision to get out of jail as quickly as possible may be a consequential but highly understandable choice. Why sit in jail for a week or two (or more) waiting for your next court date if there is a misdemeanor offer on the table that could get you out well before then?

This calculus is particularly compelling for those who have a criminal history. They may decide that another misdemeanor conviction on their record is not a particularly big deal and will carry little stigma.[11] Recall the people discussed in chapter 3 who were wrongly arrested, rearrested, and rearrested again by corrupt police officers at the Ida B. Wells housing project. When innocent people are the victims of aggressive and repeated policing, they become resigned to misdemeanor charges and speedy resolutions as part of the unfair, everyday reality of living in an overpoliced community.

Another reason innocent people plead guilty is that they are made an offer too good to refuse. An unknown proportion of no-crime misdemeanor convictions stem from cases where an innocent defendant was charged with a more serious felony but was offered an attractive misdemeanor plea. In many jurisdictions, for instance, felony drug cases that carry potential prison time are resolved quickly on "rocket dockets" through misdemeanor pleas, even before the substances are tested to confirm the presence of illegal drugs. Misdemeanor pleas by felony defendants represent at least 10 percent of all felony case dispositions in large urban counties (although the percentage of innocent defendants is not known).[12] Ironically, of course, the prosecution often offers the most lenient pleas in those felony cases where the evidence is weak or constitutionally suspect. Only the prosecution knows at the earliest stages that, for instance, the so-called eyewitness is inconsistent and unreliable, or that the police engaged in a questionable search. A defendant with the economic means to fight the charges in those cases would likely walk away with no conviction. But for the poor defendant who cannot make bail, it is far better to jump on a misdemeanor plea offer than risk a long wait in jail pending a felony trial or a potential felony conviction with felony prison time.

It is these types of practical considerations that outweigh evidentiary considerations of innocence or guilt in misdemeanor cases. Added to that pressure is the summary and rushed nature of the misdemeanor process. Misdemeanor justice is nothing of the sort. At its core, the system is an assembly line run by actors who are far too overwhelmed to do their jobs effectively in each and every case. Faced with an overflowing docket of low-level cases, courts process misdemeanor cases as efficiently as possible, with minimal reflection about principles of justice, procedural fairness, or evidentiary considerations.

For the typical misdemeanor case, the prosecution has a thin file and has conducted little or no investigation. Under pressure to quickly resolve these cases, prosecutors in many courtrooms make early, take-it-or-leave-it plea offers that require defendants to make decisions on the spot even before an attorney or anyone else has had a chance to look at the evidence. Harried and overburdened defense attorneys may offer limited advice and, after only a few minutes' conversation, encourage their clients to plead without ever evaluating the merits of the accusations. Judges also feel the heat about moving their court dockets along. Judges who take too much time with each case wind up with a courtroom backlog for which they are criticized and possibly removed from the bench.[13]

In a very real way, then, it is the police decision of whom to arrest that determines the outcome of a misdemeanor case. In "quality of life" crimes such as loitering or trespass, officers employ their discretion in deciding whether to make an arrest and for what crime. Once a person is arrested for a misdemeanor offense, prosecutors do not carefully vet the initial allegations, defense lawyers rarely challenge the charges, courts seek speedy resolutions, and the accused nearly always plead guilty without ever requiring the prosecutor to prove the case against them.

The police decision to arrest becomes the functional equivalent of a conviction.

And in contrast to most felony cases, it is rare that a misdemeanor conviction is ever appealed. The reasons are many and varied.[14]

Lack of Appellate Review in Misdemeanor Cases

In summary misdemeanor proceedings, people routinely plead guilty at their first appearance and go home. Because misdemeanor cases are so quickly resolved, with little discussion, effort, or discovery, the court record is sparse. Given the paucity of information about each case, there is little to challenge on appeal. Consider a person who pleads guilty to prostitution at arraignment. As part of the plea colloquy, the defendant admits their participation in the crime as written in the criminal complaint. They affirm that their plea is voluntary, knowing, and intelligent. And then they are released. It would be hard later to prove that the person had *not* engaged in prostitution, based on a two-page record that contains virtually no facts other than the defendant's knowing and voluntary admission of guilt under oath.

But even in the unusual case where an innocent person is convicted after a full-blown misdemeanor trial, it is still rare to see an appeal and subsequent exoneration. Most misdemeanor defendants do not know about their right to appeal and do not have an attorney to assist them. In many jurisdictions, appellate counsel is not appointed in a misdemeanor case unless there is a period of jail time involved. That leaves indigent defendants potentially without legal assistance.

In contrast to serious felony convictions, innocence projects do not typically take on misdemeanor cases, because they focus their limited resources on defendants serving lengthy prison sentences for the most serious crimes.[15] People convicted of misdemeanors cases will usually have already served any sentence before the first appellate brief is even filed, making their cases less pressing than those of defendants who remain incarcerated.

Even if a defendant has a lawyer to represent them on a misdemeanor appeal, there are additional practical impediments to challenging misdemeanor convictions. Given that it can take more than a year to perfect an appeal, would-be appellants may not consider the process worth the effort. And that assumes that appellants did not waive their right to appeal as part of the case resolution, making appellate challenges difficult to bring.

Added to those procedural hurdles is the reality that courts are loath to reopen cases resolved by guilty pleas. This is particularly true for misdemeanor cases. Were the litigation floodgates to open, misdemeanor appeals from plea convictions would bring the court system to a halt.

It is thus no surprise that exonerations in misdemeanor cases are so rare and that we know so little about them. But that doesn't mean that innocent people are never wrongly convicted of misdemeanors. It just means that it happens so far under the radar that we know little about it.

Consequences of Misdemeanors

Misdemeanor cases are often dismissed as trivial or unimportant, but they have serious consequences. Rebecca Greenberg, an attorney in the Civil Action Practice of the Bronx Defenders in New York, shared the story of a client named "Gloria." Gloria was a sixty-year-old great-grandmother who had lived in Bronx public housing her entire life. Mentally sharp, with a funky style and a warm sense of humor, Gloria suffered from debilitating physical ailments that made movement without a wheelchair or a scooter nearly impossible. After she had surgery in 2009, Gloria's great-nephew agreed to look in on her, an arrangement that went on for several months. One day, in the early morning hours, the police entered Gloria's apartment while she was in bed, armed with a search warrant for drugs. They found crack cocaine in a bag hidden deep in the entryway closet. Gloria was arrested in her nightgown for felony drug possession and was hauled off to the precinct; because she was so frail, police officers had to carry her to their police car.

Gloria was assigned an attorney at arraignment, and shortly afterward, the prosecution offered her a misdemeanor plea to drug possession. Gloria continued to deny that the crack cocaine was hers or that she knew anything about the drugs, but eventually she pled guilty because the physical strain and emotional stress of traveling to court, waiting in the security line, and then waiting hours for her case to be called were simply too taxing for her. A plea, Gloria believed, would put an end to her predicament and allow her to resume her life as she knew it.

But the plea was actually the beginning of the end for Gloria. Shortly after her misdemeanor conviction, Gloria received notice that the New York City Housing Authority (NYCHA) had scheduled a hearing about her eligibility to remain in public housing. The housing proceedings took place in downtown Manhattan, in another borough miles from Gloria's apartment. She had to depend on "access a ride," whose reliability can be hit or miss, to make the lengthy journey through New York City traffic, in all kinds of weather. Gloria then watched with increasing dismay and anxiety as she lost at every stage of her housing case. In 2014, the court finally ordered her to be evicted from her apartment because of the misdemeanor drug conviction. Gloria died of a heart attack shortly after the court's ruling, but before the city could actually evict her. To this day, Rebecca believes that Gloria's stress at the prospect of being evicted from the only home she'd ever known—all because of a misdemeanor conviction for a crime she did not commit—was a major contributor to her death.

Although not a true "no-crime" case, since drugs were in her apartment that belonged to someone else, Gloria's case painfully illustrates the significant repercussions that misdemeanors can have for the individuals convicted of them. While misdemeanor convictions cannot be punished by lengthy prison terms, they carry with them serious consequences outside the courtroom. Misdemeanor convictions create a criminal record that has significant dampening effects on prospects for jobs and admission to college and vocational programs.[16] They may generate significant fines and court fees, leaving already-poor defendants deep in debt and facing potential future jail time for failure to pay. They can impact child custody, affect food stamp eligibility, result in deportation, and, as with Gloria, lead to being banned from public housing.[17]

Misdemeanor convictions also leave a criminal justice fingerprint, making people more vulnerable in future criminal justice interactions. People with criminal records may be viewed with greater suspicion, meaning that they may lose the benefit of the doubt in exchanges with the police and other actors in the legal system. Misdemeanor convictions also may result in more severe sentences for future offenses.[18]

Yet innocent people plead guilty to misdemeanor offenses simply to get out of jail and go home, leaving them with a conviction that will follow them for the rest of their lives.

Field Tests That Result in No-Crime Wrongful Convictions in Drug Cases

In Harris County, Texas, from 2009 on, the police routinely stopped thousands of people for alleged traffic infractions. Many of the people stopped by the police were black or brown, and many had criminal records. Whenever the police found a "suspicious" substance that could be drugs, they performed a roadside field test to confirm the presence of illegal drugs. If the field test was positive, the person was arrested. Once arrested, the person went to court and almost invariably pled guilty to criminal drug possession on the basis of the field tests. Most of these pleas involved misdemeanors, including felony charges downgraded to misdemeanors, though some cases remained felonies. Defendants were sentenced to incarceration, or to probation and fines. The lab tests that could have refuted the positive field tests were not available at the time of the plea, and no one asked for them.

In 2007, twenty-year-old Corey Anthony Love was arrested and charged with possession of more than a gram of cocaine.[19] When he was offered a misdemeanor plea with a jail sentence of 210 days, he took it. He served his time and was released in June 2007. Years later, in December 2012, the Houston Crime Lab tested the substance that was seized from Love and confirmed it was not cocaine or any other illegal drug. The Harris County district attorney's Conviction Review Unit asked that an attorney be appointed for Love, and supported a petition for a writ of habeas corpus. His conviction was vacated by the Texas Criminal Court of Appeals, with an accompanying finding of innocence.[20]

Love is among the lucky ones. For most people in his situation, the case would have ended after Love pled guilty. But Harris County took an unusual next step. Unlike most jurisdictions, where the entry of a guilty plea closes the case, Harris County realized there was a backlog of unexamined field test results that had not been confirmed by a lab test, and it had them reviewed. The results were shocking. A 2016 audit revealed that almost three hundred people had been wrongly convicted based on guilty pleas in cases where the lab results came back negative for drugs.[21] The field tests were wrong, but innocent people had been convicted, after their own guilty plea, of drug crimes that never happened. Of the individuals thus wrongfully convicted in Houston, 59 percent were black—in a city whose population is just 24 percent black.[22]

Harris County then took a second unusual step. The Harris County prosecutor's Conviction Integrity Unit (CIU) tried to locate the defendants who had been wrongly convicted, and they worked with defense lawyers and the local courts to vacate the convictions. No other jurisdiction that accepts guilty pleas based on field tests without lab confirmations has ever done that. The National Registry of Exonerations has identified 136 exonerations as of June 30, 2019, in drug cases that were cleared through the efforts of the Harris County CIU; the convictions of those defendants who could not be located remain intact.[23]

Harris County, Texas, is anomalous in having followed up on old, untested field results. But field tests are used throughout the country, and they are notoriously unreliable *everywhere*. Although error rates are not exact, estimates suggest field tests produce false positives in one-fifth to one-third of all cases. Just about anything can generate a false positive. According to a report by the *Washington Post,* everyday household items that yielded a false positive from a drug field test included "sage, chocolate chip cookies, motor oil, spearmint, Dr. Bronner's Magic Soap, tortilla dough, deodorant, billiards chalk, patchouli, flour, eucalyptus, breath mints, Jolly Ranchers, Krispy Kreme donut glaze, *exposure to air* and loose-leaf tea."[24] Yet the most commonly used field tests do not even include warnings about the exceptionally high rate of false positives.

If courts accept guilty pleas based on uncorroborated field tests, innocent people will inevitably plead guilty to those charges for all the reasons discussed in this chapter. But this fact hasn't stopped the practice. In Las Vegas, for example, the crime lab warned the police department of the field tests' unreliability. Even after that warning, the police department continued using—in fact, expanded their use of—the flawed technology. Thousands of people in Las Vegas were convicted based solely on the field test results; the number of those cases involving false positives for substances that were not illegal is unknown.[25]

There are jurisdictions that allow the use of field tests as an initial screening tool for drugs, but permit only lab results as evidence in court.[26] Regrettably, that policy is of little comfort to the thousands of men and women who are arrested based on faulty field tests and then are jailed pending lab results because they are too poor to make bail. When possible, they too prefer to plead guilty to any offer that enables them to be released, including those based on field tests alone.

Even those who can make bail suffer tremendously. In Tampa, for instance, Rebecca Shaw, a mother of four, ran out of gas on the side of the road.[27] A police officer stopped, asked if he could search her car (instead of asking if she needed help), and found pills that he thought looked like oxycodone but that she said were vitamins. A drug field test yielded a positive result for oxycodone, and she was charged with drug trafficking. Shaw spent five months in jail while her husband frantically raised the $5,000 in bail money so that she could fight the charges against her. Seven months after her release on bail but before she was convicted, the state crime lab revealed that the field test had yielded a false positive, that the pills were not illegal drugs, and the charges were dismissed.

CRIME POLICIES RESULT IN ARRESTS AND CONVICTIONS FOR NO-CRIME MISDEMEANOR CASES

I start this chapter with stories about people who were arrested in New York for trespassing. These cases were part of the Trespass Affidavit Program

(TAP), formerly known as Operation Clean Halls, in the Bronx. Beginning in the early 1990s, TAP allowed officers in "high-crime" areas to patrol in- and outside certain privately owned and public housing buildings where drug dealing was allegedly occurring.[28] For a building to be part of TAP, landlords simply signed a short affidavit that gave the NYPD permission to enter enrolled buildings with an eye to arresting anyone found to be engaged in criminal activity. Many of the affidavits authorized the NYPD to enter the enrolled buildings "in perpetuity."[29] Throughout Bronx neighborhoods, nearly every private apartment building was enrolled in the TAP program. For those readers who have not been to the Bronx, this translates into hun- dreds of tall buildings with thousands of residents.

The TAP program resulted in nothing short of a full-on siege against resi- dents and their guests. The NYPD stopped people in lobbies, hallways, stair- wells, courtyards, and other common areas in Clean Halls buildings. They stopped people who were entering and exiting the buildings. They demanded that residents produce identification at any time, including when they were doing routine tasks in their own buildings like getting the mail or taking out the garbage. A federal district judge described a typical TAP stop this way:

> A person approaches or exits a Clean Halls building in the Bronx; the police suddenly materialize, stop the person, demand identification, and question the person about where he or she is coming from and what he or she is doing; attempts at explanation are met with hostility; especially if the person is a young black man, he is frisked, which often involves an invasive search of his pockets; in some cases the officers then detain the person in a police van in order to carry out an extended interrogation about the person's knowledge of drugs and weapons; and in some cases the stop escalates into an arrest for trespass, with all of the indignities, inconveniences, and serious risks that fol- low from an arrest even when the charges are quickly dropped.[30]

The police, of course, did not arrest everyone they stopped, and on occasion they would choose to issue a summons or a citation rather than place the person under arrest. But plenty of people were arrested, arraigned, and assigned a lawyer.

These trespass stops became so routine as to appear unremarkable or as a rite of passage for poor people of color who lived in certain neighborhoods. One 2008 study about the TAP program found that "approximately 30% of the residents [who lived in specified housing units run by the New York City Housing Authority (NYCHA)] reported they had been charged with trespassing, *despite the fact that they lived there.* Approximately 70% of those surveyed at the NYCHA Thomas Jefferson Houses reported that they had been repeatedly stopped by police officers when simply coming and going around their homes."[31]

The scope and impact of the program is hard to fathom.

Official NYPD data demonstrated that tens of thousands of people were stopped for trespassing each year. Between 2006 and 2010, police officers made 329,446 stops of individuals they suspected of trespassing. This represented roughly 12.2 percent of all *reported* stops for all crimes (and there were likely many stops that went unreported).[32]

And here's the thing: only 7.7 percent of reported trespass stops resulted in arrest, and about 4.9 percent in the issuance of a summons.[33] While many thousands of innocent people were stopped and forced into a police encounter that did not yield a trespassing arrest, thousands were actually arrested for trespassing. Between 2007 and 2012, there were at least 16,000 misdemeanor arrests for trespass in New York City annually.

This program did not impact all New Yorkers equally. From 2006 to 2010, about 94.4 percent of those stopped for trespassing were black or Latino, though blacks and Latinos together constituted approximately 52 percent of the New York City population. Between 2003 and 2011, blacks and Latinos made up over 90 percent of those arrested for trespassing; blacks were twelve times, and Latinos seven times, more likely to be arrested for trespassing than whites, Asians, and Native Americans combined.[34]

As I witnessed firsthand in the Bronx, people of color—particularly poor people of color—bore the brunt of these invasive policies. My clients were arrested under the TAP program for having visited a friend, or for leaving their own apartment building without identification, or for sitting in the courtyard with family and friends. In other words, they had been lawfully on the premises and had nonetheless been arrested, charged, prosecuted, and convicted after a guilty plea for a trespass that never happened.

The Clean Halls policy was not born of bad intentions. Rather, it sprang from a concept first presented in the early 1980s by criminologists George L. Kelling and James Q. Wilson, who introduced the idea of "broken windows" policing to the national consciousness.[35] They believed that neighborhoods with signs of disorder and decay, such as unrepaired broken windows, were more likely to experience criminality. Under a simplified version of broken windows policing, the police could prevent major crimes from occurring by focusing on maintaining order for the lowest quality-of-life occurrences.

Amid fears of rising crime, Rudy Giuliani swept into his new role as New York City mayor in 1993. With his newly appointed police commissioner, Bill Bratton, by his side, Giuliani championed broken windows policing. With it, came a new era of aggressive law enforcement that disparately impacted poor people of color. Crime declined, and Giuliani attributed that drop to his broken windows policy. There were other, more compelling, narratives about the crime reduction that were linked to national trends, rather than broken windows policing.[36] But the Giuliani narrative prevailed. When Mayor Michael Bloomberg took office in 2001, he continued to support aggressive policing, including a major expansion of "stop and frisk" searches.

Eventually, class action lawsuits were brought against the city. One in particular, *Ligon v. the City of New York,* was filed by the New York Civil Liberties Union, Latino Justice PRLDEF, and the Bronx Defenders. The lead plaintiff in the case, Jaenean Ligon, filed suit after her seventeen-year-old son, J.G., was stopped on his way back to his own apartment in August 2011. According to the complaint, J.G. went to the store to buy ketchup at his mother's request. As he approached the front door of his apartment building, five police officers stopped him and asked him a slew of questions, including why he was entering the building and where he was coming from. When J.G. explained he had purchased ketchup, an officer began to frisk him and then demanded that he show identification. The officers went further, insisting that J.G. show them his exact apartment. The officers rang the bell to the apartment, and when Ms. Ligon answered the intercom, she was told by an officer to come downstairs to identify her son. Panicked that her son was seriously injured or dead, she ran downstairs, only to find her son very much alive and surrounded by five police officers. She burst into tears. One of the officers laughed and, after confirming that J.G. was her child, handed over the ketchup bottle.

In a sweeping 2013 ruling in favor of the plaintiffs, the court found that "while it may be difficult to say where, precisely, to draw the line between constitutional and unconstitutional police encounters, such a line exists, and the NYPD has systematically crossed it when making trespass stops outside TAP buildings in the Bronx." The parties reached a settlement in 2017 that further specified what the police can and cannot do when people are seen entering and exiting TAP buildings. Think about that. It took until 2017—nearly twenty-five years since those trespass policies first kicked into high gear—for reform measures to be fully agreed upon, let alone start being implemented.

"Quality of life" policing for low-level crimes is not unique to New York. In Miami, for example, Earl Sampson, a black man in his twenties, was stopped and arrested more than fifty times for trespassing *at his own place of employment,* over his employer's objections, as part of the "Zero-Tolerance Zone Trespassing Program."[37] Sampson repeatedly pled guilty to the charges, even though he had committed no crime, because it was easier than fighting them. Enter any courtroom in Baltimore, Chicago, Washington, D.C., and other large city, and there will be poor people pleading guilty to low-level offenses that never happened.

Most of the time, the people targeted for low-level arrests are poor. But one does not have to be poor to be targeted for trespass prosecutions. The police decision to arrest for a crime such as trespass may be impermissibly based on race alone. In April 12, 2018, Rashon Nelson and Dante Robinson, two black men who had arrived ten minutes early to a business meeting at a Starbucks in an upscale Philadelphia neighborhood, were arrested for trespassing.[38] The men arrived at 4:35 PM, and one of them asked to use the restroom. The manger informed them the restroom was for paying customers only. They then sat down at a table, waiting to place their order until the third person arrived. A barista approached the table and asked them if they wanted something to drink—an unusual event at a Starbucks, which typically offers only counter service. At 4:37 PM, a mere two minutes after the men arrived, the manager called the police, claiming the men refused to order or leave. Their subsequent arrest was captured on video and went viral. The charges were later dropped, the Starbucks employees were fired, the CEO of Starbucks apologized, the police chief apologized, and Starbucks closed for a day of racial sensitivity training.

Just a few days after this incident garnered national headlines, on April 15, 2018, a different police department was called to an LA Fitness gym in New Jersey to remove two black men who were accused of not being lawfully on the premises.[39] One man had a long-standing, current membership at the club, and the other was there on a four-day guest pass.

Admittedly, in the situations described above, it was the management's calls, and not police policies, that triggered the trespass arrests. But the police could have declined to make the arrest. Instead, they pursued the men for "alleged crimes" that they knew, or should have known, had not happened.

The common thread in these cases is that low-level offenses are used as trip wires in monitoring and controlling members of traditionally disfavored groups. People were arrested for trespassing in places where they were lawfully present. No crimes had been committed. The trespass arrests are echoes of the not-too-distant past when police routinely arrested poor people and people of color for vagrancy and loitering.

In 1959, Sam Thompson, an African American man, went into the Liberty End Café in Louisville, Kentucky. He ordered and paid for a glass of beer and a dish of macaroni.[40] Thompson remained in the café while waiting for a bus to take him home. The police entered the café on a "routine check" and arrested Thompson for loitering and then for disorderly conduct. The owner of the café later said that Thompson was a regular customer who had been doing nothing wrong. Thompson was likely not surprised by his arrest, as he had been stopped and arrested more than fifty times for loitering and vagrancy. But Thompson finally decided that enough was enough. Represented by an attorney from the newly minted Kentucky ACLU, Thompson challenged his arrest. He was convicted after a trial and sentenced to pay a fine. The U.S. Supreme Court eventually heard his case and ruled in favor of Thompson under the Due Process Clause of the U.S. Constitution; the Court found no evidence that Thompson had been loitering.

Thompson's conviction for a crime that never happened was overturned.

But police continued to use loitering and vagrancy laws as a means of social control. This all changed, at least in theory, with the U.S. Supreme Court decision in *Papachristou v. City of Jacksonville* (1972).[41] At issue in *Papachristou* was the arrest for vagrancy of two black men and two white women who were out together one evening in Jacksonville, Florida. Jacksonville's broad vagrancy ordinance captured within its ambit wide swaths of people and relatively innocuous behaviors:

> Rogues and vagabonds, or dissolute persons who go about begging, common gamblers, persons who use juggling or unlawful games or plays, common drunkards, common night walkers, thieves, pilferers or pickpockets, traders in stolen property, lewd, wanton and lascivious persons, keepers of gambling places, common railers and brawlers, persons wandering or strolling around from place to place without any lawful purpose or object, habitual loafers, disorderly persons, persons neglecting all lawful business and habitually spending their time by frequenting houses of ill fame, gaming houses, or places where alcoholic beverages are sold or served, persons able to work but habitually living upon the earnings of their wives or minor children shall be deemed vagrants and, upon conviction in the Municipal Court, shall be punished as provided for Class D offenses.[42]

The Supreme Court struck down Florida's vagrancy law as unconstitutionally vague because it gave the police unfettered discretion to discriminate against people who they labeled "vagrant." Police could and did arrest disfavored people based on race or economic status while hiding behind charges of vagrancy.

Although *Papachristou* theoretically put an end to overly vague vagrancy laws, the practice continued to thrive. As what happened to Evan Howard and Tyrone Braxton illustrates, the Baltimore police routinely ordered people who were standing around to "move on." When people refused, the police would arrest them for loitering, which is defined as "interfering, impeding, or hindering the free passage of pedestrian or vehicular traffic after receiving a warning." The police made these arrests despite the Maryland Supreme Court's clear ruling in 2000 that standing around, even when ordered to move on, does not constitute loitering.[43] In 2016, the U.S. Department of Justice issued a scathing report about the police department's discriminatory practices;[44] in 2017, the Baltimore Police Department and the city of Baltimore entered into a consent decree with the Department of Justice to address, among other issues, their discriminatory application of "quality of life" ordinances, including those that outlawed loitering, in ways that targeted young men of color.[45]

PROSECUTORS COULD PREVENT NO-CRIME MISDEMEANOR WRONGFUL CONVICTIONS— BUT THEY DON'T

One final point is worth making here. Prosecutors have the power to decline to prosecute in cases where no crime occurred. But they use their power sparingly—in some jurisdictions, the prosecution declination rate is as low as 2 percent.[46] Instead, they proceed with cases that are weak or specious, thereby causing innocent people to face criminal charges in cases that should never have been brought in the first place. For the innocent person caught in this web, the prosecutor's refusal to use their discretion early on can have consequences that range from an unjust plea conviction to the tedium and inconvenience of having to fight charges that should never have been brought.

Gina DeVito, a criminal defense attorney in New Jersey, recounted to me a particularly egregious story of the prosecution's refusal to dismiss a case without merit. Ms. DeVito was assigned by the county public defender's office to represent "John Smith." Smith lived in a small apartment that he shared with "David Jones." Smith and Jones had an argument, and Jones stabbed Smith with a kitchen knife. Smith was rushed to the hospital, where he stayed in recovery for nearly a month after undergoing abdominal surgery.

Jones was arrested and charged with aggravated assault. While Jones was in jail awaiting his court date, he claimed that items had been taken from his apartment, which had been left unattended after his arrest. He subsequently filed a citizen's complaint naming Smith as the thief, though no evidence was offered that the items were actually missing.

After DeVito reviewed the discovery, it was clear that Smith had been in the hospital at the time Jones claimed his items were taken. Meeting Smith for the first time in court to answer to the theft charge, DeVito was struck by his frailty and by the surgical scars he freely showed her, but even more striking was the fact that he was flanked by victim advocates from the *prosecutor's office*. Remarkably, the advocates wondered aloud to DeVito why the prosecution (their office) was going forward with a case against Smith. Despite the attendant circumstances clearly indicating that Jones had falsely accused Smith of stealing his property, the prosecution refused to dismiss the charges. Instead, the prosecutor remanded the case to municipal court, where misdemeanor cases, known in New Jersey as disorderly persons offenses, are heard.

Weeks later, DeVito appeared on behalf of Smith in municipal court, and detailed the case to the municipal prosecutor and the judge, who ultimately dismissed the case. When she explained that she had requested a dismissal in superior court, where felonies—known in New Jersey as indictable offenses—are handled, the municipal court judge scoffed and said, "Don't hold your breath; they never dismiss anything."

DeVito expressed frustration with the prosecution's refusal to scrutinize the evidence and use its prosecutorial discretion to dismiss: "Rather than admit they cannot meet the high burden of proof beyond a reasonable doubt and dismiss the case, prosecutors at the superior court level abdicate their responsibility to the municipal prosecutor. In more serious cases that do not lend themselves to remand, the prosecutors will either extend a plea offer that is difficult to refuse or, if the defendant does refuse, leave it to the jury to sort out. Rather than seeking justice as they are sworn to do, prosecutors seem more invested in keeping cases, even those deeply flawed, afloat, and if they crash, it won't be on their heads."

Law enforcement policies that result in indiscriminate and discriminatory arrests matter a great deal. In essence, a police officer's decision about whom to arrest ultimately determines who will be convicted. That's because people plead guilty to charges that are never scrutinized by anyone—not the prosecutors, the defense lawyers, or even the judges. This is particularly troubling when the arrests themselves are products of "quality of life" policing policies designed to maintain order, or because of quotas or corruption (as discussed in chapter 4), rather than actual crimes with an evidentiary basis.

And once a person is arrested, as shown throughout this chapter, they often plead guilty to go home or to quickly resolve the case. They do so even though there is no evidence that they committed a crime, or that any crime was committed. The system churns people through with little attention paid to evidence or guilt. In truth, the misdemeanor process does not have the bandwidth to properly adjudicate the volume of low-level crimes that appear every day. Whether it be loitering or trespass, we see time and again innocent people pleading guilty to crimes that never happened.

Misdemeanors may be called petty offenses, but they carry with them serious consequences. Most of those consequences, particularly in urban settings, are borne by poor people and people of color, who are disproportionately saddled with misdemeanor convictions. The misdemeanor system is marred by "malign neglect,"[47] and a breathtaking carelessness and casualness about who is arrested, charged, and convicted based on inadequate or nonexistent evidence. The system has become inured to the hyperefficient criminal justice processing of poor black and brown people, often young men, based on petty offenses that are never properly screened by anyone: not the prosecutor, not the defense lawyer (if one is provided), and not the judge.

No-crime wrongful misdemeanor convictions have never been—and likely never will be—counted. But one does not need a hard number to know that they happen far too frequently, in poor communities and for people of color, in ways that are profoundly and deeply troubling.

Conclusion

CLEARING THE SMOKE

THIS BOOK ADDRESSES THE PHENOMENON of no-crime wrongful convictions. It begins by considering the various "triggering" events that cause no-crime convictions to occur in the first place: the mislabeling of accidental or naturally occurring events as crimes, false accusations, and police misconduct. It then examines the criminal justice actors in the legal system—prosecutors, defense lawyers, and judges—who enable no-crime wrongful convictions to occur and fester unchecked. Finally, this book looks at the pervasive but often overlooked issue of misdemeanor no-crime wrongful convictions.

No-crime wrongful convictions have multiple and co-occurring causes. In this chapter, I offer modest but concrete proposals for reforms that specifically target no-crime wrongful convictions. Some of these suggestions overlap reforms that can reduce wrongful convictions in all cases, and perhaps even improve the criminal justice system for the innocent and guilty alike. But the proposals home in on policy recommendations that could make a real difference in preventing no-crime wrongful convictions.

REFORMING THE USE OF FORENSIC SCIENCE

As demonstrated throughout this book, forensic error can lead to no-crime wrongful convictions. Sabrina Butler was wrongly convicted of murder after an expert determined that her child had died from shaken baby syndrome. Herbert Landry was wrongly convicted of arson after an expert mislabeled an accidental fire as one that had been deliberately set. In each of these cases, experts initially misdiagnosed an event as a crime, which in turn caused the police to solve the "crime" by arresting an innocent suspect. But for the expert's erroneous analysis, there would have been no erroneous crime designation and ultimately no wrongful conviction. In addition to forensic error, forensic misconduct causes no-crime wrongful convictions. As demonstrated by the scandals in crime labs throughout the country, analysts have falsified test results, inventing outcomes in hair, blood, drug, and breathalyzer tests. The outright fabrications by forensic scientists have caused countless wrongful convictions, and led to the reversal of thousands of convictions.[1]

Given that bad forensic science causes no-crime wrongful convictions, we should work diligently to prevent the use of such "science" in the first place. In 2009, the National Academy of Sciences (NAS) issued a landmark report on the state of forensic science and its use in court.[2] In clearly stating that nuclear DNA evidence is the only reliable forensic method to connect individuals to evidentiary samples, the report turned the common understanding of forensic science upside down.[3] In 2016, the President's Council of Advisors on Science and Technology (PCAST) echoed these findings in another landmark report that specifically examined forensic feature-comparison methods.[4]

Since the NAS report was first issued, a whole range of "forensic science" has been discredited. But prosecutors keep trying to introduce it anyway. Take, for instance, bite mark testimony. The NAS report rejected bite mark evidence because it lacked foundational research and scientific validity. The PCAST report also blasted bite mark evidence, lamenting the absence of reliable scientific research to support it and noting that the technique is so random and problematic that experts at the outset "cannot even consistently agree on whether an injury is a human bitemark."[5] Across the United States, at least thirty-one people have been exonerated from convictions based on faulty bite mark testimony.[6] Yet, despite the clear scientific consensus that bite mark evidence is nothing more than pseudo-science, prosecutors continue to insist on using it. Only one day after exoneree Keith Harward described at a 2017 meeting of the National Commission on Forensic Science how bite mark evidence contributed to his wrongful conviction and thirty-three-year incarceration for a crime he did not commit, the chair of the National District Attorneys Association reiterated his organization's stance that bite mark evidence is a "reliable science."[7] Richard A. Consiglio, the Pennsylvania county attorney in the pending retrial of Aaron Ross, whose 2004 murder conviction relied on bite mark testimony, insisted at a 2016 hearing that bite mark evidence was valid and should be admissible in court. The issue of bite mark admissibility is wending through the

Pennsylvania courts while Ross, who insists on his innocence, remains incarcerated awaiting a chance to clear his name.[8]

Prosecutors have an ethical obligation to seek only those convictions that are based on reliable evidence. Yet they continue to rely on discredited pseudoscience to prove their cases. They do so, in part because no one stops them. Judges have the authority to exclude unreliable evidence, but don't. The NAS report directly chastises the judiciary for failing to perform its gatekeeping function in the courtroom: "The bottom line is simple: In a number of forensic science disciplines, forensic science professionals have yet to establish either the validity of their approach or the accuracy of their conclusions, and *the courts have been utterly ineffective in addressing this problem.*"[9]

This is not entirely surprising. Judges are not scientists. As one commentator remarked:

> We don't ask judges to perform regression analyses. We don't ask them to design sewer systems, hit fastballs or compose symphonies. We know they aren't qualified to do any of those things. Judges are trained to perform legal analysis. No one goes to law school to become a scientist. Few go to medical school or enroll in a Ph.D. program in the sciences because they have a penchant for law. The two fields represent two entirely different ways of thinking, are governed by two entirely different epistemologies and employ two nearly incompatible methods of analysis. And yet for some reason, we have decided that when it comes to the critically important issue of assessing the validity of expert testimony that could send someone to prison, or to the execution chamber, we will defer to the scientific knowledge of . . . judges.[10]

So what can be done to reduce forensic errors and misconduct that lead to no-crime wrongful convictions?

First, judges need to enforce evidentiary standards by ensuring that any testimony about forensic science is rooted in foundational research and has appropriate indicia of scientific validity. Relating to forensic evidence in the courtroom, the PCAST report recommends that judges carefully consider the "appropriate scientific criteria for assessing scientific validity," and apply specific criteria (set out in the report) when considering the "foundational validity" and the "validity as applied" of the proffered forensic evidence and experts' qualifications.[11]

Even when experts are permitted to testify, judges need to be vigilant against expert testimony that is exaggerated and inaccurate. Judges "should ensure that testimony about the accuracy of the method and the probative value of proposed identifications is scientifically valid" and is not exaggerated or "scientifically indefensible."[12] Great caution should be taken to ensure that experts don't overstate the significance of evidence or make claims that are not based in reality. Remember the case where Fred Zain wildly overstated the likelihood that defendant Gerald Davis had contributed the semen? Or the dog handler who testified that Oscar's nose was more sensitive and accurate than existing lab technology, an assertion that had no basis in science or truth? Experts should not be permitted to make claims about "zero error rates" or "infallibility," because such claims are empirically unfounded and inaccurate and will mislead the jury.

Because most judges are not scientists, judges should be provided with legal education and training relating to forensic evidence and its admissibility.[13] Alternatively, judges should call upon independent experts in individual cases to help evaluate whether the proffered forensic evidence meets rigorous scientific standards.

Where it does not, judges should exclude the testimony. Period.

Second, prosecutors should decline to pursue cases that rely exclusively on forensic evidence. In cases involving shaken baby syndrome, for instance, it is generally accepted that a conviction should never be based solely on expert testimony.[14] If a case is made of nothing more than forensic scientific evidence, the prosecutor should rethink the prosecution. Prosecutors should also refrain from introducing evidence by experts who are little more than "witch doctors."[15] Think here of Michael West, the odontologist who had been discredited in a number of news reports in the mid-1990s, but was called in by the prosecution in 2000 to assist in the case against Leigh Stubbs and Tammy Vance.[16] At trial, West had the seemingly magical powers to match suspects to bite marks that no one else saw and to enhance a video recording to prove culpability, the latter a capability even the FBI lacked. Prosecutors have an obligation to present reliable evidence of a defendant's guilt, not dubious or fantastic testimony based on pseudoscience.

Third, defense lawyers need better training in *Daubert*'s requirements and in forensic science generally. A 2009 study of 137 cases involving DNA exonerations found that "[d]efense counsel rarely made any objections to the invalid forensic science testimony in these trials and rarely effectively cross-examined forensic analysts who provided invalid science testimony."[17] Defense lawyers need to protest loudly when presented with questionable forensic evidence, but they often fail to do so.

One way to ameliorate this defense forensic deficit is to provide defense lawyers with funding for expert witnesses. A recent near-miss no-crime case highlights just how important it is for defendants to have access to their own experts. Ronnie Winfield was accused of strangling his seventy-six-year-old neighbor Leannia Hall in their Chicago neighborhood in March 2014.[18] Winfield, who was sixty-five-years old, at the time, insisted he was innocent. According to Winfield, Hall invited him across the street to her home. She initiated sex but Winfield was unable to continue. Winfield explained that Hall began to cough, laid down on her bed, began snoring, and then stopped breathing.

Dr. Adrienne Segovia, an assistant Cook County medical examiner who had failed her certification exams three times, believed otherwise. She performed the autopsy on Hall and determined that the woman had been strangled. Because Segovia ruled that Hall's death was a homicide, Winfield—the last person to be with Hall—was charged with murder. He was interrogated for four days, lied to by detectives, and held in pretrial detention for nineteen months on $5 million bail.

Winfield, however, was able to defend himself against Segovia's designation of Hall's death as a homicide because the court appointed Dr. Shaku Teas, a board-certified pathologist, to serve as a defense expert at the county's expense. Teas testified that Segovia got it entirely wrong. According to Teas, Segovia missed critical signs that Hall had *not* been killed by strangulation but had died of heart failure. Segovia overlooked the fact that Hall had no marks on her neck, no defensive wounds, no exterior signs of trauma or injury, no signs that Hall had put up any fight. She missed that Hall's hyoid bone was intact—in cases of strangulation, the hyoid is often broken. She also neglected to explore whether Hall, a four foot, ten inch woman who weighed 215 pounds, had died of heart failure due to an abnormally enlarged heart. Teas went on to testify that Segovia had not only failed to measure the damage to Hall's enlarged heart but also refused Teas's request to perform the test herself. Concluding her testimony, Teas declared "Leannia Hall died a natural death as a result of hypertensive cardiovascular disease."[19] Winfield was acquitted. Without the benefit of a court-appointed, publicly funded expert to vigorously challenge Segovia's findings, Winfield could well have been convicted of a murder that did not happen.

Fourth, crime labs should be independent and removed from the purview of law enforcement agencies. In their groundbreaking book, *Actual Innocence* (2000), Innocence Project founders Barry Scheck and Peter Neufeld sounded a clarion call for the creation of independent crime labs:

Scientific evidence, when properly handled, can be the best evidence in a case. Clearly, forensic science has yet to achieve the status of an independent third force, unbeholden to prosecutors or defense lawyers, consisting of professionals who will not misrepresent or slant data for either side. The abuses of Fred Zain and those like him simply could not exist in a truly independent forensic science community, fostered in institutions that carry out only scientific agendas. Neither the [forensic] laboratory nor its budget should be under the supervision of the police department of a prosecutor's office.[20]

This was also a key, albeit controversial, recommendation of the NAS report: "The best science is conducted in a scientific setting as opposed to a law enforcement setting. Because forensic scientists often are driven in their work by a need to answer a particular question related to the issues of a particular case, they sometimes face pressure to sacrifice appropriate methodology for the sake of expediency."[21]

When crime labs are not independent of law enforcement, there is a real and documented danger that forensic scientists will view themselves as working with and for the police and prosecution. This leads to biased analyses and outcomes in what should otherwise be an entirely objective process.

In addition to crime lab independence, a national independent forensic science commission should be created to evaluate forensic disciplines on an ongoing basis. The commission could serve several important functions. It could issue guidance on which forensic methods are accurate and reliable. It could set national standards for crime labs, provide national accreditation for independent crime labs, and subject them to regular oversight.

The national forensic commission could also create national certification standards for forensic scientists. Currently, the certification of scientists varies widely. At minimum, lab employees should meet educational requirements and be consistently certified, and their certifications should be renewable and based on both professional evaluations and participation in continuing education. Corruption could be stemmed by better and more rigorous oversight. Rogue forensic scientists—like Fred Zain and Annie Dookhan—were able to falsify lab results for crimes that simply did not happen because there was no one checking their work.[22] In fact, Annie Dookhan falsified her credentials when she was hired, a fact that also went unnoticed.

These proposals are obviously subject to funding and the vagaries of politics. President Obama authorized the creation of an independent National Commission on Forensic Science, which was promptly disbanded under President Trump in 2017 by then attorney general Jeff Sessions.[23] Sessions then announced the creation of a Forensic Science Working Group, to be housed within the Justice Department. That's not exactly an independent entity. Further, the group was to be led by Ted Hunt, a career prosecutor who has questioned important forensic reform recommendations.[24]

A few jurisdictions have taken seriously the call for the creation of independent labs. Washington, D.C., for instance, created the Department of Forensic Sciences, the first independent crime lab in the nation to deliberately implement a number of the NAS reform recommendations.[25] Other cities and states should follow suit.

Finally, there needs to be more and better training about cognitive biases in the context of forensic analysis. Consider the case of Rodricus Crawford, convicted of murdering his infant son, who actually died of pneumonia. The EMTs who made disparaging comments as they unhurriedly made their way to the scene arrived at Crawford's residence expecting the worst, and they acted accordingly. Later, the medical examiner minimized the significance of pneumonia and instead went straight to a diagnosis of murder by suffocation. Training about cognitive biases, including confirmation bias and expectation bias, could be folded into medical education for doctors, nurses, and emergency technicians, as well as for forensic analysts. Such training could enable these professionals to take countermeasures against unconscious assumptions that might influence their initial diagnosis, and thus help reduce misdiagnoses of crimes that never happened.

Most of the time, misdiagnoses occur in the difficult cases where the cause of death is not readily apparent. Medical personnel could be trained to engage in devil's-advocate analysis whenever their diagnosis is critical to a crime designation, carefully considering which medical factors run counter to their conclusions. By deliberately taking a contradictory view of their own conclusions, medical personnel would be forced to confront and consider the weakness of their diagnosis. Alternatively, at least in ambiguous cases involving the most serious of crimes where homicide is designated as the cause of death, protocols could be established for a second review of the medical evidence by independent personnel who are not involved in the case.

PROPOSALS FOR POLICE REFORM

Police officers are on the front end of no-crime wrongful convictions and play a role throughout the case in providing evidence against people later proven to be innocent. Reform proposals that target existing police policies could go a long way in reducing their occurrence.

Detecting False Accusations

No-crime wrongful convictions can be caused by false accusations by civilian accusers. Whether the witnesses fabricate the existence of a crime for motives of exacting revenge, securing child custody, winning sympathy, or diverting attention elsewhere, the police and prosecution play an important role in vetting such allegations. This is no easy task. Police have been much criticized for failing to take seriously genuine accusations of rape and sexual assault. But when the police wrongly pursue false accusations as true, they risk the lives of innocent people for crimes that never happened.

Police training can help improve officers' evaluation of accusations. First, police need to be taught—early and often—that their ability to detect lies is highly fallible; such awareness could reduce the overconfidence that is often seen in lie detection and that in turn can produce errors. Police also should receive training based on empirical data about why people make false accusations, such as to create an alibi, seek revenge, or obtain an emotional or financial gain. The presence of these markers may provide the police both with guidance in their initial assessment of an accusation and with a basis for further examination of the allegation.[26]

Police also need training about the dangers of tunnel vision and belief perseverance, which are often exacerbated by departmental pressures to close cases. They should be routinely and consistently encouraged to pursue all evidence, rather than those facts that confirm their initial theory. Police should be trained to understand that facts rather than gut feelings should govern the determination of whether a crime has occurred. If the complainant's story is contradictory or inconsistent, the police should carefully consider all explanations, including whether a crime has been committed.

Investigative checklists can help the police reduce the effects of tunnel vision, because they help remind the police about investigative procedures and help steer them away from using shortcuts based on unconscious biases.[27] The checklists could include, for instance, a record of what evidence the police found and what evidence they expected to find; evidentiary and witness inconsistencies; and steps to identify other possible theories in the case. Checklists have been adopted by police departments and prosecutor offices in other contexts and could provide a blueprint for investigative procedures. They have the added benefit of creating a record that can later be reviewed.[28]

Prosecutors also work with the police in screening false accusations. The police need only have probable cause to make an arrest, which means they need only determine that it is more probable than not that a crime was committed and that a particular individual committed that crime. The prosecution, however, is required to prove its case beyond a reasonable doubt—a much higher burden of proof. The prosecution needs to carefully consider the complainant's story, any inconsistencies, and markers that may indicate a falsehood in the case. Rather than moving forward with cases by shoring them up with questionable evidence, prosecutors should decline to prosecute cases that do not pass careful scrutiny.

In addition to checklists, police should refrain from using guilt-presumptive techniques in questioning. In the United Kingdom, police now employ the PEACE model of questioning,[29] a protocol that encourages officers to keep an open mind to all the differing narratives and that can be applied equally to suspect and witnesses. Application of the PEACE method could also reduce false confessions. While false confessions occur only infrequently in no-crime exonerations, they can be damning to the innocent defendant. In addition, the police should video record interrogation sessions, from the start of questioning through the final statement, in order to help fact finders evaluate the reliability of a statement. At least twenty-six states have implemented video recording of interrogations, and more than a thousand jurisdiction have voluntarily adopted the practice.

Reducing Police Misconduct

Police misconduct also directly causes no-crime wrongful convictions. One major obstacle to reducing police misconduct is the "blue wall of silence." The code of silence has been difficult to penetrate, because officers are informally taught to protect their own even in the face of lawbreaking.

But innovations are on the horizon. In 2017, the New Orleans Police Department, which had been wracked by complaints about police misconduct, implemented a peer intervention program called Ethical Policing Is Courageous, or EPIC.[30] EPIC fosters the expectation that police officers will step in whenever they see their colleagues about to engage in an act of misconduct, and that they will report bad acts.[31] Since EPIC was implemented, citizen complaints against the police have dropped. Anecdotal evidence demonstrates that the program is having an effect. In one case, one officer arrested another officer who kicked a handcuffed man in the face, admonishing that officer that times had changed. In another incident, a handcuffed man spit in the face of an officer, who walked away instead of responding with force. Michael S. Harrison, former superintendent of the New Orleans Police Department, was recently hired by the city of Baltimore to serve as its police commissioner. Harrison will be taking EPIC with him.[32] Other cities around the country are also considering implementation of EPIC.

Body cameras may also reduce police misconduct.[33] If police officers are required to wear body cameras that are recording any time they interact with the public, there will be a better and more accurate record of the interactions leading up to an arrest. In turn, this might reduce police officers' willingness to trump up charges in the first instance. Further, prosecutors can easily review the camera footage and dismiss charges for crimes created by the police. Recall from chapter 5 the prosecutor in Pennsylvania who reviewed dash cam footage of a corrupt officer planting drugs on innocent suspects, and thereby prevented no-crime wrongful convictions from occurring.

But programs like EPIC and even the implementation of body cameras need to be accompanied by police leadership that demonstrates a deep commitment to improving training, supervision, and investigation of police misconduct. Change will happen only when new programs and strategies for preventing misconduct are combined with accountability for those officers who abuse their power.

Policymakers could aid in reducing police misconduct by changing the rhetoric and policies that have fostered mass incarceration. Declaring a "war on drugs" and providing the police with accompanying paramilitary gear signify an emergency that does not exist but that engenders rapid and punitive responses by police against the "enemy." Often, the "enemy" is deemed to be poor people or people of color, as we have seen time and again in the drug raids of Tulia and elsewhere that have yielded arrests but uncovered no actual crimes. Policymakers need to be far more thoughtful about how they define crime, and about how they want those laws to be enforced. At the low end— for instance, in the trespassing sweeps in New York City—the very nature of policing was subverted as officers did not conduct individualized investigations based on probable cause, but rather arrested large groups of individuals who were then collectively prosecuted and punished regardless of their actual guilt or innocence. Many of the innocent defendants caught up in these policies have pled guilty to avoid the costly process of fighting their case, even though there was no wrongdoing.

It is also time to rethink aggressive policies that incentivize law enforcement officers to make arrests. Quotas and financial incentives in the forms of forfeiture laws and fines and fees can result in indiscriminate sweeps of poor and marginalized members of the community, irrespective of guilt or innocence. Policing initiatives are most effective when developed in partnership with the affected communities, and should be implemented with an eye to reducing arrests for low-level, nonviolent offenses.

If we stop arresting people for crimes that never happened, if we are more careful and deliberate about what we define as criminal and what we arrest and prosecute people for, we could find ourselves with a smaller, less crowded criminal justice system. Police could have more time to investigate real crimes, prosecutors to pursue actual perpetrators, and defense lawyers to adequately do their jobs. And errors would likely be uncovered sooner.

PROVIDE COGNITIVE BIAS TRAINING TO POLICE, PROSECUTORS, AND JUDGES

As we have seen throughout this book, cognitive biases, including tunnel vision, belief perseverance, confirmation bias, expectation bias, and hindsight bias, are significant contributors to no-crime wrongful convictions that play out at every stage of the criminal justice process. Take the guilt-presumptive bias. Alan Dershowitz, a Harvard law professor and criminal defense attorney, conceptualized the criminal justice system as a game that begins with two rules:

> Rule I: Almost all criminal defendants are in fact guilty.
>
> Rule II: All criminal defense lawyers, prosecutors, and judges understand and believe Rule I.[34]

The guilt-presumptive bias starts with the police approach to an event as a crime and to a suspect as its perpetrator, to a prosecution's decision to charge and pursue a case, to a defense lawyer's harried approach to a case, to a judge's way of ruling on motions, assessing credibility, and using their discretion. The guilt-presumptive approach makes people look the other way from police overreach, prosecutorial impropriety, or bad lawyering. It infects the entire process, but very few actors recognize its impact.

Although cognitive biases are difficult to control, research suggests that education and training can mitigate their influence.[35] Awareness of the effect of cognitive biases is particularly important because criminal justice actors often perceive themselves as highly objective. In one survey of thirty-six judges who attended a conference, 97 percent believed they were in the top quarter in "avoid[ing] racial prejudice"—a mathematical impossibility.[36] Legal scholar Jerry Kang suggests that people who believe themselves to be unbiased may actually be *more* prone to biased decision making, but he also argues that training about cognitive biases reduces bias.[37] As chapter 7 shows, judges—both black and white—who took the Implicit Bias Test showed a bias in favor of white defendants, but could self-correct when they knew they were being evaluated for race biases. Taking steps to improve the diversity of judges on the bench—who in most communities are still mostly white and male—could also make a difference in de-biasing them.[38]

But research demonstrates that simply informing a person about their biases and urging them to overcome them is not enough. The next step is to develop actionable steps designed to change behavior. Studies have shown that forcing decision makers to consider the opposite of their conclusion—in these cases, to consider the idea that defendants are innocent or that no crime happened—could prove effective.[39]

To mitigate against the influence of belief perseverance and tunnel vision, police actors could be required to present their cases to supervisors or other investigators with no connection to the case, who could serve as devil's advocates, forcing the primary investigators to articulate how and why the results could have been different. For instance, in the near-miss no-crime conviction involving Ronnie Winfield, the police and the prosecutor should not have just accepted that Hall was strangled. Each actor should have looked at the homicide label and asked themselves what evidence was absent that they would otherwise have expected to find. As the defense expert pointed out, there were virtually no signs of strangulation. Had they been willing to consider disconfirming evidence, they might have realized that the case for Hall's strangulation was quite weak and circumstantial, while the evidence that she died of natural causes was quite strong and direct.

Prosecutors should conduct a similar evaluation when a case is brought to their offices. But prosecutors often receive their evidence from police investigators, which means their understanding of a case may be contaminated by the investigator's cognitive biases. These add to whatever cognitive biases prosecutors themselves bring to the table.[40]

In theory, when criminal justice actors have failed to screen out no-crime cases in the first instances, jurors serve as a backstop. But contradictory evidence is almost never considered by any fact finder, because cases almost never go to trial. In the context of plea bargains, through which almost every case is resolved, it is the *prosecutor* who first needs to put on a defense hat and engage in a critical assessment of the weaknesses in the case. If prosecutors are unwilling to conduct that review, it will never happen. To facilitate this process, prosecutor offices could adopt a second-look procedure in which supervisors or other team members come in blindly on a case and raise hard-to-ask questions about case flaws with an eye to ferreting out valid innocence claims. Doing so might weed out cases that should never be brought in the first place.

REFORMING THE PLEA PROCESS FOR INNOCENT NO-CRIME DEFENDANTS

As this book shows, innocent defendants plead guilty to crimes that never happened. Even when a defendant's decision to plead guilty is the most rational one given the current realities of the criminal justice system and its practices, that does not mean that the outcome is just or that we cannot do better. Plea bargaining has its place in the prosecution of the guilty, who are awarded a benefit in exchange for admitting guilt, accepting punishment, and conserving state resources. In contrast, no public interest, other than expediency, is served by plea convictions in cases where nothing criminal happened in the first place. A plea hides police wrongdoing, cloaks weaknesses in the prosecution's case, gives a pass to harried defense lawyers who have no time to provide real representation, and enables judges to keep their dockets moving. Further, pleas to crimes that never happened waste precious taxpayers' resources, with the police and prosecutor investigating fictional events and defense lawyers, mostly at taxpayer expense, trying to stave off the state. Worst of all, they harm innocent defendants who become permanently branded a criminal after serving whatever sentence they receive

Because the plea system circumvents the fact-finding function of a trial, a defendant's willingness to plead guilty is treated as evidence that he or she *is* guilty. This is, of course, simply untrue. As this book discusses at length, innocent people plead guilty all the time for reasons that have nothing to do with actual guilt.

We might imagine the elimination of plea bargaining. Some reformers have in fact floated the idea of defenders who refuse all pleas and "crash the courts."[41] No doubt the system would grind to a halt. But in truth, a complete and radical overhaul of plea bargaining is unlikely to happen. As the U.S. Supreme Court declared in 1970, plea bargains have become "inherent in the criminal law and its administration."[42] All players in the system—prosecutors, defense lawyers, judges, and even defendants who are in fact guilty—have a vested interest in plea bargaining.

So what, then, can be done to reduce the prevalence of innocent people who plead guilty to crimes that never happened?

First, bail reform would help reduce the number of no-crime wrongful convictions based on guilty pleas by poor defendants who admit guilt to avoid pretrial detention. If innocent defendants, particularly in low-level offenses, were not held in jail because they are too poor to post bail, they might be far less willing to plead guilty. Prosecutors would be forced to grapple with the strengths or weaknesses of their cases and decide whether a crime actually occurred.

Remember Erma Faye Stewart from chapter 3? Had she not been so desperate to go home to her children, she would not have pleaded guilty to a drug crime that never happened. Had she had the money to do so, she would have made bail. Had she had the ability to wait it out in jail, she would have been among the defendants against whom the prosecution dismissed the charges once they realized the informant was a liar. But she did not. And her drug conviction for a crime that never happened haunts her to this day.

Bail reform has gained momentum. In 2017, New Jersey implemented major bail reform, eliminating cash bail for most defendants. In 2019, New York State passed sweeping bail reform measures. In 2019, California passed a bill to eliminate cash bail that will be subject to a referendum in November 2020.[43] Nonprofit organizations such as the Bail Project and the Bronx Freedom Fund have sprung up to pay for bail when defendants cannot.[44] States and cities should adopt bail reform in order to relieve the pressure on innocent people to plead guilty, to allow low-level offenders to remain with their families at no sacrifice to public safety, and to save taxpayer dollars.

Second, as a blanket policy measure, prosecutors should not make plea offers in drug cases based solely on field tests—particularly not "exploding" offers that require defendants to accept the deal immediately. For their part, judges should not accept plea convictions until lab results confirm the existence of an illegal substance. This change would work best in tandem with bail reform measures so that defendants do not languish in jail while awaiting lab results. Field tests are notoriously unreliable, and defendants should not be forced to choose between pretrial detention and pleading guilty until the presence or absence of drugs is confirmed.

Third, the plea system is opaque and suffers from an informational imbalance. Particularly in the early stages of a case, it is difficult for a defendant to assess the strength of the prosecution's evidence. While a guilty defendant may have at least a sense of what proof the prosecution has at their disposal, an innocent defendant who committed no crime is unlikely to have any clue. Jurisdictional rules and policies could be changed to allow for earlier and more open sharing of information before plea resolutions. The liberalization of discovery would improve information and accuracy by allowing defendants and their lawyers to better assess the strength of the case. If liberalization rules were reciprocal, prosecutors might evaluate earlier any evidence that contradicts their presumption of guilt, which in turn could result in more robust screening of cases before an innocent defendant is convicted of a crime that never happened.

Fourth, we could rethink the role of judges in plea bargaining. Judges typically play no part in plea negotiations, and the deal making is almost always done off the record. Unlike a criminal trial, where prosecutors have to prove their case beyond a reasonable doubt, plea bargaining has no similar requirement. A prosecutor makes an offer and the defendant decides whether to take the deal without ever knowing if the prosecution can prove its case.

Judges could be permitted to play a more active role in the plea process. Research suggests that a judge's early input into plea negotiations can render the final disposition more accurate and procedurally just.[45] In Connecticut, judges are actively involved in the negotiations as moderators.[46] They provide input on the merits of the case and on the ultimate sentence acceptable to the court. In their role as "information mediator," judges can provide a neutral assessment of the case's merits. They can also help the defense and the prosecution come to a fair resolution that reflects the strengths and weaknesses of the evidence. More specifically, judges would ideally have access to the evidence that forms the factual basis for the plea; if it is inadequate because no crime was committed, judges could intervene. To avoid potential future conflicts, the judge who participates in pretrial negotiations where no plea agreement is reached could be prohibited from presiding over any future trial involving the same defendant.

Of course, greater involvement of judges is no panacea. They too are plagued by large caseloads and are often beholden to politics. But they can serve as a check on prosecutors, who in the current plea-driven structure have virtually unfettered power to induce pleas.

Fifth, increasing the availability of trials could reduce pleas in no-crime cases. In Philadelphia, defendants frequently waive their right to a jury trial and allow a judge in a bench trial to determine whether the prosecution has proven its case beyond a reasonable doubt. This change appears to have gained traction. In 2015, only 72 percent of defendants in Philadelphia pled guilty, while 15 percent pursued a bench trial.[47] Bench trials avoid the time consumed by jury selection and allows defendants to have their cases heard expeditiously. While a bench trial requires defendants to forgo a review of the evidence by their peers, it does offer a way for the accused to hold the prosecution to their evidentiary burden.

A final point is worth making here. Misdemeanor cases are nearly always resolved by plea bargains. "Petty offenses" carry with them significant, life-long consequences. We do not know how many innocent people have pled guilty to crimes that never happened, but one need only look at the trespass-ing cases in the Bronx or the loitering cases in Baltimore to know it happens far too frequently. Misdemeanor cases deserve more attention than they get. They matter. If we are going to arrest people for them, more funding needs to be provided to defense lawyers to ensure that misdemeanants receive the representation that they deserve. Or we could stop arresting people in crime sweeps that capture innocent people in their net for crimes that never happened.

PROMOTE OPEN DISCOVERY RULES AND ENFORCE EXISTING *BRADY* OBLIGATIONS

Prosecutors routinely violate their discovery obligations under *Brady,* as this book discusses in regard to many no-crime cases. It is time to stem the epi-demic of *Brady* violations.

Courts can play a significant role in ensuring the prosecution meets its obligations. Trial courts, for instance, have a range of tools they could employ, and they are ideally situated to use them. For instance, trial judges can issue a standing order that all prosecutors must comply with *Brady.* They can develop *Brady* checklists, in writing, that detail the different types of exculpatory and impeachment evidence that the prosecution is required to turn over. As part of their pretrial conferences or, even more ideally, as part of a hearing on the record, they can review the *Brady* checklist with both parties to ensure that the obligations have been met.

When prosecutors nonetheless fail to meet their *Brady* obligations at trial, trial judges can impose an array of sanctions. They can order the evidence turned over to the defense and issue an instruction to the jury. They can hold the prosecutor in contempt or even bar them from their courtroom. They can report the prosecutor for ethical violations.

But most *Brady* violations come to light only after a trial in which a defendant has been convicted. If a trial judge does not prevent a *Brady* violation, the use of a checklist and an on-the-record hearing will better enable appellate judges to evaluate the trial record. Appellate judges also have the ability to impose sanctions for *Brady* violations, but they rarely do so, even when the prosecutor intentionally and deliberately withheld *Brady* material. If courts held prosecutors accountable for their deliberate failures to comply with *Brady* disclosure obligations, prosecutors might rethink the way they approach those obligations.

One way to affirmatively end this *Brady* morass is to change the law concerning the prosecution's disclosure obligations. One reason for *Brady*'s ineffectiveness is that prosecutors are required to turn over "material" evidence, that is, the very evidence that most damages their case. This conflict of interest between meeting *Brady* obligations and undercutting their ability to "win" is often resolved to the detriment of the defendant. This is particularly true since prosecutors are rarely held accountable for their errors.

A policy change that could help avoid the wrongful conviction of innocent people, and the endless litigation that *Brady* claims spawn, is open-file discovery. Open-file discovery means what its name suggests: the defense would have access to the prosecution's entire case file and the files of the investigative bodies working with the prosecution. Prosecutors would have the right to make a motion for an in camera inspection of material they do not want to disclose because of confidentiality or public safety concerns. Open-file discovery levels the playing field by creating an informational flow that might well allow innocent defendants to adequately defend themselves. While prosecutors could play fast and loose with this rule by keeping exculpatory evidence outside their files, in violation of the spirit of this *Brady* reform, or by dumping excessive documents on defense lawyers in an effort to bury the evidence, open discovery would likely narrow *Brady* violations to only those committed by prosecutors bent on circumventing the law at all costs.

Appellate judges also need to do their jobs with greater awareness and diligence. In Brandon Garrett's study of the first two hundred cases of innocence, appellate judges often found compelling evidence of guilt in applying the "harmless error" doctrine to people who were actually and factually innocent. At minimum, appellate judges should be made aware of the dangers of hindsight bias, and engage in careful scrutiny of the record below. Rather than assume a conviction was inevitable and therefore an error was harmless, courts could focus on the actual error at hand.

CHANGING PROSECUTION PRACTICES AND CULTURE FROM THE INSIDE AND THE OUTSIDE

To change prosecutorial practices from the inside, we need to transform prosecutorial culture.[48] It is axiomatic that prosecutors, as "ministers of justice," should be held to high ethical standards. The Prosecution Standards of the National District Attorneys Association assert: "The prosecutor is an independent administrator of justice. The primary responsibility of a prosecutor is to seek justice, which can only be achieved by the representation and presentation of truth."[49] Chief prosecutors could embrace a vision of their office as driven by justice rather than convictions. They could cultivate an office environment that prioritizes and celebrates ethical behavior. They could call out or shame prosecutors within the office who fail to live up to ethical standards. They could reassess prosecutorial priorities and decline to prosecute low-level "quality of life" offenses.

There are signs of change in the air. Reform-minded prosecutors swept into office around the nation after campaigning on platforms that included bail reform, diversion of low-level offenses out of the system, racial equality, and the decriminalization of marijuana. One need only consider the impressive array of newly elected reformers to see that momentum, at least in certain jurisdictions, is swinging away from prosecution as usual to a more inclusive, less punitive vision of the prosecutor's role. Kim Ogg was elected DA in Houston, Texas, after campaigning on a platform of restoring prosecutorial integrity and ensuring the robust protection of constitutional rights. Kim Foxx, an African American woman who grew up in the Cabrini-Green housing projects in Chicago and was elected as the Cook County state attorney general in 2016, campaigned to reduce racial disparities and improve police misconduct investigations. Mark Gonzalez, a former defense attorney with the words "not guilty" tattooed across his chest, was elected DA in Nueces County, Texas, whose seat is Corpus Christi. Gonzalez promised to be more selective in the cases his office prosecutes, including marijuana crimes. Larry Krasner, a reformist attorney who previously represented Occupy Wall Street and Black Lives Matter activists, was elected as Philadelphia's district attorney after promising to end mass incarceration and never to seek the death penalty.

Of course, electing reformers is only the beginning. Progressive DAs have their work cut out for them in gaining the trust and cooperation of police departments when they seek to implement such reforms as decriminalization of marijuana or other low-level offenses. Prosecutors also have an uphill road in changing the office culture and the mentality of career prosecutors who do not necessarily see eye to eye with their new bosses. Perhaps in recognition of the need for buy-in, DA Ogg in Harris County cleaned house, firing thirty-seven prosecutors and bringing in defense lawyers to fill their places.[50] Culture change could be hastened along with changes in hiring and training, and with mentorship by like-minded prosecutors to newly minted attorneys.

But changes in culture take time. To reduce the risk that prosecutors are pursuing convictions based on crimes that did not happen, practical measures can be implemented in the meantime.

First, prosecutors could build into their practice a rigorous screening of the evidence—interviewing key witnesses and asking the police to investigate alibis and patent weaknesses in cases—before issuing charges. This may seem obvious to a layperson, but it does not often happen. Because prosecutors are also overwhelmed by large caseloads, in a case's early stages, they often rely on police narratives without sifting the evidence. The result is that more cases are filed than prosecutors can responsibly handle. Individual prosecutors sometimes carry hundreds of open cases at any given time, many of them serious felonies. In Houston, for instance, prosecutors may have five hundred open cases at one time and handle more than fifteen hundred cases in a single year. In Las Vegas in 2009, prosecutors handled eight hundred cases in a year.[51] Such heavy caseloads leave prosecutors with virtually no time to engage in the careful scrutiny of each case on their docket that justice would demand. Cases that should be dismissed languish on the docket simply because no prosecutor has dug deep into the file.[52] As cases are passed between prosecutors juggling large caseloads, it is possible that no one has engaged in a meaningful review of the existing evidence. Cases, even ones that should be dismissed, end in pleas because defendants are desperate to minimize their jail time and go home.

Prosecutors should initiate better screening up front in order to sort out the viable cases involving actual crimes from the trespassing and other low-level offenses that never happened. Screening does occur today, but it is not always effective. More needs to be done early on so that no-crime cases do not gain momentum.

Second, prosecutor offices should develop robust second-look programs. Prosecutor offices could create preconviction procedures through which defense lawyers (or even judges) could request a "second look" from a supervisor (or at least a different prosecutor) in cases where the specter of actual innocence lurks. Prosecutor offices should also create conviction integrity units (CIUs), which have been recognized as a best practice.[53] At the end of 2018, CIUs operated in forty-four jurisdictions.[54] The CIU should be structurally independent of the rest of the office and be adequately staffed and funded to ensure its members can do their jobs.

We know that wrongful convictions happen. With effective CIUs, prosecutors can be part of the solution. CIUs provide an opportunity for prosecutor offices to take a systems approach to learning from their mistakes. Much like the "sentinel event" analysis that occurs after an airplane crash, the work of CIUs can help prosecutor's offices examine what went wrong in any individual case and develop policies to prevent those errors from recurring. Such analyses also provide an opportunity for prosecutors to reassure the public that they are serving all members of the community. As forty-four elected prosecutors recently wrote in support of the St. Louis CIU: "CIUs serve as vehicles for building . . . public trust, by demonstrating an elected prosecutor's commitment to ensuring each case is handled in an ethical manner and that each conviction was rightfully obtained. On the other hand, wrongful convictions—especially those involving prosecutorial misconduct—erode community trust in the justice system."[55] Prosecutors should zealously pursue justice, before and after a conviction is obtained. CIUs can help prosecutors achieve this objective.

Third, as discussed previously, prosecutors need to provide better discovery. Even without a change in law requiring open discovery, prosecutors can still do far better than what *Brady* requires. Prosecutors should turn over evidence that *might* be relevant at trial—even if it is not technically "material" under *Brady*. This generous standard undoubtedly exceeds what is legally required by law, but may be what is required to fulfill the mandates of justice.

Finally, to change prosecutor practices from the outside, courts and legislators have to change immunity for prosecutors. Prosecutors currently enjoy absolute immunity from civil damages for misconduct performed in their advocacy function.[56] This rule has insulated prosecutors—even those who deliberately and intentionally engage in the most egregious forms of misconduct that resulted in wrongful convictions—from being held liable for their actions. Absolute immunity should, at minimum, be replaced by qualified immunity, which arguably "would protect honest prosecutors from unwarranted litigation while affording victims of deliberate prosecutorial misconduct a remedy for the willful violation of their civil rights."[57]

DEFENSE LAWYERING

That defense lawyers have overwhelming caseloads and a chronic lack of funding, as detailed in chapter 6, is not a new complaint. It is also not a problem unique to wrongful convictions, but has structural implications for the entire criminal justice system. Supreme Court justice Hugo L. Black warned in 1956 that there "can be no equal justice where the kind of trial a man gets depends on the amount of money he has." Indeed.

Even though poorly funded, overworked defense lawyers are not unique to no-crime wrongful convictions, they certainly contribute to them. Defense lawyers, particularly in misdemeanor cases, cannot ferret out the fact that no crime occurred if they have only minutes to meet with their clients before they are on to the next case. They cannot consider whether a crime occurred, let alone mount a robust defense, investigate alibis, challenge prosecution witnesses, track down defense witnesses, file motions, and otherwise fulfill their constitutional mandates if they don't have manageable caseloads and funding to do their jobs. They can't be strategic and thoughtful if they are in a constant state of triage.

To reduce caseloads, state and local governments need to provide additional funding for the hiring and training of additional lawyers. They need to learn more about forensic evidence so they can mount effective defenses, and they need greater access to experts. To meet these goals, lawmakers need to increase funding for defense lawyers. If they do not, public defender officers should refuse to take new cases when caseloads exceed recommended levels for existing staff.

But the root of the problem is not just caseloads, and not just funding. As noted throughout this book, defense lawyers are forced to rely on the prosecution to act in good faith, to provide them with discovery in a timely manner, to turn over exculpatory evidence to the defense, to put on reliable and truthful evidence. It is often nearly impossible for a defense lawyer to discover that the prosecution did not do what it was required to do. Under current law, when prosecutors violate their obligations, the only person who suffers the consequences is the innocent defendant. That needs to change.

One final note about the legal profession and its obligation to provide quality representation to all defendants. If good defense lawyering matters—and I believe it does—then we need to do more to ensure that lawyers are doing their jobs competently. It is not enough to have a defense lawyer seated at the table. Judges and even prosecutors are officers of the court. They have an ethical obligation to call out bad lawyers who are sleeping or intoxicated or are seemingly ignorant of the law, and they should make a record of negligent lawyering. Poor defendants should not lose their life and liberty simply because they had the misfortune of being assigned a bad lawyer; it is up to all actors in the system to ensure that a defendant is receiving appropriate representation.

When defense lawyering is done properly, the criminal justice system functions better. When defense lawyers have the time and resources to provide proper representation, they can prevent no-crime wrongful convictions in the first instance.

When a crime occurs, society has a vested interest in finding the perpetrator and seeing that justice is done. With actual-crime wrongful convictions, our duty is to reduce the frequency of error by improving police and prosecutor practices, by changing the system's responsiveness time, and by being prepared to remedy the harm caused by convicting the wrong person for the crime of another.

But no-crime convictions do not even start with a vested societal interest in solving a crime—because the crime never happened. Nothing criminal happened at all.

Yet, despite the absence of a crime, people are convicted. In more serious cases, men and women endure months or years locked in filthy, overly hot or cold steel cages, in violent and hostile conditions, separated from family and friends, labeled a felon and a monster. In some no-crime cases, innocent people have even been executed. In low-level misdemeanor cases, innocent defendants may escape with "only" the stigma of a misdemeanor conviction and the multitude of consequences that stem from a criminal record. They are mostly poor, and mostly people of color.

All have lost so much to the criminal justice system. Even though no crime ever occurred.

What a colossal waste of time. Of energy and resources. Of human spirit.

No-crime wrongful convictions are deeply disturbing. They need to be taken seriously. The modest proposals outlined in this conclusion offer concrete steps that system actors can take to reduce the occurrence of no-crime wrongful convictions.

No-crime convictions represent the perfect storm of errors and indifference.

We can, we must, do better.

NOTES

INTRODUCTION

1. Maurice Possley, "Rodricus Crawford," *National Registry of Exonerations* (hereinafter *NRE*), posted April 18, 2017, https://www.law.umich.edu/special /exoneration/Pages/casedetail.aspx?caseid=5123.

2. The following discussion of Rodricus Crawford's case and its aftermath is based on Rachel Aviv, "Revenge Killing," *New Yorker,* June 29, 2015, https://www .newyorker.com/magazine/2015/07/06/revenge-killing; Rachel Aviv, "A Death Sentence Overturned in Louisiana," *New Yorker,* November 23, 2016, https://www .newyorker.com/news/news-desk/a-death-sentence-overturned-in-louisiana; Sarah Crawford, "From Death Row to Freedom: Rodricus Crawford Looks to Future," *Shreveport Times,* April 21, 2017, https://www.shreveporttimes.com/story /news/2017/04/21/death-row-freedom-rodricus-crawford-looks-future-but-cant-forget-past/100620380/; and Tracy Connor, "Charges Dropped against Former Death-Row Inmate Rodricus Crawford," WNBC, April 17, 2017, https://www .nbcnews.com/news/us-news/charges-dropped-against-former-death-row-inmate-rodricus-crawford-n748551.

3. *Rodricus Crawford v. Caddo Par. Coroner's Office,* Civil Action No. 17-01509, Memorandum Ruling (February 25, 2019), 4 n. 3.

4. Aviv, "Revenge Killing."

5. *Crawford et al. v. Caddo Parish Coroner et al.,* Civil Complaint, Docket No. ₅₁₇ CV ₀₁₅₀₉, para. ₁₄ (filed November ₀₆, ₂₀₁₇) (copy in author's possession).

6. *Crawford et al.,* Civil Complaint, para. 28.

7. *Crawford et al.,* Civil Complaint, paras. 33, 34

8. Aviv, "Revenge Killing."

9. Campbell Robertson, "The Prosecutor Who Says Louisiana Should 'Kill More People,'" *New York Times,* July 8, 2015, https://www.nytimes.com/2015/07/08 /us/louisiana-prosecutor-becomes-blunt-spokesman-for-death-penalty.html?smid= pl-share.

10. *State v. Crawford,* 218 So.3d 13 (La. 2016).

11. Aviv, "Revenge Killing."

12. Aviv, "Revenge Killing."

13. Aviv, "Revenge Killing."

14. *Crawford,* 218 So.3d at 16.

15. *Crawford,* 218 So.3d at 36 (Crichton, J., concurring).

16. "Rodricus Crawford Becomes 158th Death-Row Exoneree," *Death Penalty Information Center,* posted April 18, 2017, https://deathpenaltyinfo.org/node/6736.

17. A recent suit filed on behalf of people held on Angola's death row details the conditions of extreme deprivation and hardship. See *Hamilton et al. v. Vannoy et al.,* Class Action Complaint, 3:17-cv-00194-SDD-RLB (M.D. La.), filed March 29, 2017, available at https://cardozo.yu.edu/sites/default/files/Angola%20filed%5DNEW .pdf.

18. *Hamilton et al. v. Vannoy et al.,* Class Action Complaint.

19. Sarah Crawford, "From Death Row to Freedom: Rodricus Crawford Looks to Future," *Shreveport Times,* April 21, 2017, https://www.shreveporttimes.com /story/news/2017/04/21/death-row-freedom-rodricus-crawford-looks-future-but-cant-forget-past/100620380/

20. *NRE,* data from June 30, 2019 (on file with author).

21. Gerald McFarland, *The "Counterfeit" Man: The True Story of the Boorn-Colvin Murder Case* (Amherst: University of Massachusetts Press, 1993).

22. McFarland, *The "Counterfeit" Man.*

23. Meghan Barrett Cousino, "William Jackson Marion," *NRE,* accessed September 27, 2018, https://www.law.umich.edu/special/exoneration/Pages/casedetailpre 1989.aspx?caseid=212.

24. Bill Kelly, "1887 Hanging Remains Nebraska's Most Controversial Execution," *NET Nebraska* (National Public Radio), February 7, 2013, http://netnebraska .org/article/news/1887-hanging-remains-nebraskas-most-controversial-execution.

25. For discussions of the Salem witch trials, see Mary Beth Norton, *In the Devil's Snare: The Salem Witchcraft Crisis of 1692* (New York: Knopf, 2002); Marilynne K. Roach, *The Salem Witch Trials: A Day-by-Day Chronicle of a Community under Siege* (Lanham, MD: Taylor Trade, 2004)

26. Barry C. Edwards, "Why Appeals Courts Rarely Reverse Lower Courts: An Experimental Study to Explore Affirmation Bias," *Emory Law Journal Online* 68 (2019): 1035, 1037–40.

27. Samuel Gross et al., "Rate of False Conviction of Criminal Defendants Sentenced to Death," *Proceedings of the National Academy of Sciences of the United States of America* 111 (2014): 7230–35.

28. Danielle Kaeble and Mary Cowhig, "Correctional Populations in the United States, 2016," Bureau of Justice Statistics, April 2018, https://www.bjs.gov/content /pub/pdf/cpus16.pdf.

29. "Mass Exonerations and Group Exonerations since 1989," *NRE,* April 9, 2018, http://www.law.umich.edu/special/exoneration/Documents/NREMass ExonConf4418.pdf.

30. "Mass Exonerations and Group Exonerations since 1989."

31. Alexandra Natapoff, "Why Misdemeanors Aren't So Minor," *Slate,* April 27, 2012, http://www.slate.com/articles/news_and_politics/jurisprudence/2012/04/misdemeanors_can_have_major_consequences_for_the_people_charged_.html.

32. Jed S. Rakoff, "Why Innocent People Plead Guilty," *New York Times Book Review,* November 20, 2014, https://www.nybooks.com/articles/2014/11/20/why-innocent-people-plead-guilty/.

33. *NRE,* data from June 30, 2019 (on file with author).

34. Candace McCoy, "Plea Bargaining as Coercion: The Trial Penalty and Plea Bargaining Reform," *Criminal Law Quarterly* 50 (2005): 67, 72.

35. For a general discussion, see Nate Blakeslee, *Tulia: Race, Cocaine, and Corruption in a Small Texas Town* (New York: PublicAffairs, 2006).

36. For an excellent overview about how these factors lead to wrongful convictions, see Barry Scheck, Peter Neufeld, and Jim Dwyer, *Actual Innocence: When Justice Goes Wrong and How to Make It Right,* 2d ed. (New York: Doubleday, 2001).

37. Edwin M. Borchard, *Convicting the Innocent* (New Haven: Yale University Press, 1932), 375–78.

38. "Eyewitness Misidentification," *Innocence Project,* accessed November 24, 2019, https://www.innocenceproject.org/causes/eyewitness-misidentification/.

39. The data in table 2 include only the "worst conviction" associated with an exonerated defendant in a no-crime wrongful conviction case. For instance, if a defendant is convicted of murder that was caused by arson, only the murder conviction would appear in this data.

40. Samuel Gross et al., "Race and Wrongful Convictions in the United States," *NRE* (March 7, 2017), 18–19, http://www.law.umich.edu/special/exoneration/Documents/Race_and_Wrongful_Convictions.pdf.

41. "Exonerations in 2016," *NRE,* March 7, 2017, pp. 7–8, https://www.law.umich.edu/special/exoneration/Documents/Exonerations_in_2016.pdf (predicting that child sex abuse hysteria cases "most likely . . . have run their course").

42. "Briefing Paper: The Dangerous Overuse of Solitary Confinement in the United States," ACLU, August 2014, https://www.aclu.org/other/stop-solitary-briefing-paper?redirect=criminal-law-reform-prisoners-rights/stop-solitary-briefing-paper.

43. James R. Ackers, "The Flipside Injustice of Wrongful Convictions: When the Guilty Go Free," *Albany Law Review* 76 (2013): 1629, 1632.

44. Aaron Martinez, "Investigation: DPS Analyst Falsified El Paso DWI Blood Tests but Not Intentionally," *El Paso Times,* July 27, 2018, https://www.elpasotimes.com/story/news/crime/2018/07/27/investigation-texas-dps-analyst-falsified-el-paso-dwi-blood-alcohol-tests-but-not-intentionally/844257002/.

45. Maurice Possley, "Gregory Counts," *NRE,* May 10, 2018, https://www.law.umich.edu/special/exoneration/Pages/casedetail.aspx?caseid=5323; Jan Ransom, "26 Years Later, Justice for Men Imprisoned for a Bogus Rape," *New York Times,* May 7, 2018, https://www.nytimes.com/2018/05/07/nyregion/innocence-project-manhattan-rape.html.

1. The facts presented here come from a variety of sources, including the Fourth Circuit Court of Appeals decision vacating Beverly Monroe's conviction in *Monroe v. Angelone,* 323 F.3d 286 (4th Cir. 2003); John Taylor, *The Count and the Confession* (New York: Random House, 2002); Ralph Blumenthal, "A Virginia Tale of Love and Death, Suspicions and Doubt," *New York Times,* February 22, 2000, https://www.nytimes.com/2000/02/22/us/a-virginia-tale-of-love-and-death-suspicions-and-doubt.html; and Stephanie Denzel, "Beverly Monroe," *NRE,* https://www.law.umich.edu/special/exoneration/Pages/casedetail.aspx?caseid=3482.

2. Blumenthal, "A Virginia Tale of Love and Death."

3. *Monroe,* 323 F.3d at 290.

4. *Monroe,* 323 F.3d at 293.

5. Dan Simon, *In Doubt: The Psychology of the Criminal Justice Process* (Cambridge, MA: Harvard University Press, 2012), 21.

6. NRE, data from June 30, 2019 (on file with author).

7. Andrea Lewis and Sara Sommerveld, "Death, but Is It Murder? The Role of Stereotypes and Cultural Perceptions in the Wrongful Conviction of Women," *Albany Law Review* 78 (2015): 1035, 1039.

8. Lewis and Sommerveld, "Death, but Is It Murder? 1039–1050 (quote at 1046).

9. By at least one estimate, more than 150 types of cognitive biases exist, though that number varies greatly depending on how cognitive biases are defined and categorized. See, for example, Jeff Desjardins, "Every Single Cognitive Bias in One Infographic," *Visual Capitalist,* September 25, 2017, http://www.visualcapitalist.com/every-single-cognitive-bias/.

10. Keith A. Findley and Michael S. Scott, "The Multiple Dimensions of Tunnel Vision in Criminal Cases," *Wisconsin Law Review* 2 (2006): 209.

11. Daniel Kahneman and Amos Tversky, "Subjective Probability: A Judgment of Representativeness," *Cognitive Psychology* 3 (1972): 1124–31.

12. Findley and Scott, "Multiple Dimensions of Tunnel Vision," 292.

13. Findley and Scott, "Multiple Dimensions of Tunnel Vision," 292.

14. Simon, *In Doubt,* 23.

15. Jennifer L. Hillman, *Crisis Intervention and Trauma: New Approaches to Evidence-Based Practice* (New York: Springer Science and Business Media, 2013), 124.

16. M. L. Rosenberg et al., "Operational Criteria for the Determination of Suicide," *Journal of Forensic Science* 33(6) (1988): 1445–56.

17. Rosenberg et al., "Operational Criteria for the Determination of Suicide," 1448.

18. Vernon Geberth, "Seven Mistakes in Suicide Investigation," *Law & Order Magazine,* 61(1) (2013), http://www.practicalhomicide.com/Research/7mistakes.htm.

19. Simon, *In Doubt,* 24.

20. Jon B. Gould et al., "Predicting Erroneous Convictions," *Iowa Law Review* 99 (2014): 471, 504 (quoting Findley and Scott, "Multiple Dimensions of Tunnel Vision," 292).

21. *Monroe,* 323 F.3d at 295.

22. *Monroe,* 323 F.3d at 315.

23. *Monroe,* 323 F.3d at 286.

24. I searched the term *suicide* in the NRE database. I analyzed the cases that contained *suicide* and determined that, as of September 1, 2018, six defendants had been exonerated after wrongful convictions for murders later revealed to be suicide: Virginia LeFever, Fredda Susie Mowbray, Cesar Munoz, Carolyn June Peak, John Tomaino, and Lon Walker.

25. "Category Archives: Suicide-Mistaken-For-Murder," *Wrongly Convicted Group Website,* accessed July 18, 2019, https://wronglyconvictedgroup.wordpress.com/category/3-case-type/no-crime/suicide-mistaken-for-murder/.

26. Poppy Harlow and Amanda Hobor, "10 Years of Guilt over GM Crash That Killed Her Boyfriend: It May Not Have Been Her Fault," *CNN Money,* August 15, 2014, https://money.cnn.com/interactive/news/candice-anderson/index.html.

27. Harlow and Hobor, "10 Years of Guilt over GM Crash."

28. Findley and Scott, "Multiple Dimensions of Tunnel Vision," 308–9.

29. Rebecca R. Ruiz, "Woman Cleared in Death Caused by GM's Faulty Ignition Switch," *New York Times,* November 24, 2014, https://www.nytimes.com/2014/11/25/business/woman-cleared-in-death-caused-by-gms-faulty-ignition-switch.html.

30. Anderson is not alone. Kuao Fong Lee experienced a similar situation when his Toyota inexplicably accelerated, causing an accident in which multiple people were killed. Lee was sentenced to eight years in prison, but was exonerated after it was revealed that Toyota had recalled cars that had experienced sudden accelerations. Maurice Possley, "Kuao Fong Lee," *NRE,* last updated April 22, 2017, https://www.law.umich.edu/special/exoneration/Pages/casedetail.aspx?caseid=3376 experienced.

31. Ruiz, "Woman Cleared."

32. Deborah Tuerkheimer, "The Next Innocence Project: Shaken Baby Syndrome and the Criminal Courts," *Washington University Law Review* 87 (2009): 1, 4.

33. American Academy of Pediatrics, Committee of Child Abuse and Neglect, "Shaken Baby Syndrome: Inflicted Cerebral Trauma," *Pediatrics* 92 (1993): 872.

34. American Academy of Pediatrics, Committee of Child Abuse and Neglect, "Shaken Baby Syndrome: Rotational Cranial Injuries—Technical Report," *Pediatrics* 108 (2001): 206.

35. Edward J. Imwinkelried, "Shaken Baby Syndrome: A Genuine Battle of the Scientific (and Nonscientific) Experts," *Criminal Law Bulletin* 46 (2010): 156 ("[I]t seems clear that during the past two decades, prosecution expert testimony about shaken baby syndrome has contributed to thousands of convictions"); Tuerkheimer, "The Next Innocence Project" (estimating number of SBS prosecutions and convictions); Debbie Cenziper, "A Disputed Diagnosis Imprisons Parents," *Washington Post,* March 20, 2015, https://www.washingtonpost.com/graphics/investigations/shaken-baby-syndrome/In-Maryland-a-baby-collapses-and-a-babysitter-is-blamed.html.

36. Tuerkheimer, "The Next Innocence Project," 32.

37. The facts of Edmunds's case are based on a variety of sources, including "Audrey Edmunds," Center for Wrongful Convictions, Northwestern University, accessed November 18, 2019, http://www.law.northwestern.edu/legalclinic/wrongfulconvictions/exonerations/wi/audrey-edmunds.html; and Alexandra Gross, "Audrey Edmunds," *NRE*, June 2, 2018, https://www.law.umich.edu/special/exoneration/Pages/casedetail.aspx?caseid=3201. For Audrey Edmunds's firsthand account, see Audrey Edmunds with Jill Wellington, *It Happened to Audrey: From Loving Mum to Accused Baby Killer* (Green Bay, WI: TitleTown, 2012).

38. Edmunds and Wellington, *It Happened to Audrey*.

39. Cindy W. Christian et al. and Committee on Child Abuse and Neglect of the American Academy of Pediatrics, "Abusive Head Trauma in Infants and Children," *Pediatrics* 123(5) (2009): 1409.

40. Swedish Agency for Health Technology Assessment and Assessment of Social Services, *Traumatic Shaking: The Role of the Triad in Medical Investigations of Suspected Traumatic Shaking—A Systematic Review* (2016), available at National Center for Biotechnology Information, https://www.ncbi.nlm.nih.gov/books/NBK448031/pdf/Bookshelf_NBK448031.pdf.

41. Nonhomicidal causes of death misdiagnosed as SBS and resulting in no-crime wrongful convictions include sudden infant death syndrome (SIDS), venous sinus thrombosis, and sickle cell anemia. See Maurice Possley, "Teresa Engberg-Lehmer" (SIDS), *NRE*, July 29, 2012, https://www.law.umich.edu/special/exoneration/Pages/casedetail.aspx?caseid=3952; Maurice Possley, "Joel Lehmer" (SIDS), *NRE*, July 29, 2012, https://www.law.umich.edu/special/exoneration/Pages/casedetail.aspx?caseid=3953; Stephanie Denzel, "Julie Baumer" (venous sinus thrombosis), *NRE*, posted before June 2012, https://www.law.umich.edu/special/exoneration/Pages/casedetail.aspx?caseid=3017; Alexandra Gross, "Melonie Ware" (sickle cell anemia), *NRE*, posted before June 2012, https://www.law.umich.edu/special/exoneration/Pages/casedetail.aspx?caseid=3814.

42. Faris A. Bandak, "Shaken Baby Syndrome: A Biomechanics Analysis of Injury Mechanisms," *Forensic Science International* 151 (2005): 71, 76–79; Ann-Christine Duhaime et al., "The Shaken Baby Syndrome: A Clinical, Pathological, and Biomechanical Study," *Journal of Neurosurgery* 66 (1987): 409.

43. Keith A. Findley, et. al., "Shaken Baby Syndrome, Abusive Head Trauma, and Actual Innocence: Getting It Right," *Houston Journal of Health Law and Policy* 12 (2012): 209, 302–6.

44. Innocence Network, "Statement of the Innocence Network on Shaken Baby Syndrome/Abusive Head Trauma," June 14, 2019, https://innocencenetwork.org/statementoftheinnocencenetworkonshakenbabysyndrome/.

45. Innocence Network, "Statement of the Innocence Network on Shaken Baby Syndrome/Abusive Head Trauma."

46. *NRE*, Detailed View of Cases, sorted by SBS filter (retrieved June 30, 2019).

47. Sabrina Butler, "I Spent More than Six Years as an Innocent Woman on Death Row," *Time*, May 30, 2014, http://time.com/2799437/i-spent-more-than-six-

years-as-an-innocent-woman-on-death-row/; Maurice Possley, "Sabrina Butler," *NRE*, updated August 21, 2019, https://www.law.umich.edu/special/exoneration /Pages/casedetail.aspx?caseid=3078; *Butler v. State*, 608 So.2d 314 (Miss. 1992), https://www.law.umich.edu/special/exoneration/Pages/casedetail.aspx?caseid=3078

48. *Butler*, 608 So.2d 314.

49. Possley, "Sabrina Butler."

50. Rob Warden, "Patricia Stallings: Sentenced to Life without Parole for a Crime That Didn't Happen," Center on Wrongful Convictions, Northwestern University, http://www.law.northwestern.edu/legalclinic/wrongfulconvictions /exonerations/mo/patricia-stallings.html.

51. Michael S. Perry, "Patricia Stallings," *NRE*, posted before June 2012, https:// www.law.umich.edu/special/exoneration/Pages/casedetail.aspx?caseid=3660.

52. Stephani Clifford, "3 Men Imprisoned in 1980 Brooklyn Arson Case Are Exonerated," *New York Times*, December 16, 2015, https://www.nytimes.com/2015 /12/17/nyregion/3-men-imprisoned-in-1980-brooklyn-arson-case-are-exonerated .html.

53. John Lentini, "Report: Fire loss of February 7, 1980," December 4, 2014, in *In the matter of The People of the State of New York, Plaintiff, v. William Rodriguez, a/k/a William Vasquez, Amaury Villalobos and Raymond Mora, Defendants* (copy in author's possession).

54. Lentini, "Report: Fire loss of February 7, 1980."

55. Maurice Possley, "Amaury Villalobos," NRE, updated February 23, 2018, https://www.law.umich.edu/special/exoneration/Pages/casedetail.aspx?caseid=4813.

56. Clifford, "3 Men Imprisoned."

57. Parisa Dehghani-Tafti and Paul Bieber, "Folklore and Forensics the Challenges of Arson Investigations and Innocence Claims," *West Virginia Law Review* 119 (2017): 549, 551.

58. Dehghani-Tafti and Bieber, "Folklore and Forensics," 551.

59. National Research Council, *Strengthening Forensic Science in the United States: A Path Forward* (Washington, DC: National Academies Press, 2009), 23.

60. Dehghani-Tafti and Bieber, "Folklore and Forensics," 581–82.

61. Dehghani-Tafti and Bieber, "Folklore and Forensics," 557.

62. David Grann, "Trial by Fire," *New Yorker*, September 7, 2009, https://www .newyorker.com/magazine/2009/09/07/trial-by-fire.

63. Grann, "Trial by Fire."

64. Clifford Coonan, "Zhao Zouhai: Beaten, Framed, and Jailed for a Murder That Never Happened," *Independent*, May 14, 2010, https://www.independent .co.uk/news/world/asia/zhao-zuohai-beaten-framed-and-jailed-for-a-murder-that-never-happened-1973042.html.

65. "Alleged Australian Murder Victim Found Alive," *Guardian*, April 11, 2003, https://www.theguardian.com/world/2003/apr/11/australia.

66. Bob Herbert, "An Imaginary Homicide," *New York Times*, August 15, 2002, https://www.nytimes.com/2002/08/15/opinion/an-imaginary-homicide.html.

67. Herbert, "An Imaginary Homicide."

68. Maurice Possley, "Medell Banks," *NRE,* updated April 22, 2014, https://www.law.umich.edu/special/exoneration/Pages/casedetail.aspx?caseid=3010.

69. For an in-depth account of the Dookhan and Farak forensic scandals, see Shawn Musgrave, "The Chemist and the Cover-Up," *Reason.com,* March 2019, https://reason.com/2019/02/09/the-chemists-and-the-cover-up.

70. Maurice Chammah, "After Drug Lab Scandal, Court Continues to Reverse Convictions," *The Texas Tribune,* March 27, 2013, https://www.texastribune.org/2013/03/27/after-drug-lab-scandal-court-reverses-convictions/.

71. Aaron Martinez, "Defense Lawyers Allege Ex-DPS Analyst Had History of Falsifying Drug, Blood Tests," *El Paso Times,* June 12, 2018, https://www.elpasotimes.com/story/news/crime/2018/06/13/drug-blood-test-dps-forensic-analyst-accused-errors/664167002/.

72. *New Jersey v. Cassidy,* 197 A.3d 86 (N.J. 2018).

73. *Cassidy,* 197 A.3d at 97.

74. "Gerald Davis," Innocence Project, accessed November 18, 2019, https://www.innocenceproject.org/cases/gerald-davis/; "Dewy Davis," The Innocence Project, accessed November 18, 2019, https://www.innocenceproject.org/cases/dewey-davis/.

75. "Gerald Davis," Innocence Project, accessed November 18, 2019, https://www.innocenceproject.org/cases/gerald-davis/.

76. *Matter of W. Va. State Police Crime Lab,* 438 S.E.2d 501, 506 (W. Va. 1993)

CHAPTER 2. FALSE ACCUSATIONS

1. This narrative is largely based on an article by Rob Warden, "First DNA Exoneration: Gary Dotson," Center on Wrongful Convictions, Northwestern University, accessed July 3, 2019, http://www.law.northwestern.edu/legalclinic/wrongfulconvictions/exonerations/il/gary-dotson.html. For more about the story, see Cathleen Crowell Webb and Marion Chapion, *Forgive Me: An Innocent Man Jailed for Rape and a Young Girl's Journey to Youth* (Old Tappan, NJ: Fleming H. Revell, 1985). This case was the subject of a media frenzy and was prominently featured in magazines and newspapers around the country. For one example, see "Cathleen Webb," *People Magazine,* December 23, 1985, https://people.com/archive/cathleen-webb-vol-24-no-26/.

2. B. DePaulo et al., "Lying in Everyday Life," *Journal of Personality and Social Psychology* 70 (1996): 979–95. For a full discussion, see Aldert Vrij, *Detecting Lies and Deceit: Pitfalls and Opportunities,* 2d ed. (West Sussex, UK: Wiley-Interscience, 2008).

3. Vrij, *Detecting Lies and Deceit,* 162–63; Simon, *In Doubt,* 125–26.

4. Vrij, *Detecting Lies,* 153.

5. Paul Ekman and Maureen O'Sullivan, "Who Can Catch a Liar?" *American Psychologist* 46 (1991): 913–20.

6. Paul Ekman, Maureen O'Sullivan, and Mark Frank, "A Few Can Catch a Liar," *Psychological Science* 10 (1999): 263–66.

7. Maria Hartwig and Charles F. Bond Jr., "Lie Detection from Multiple Cues: A Meta-analysis," *Applied Cognitive Psychology* 28(5) (2014): 661.

8. A search of Amazon Books on the phrase "lie detection" yielded 114 results (October 18, 2018).

9. Vrij, *Detecting Lies,* 293.

10. Simon, *In Doubt,* 127–32.

11. National Research Council, Committee to Review the Scientific Evidence on the Polygraph, *The Polygraph and Lie Detection: Executive Summary* (Washington, DC: National Academies Press, 2003), 3.

12. National Research Council, *The Polygraph and Lie Detection,* 139–40.

13. Elizabeth Flock, "NSA Whistleblower Reveals How to Beat a Polygraph Test," *U.S. News and World Report,* September 25, 2012, https://www.usnews.com /news/blogs/washington-whispers/2012/09/25/nsa-whistleblower-reveals-how-to-beat-a-polygraph-test.

14. National Research Council, *The Polygraph and Lie Detection,* 224.

15. Anthony Wagner et al., "fMRI and Lie Detection," Vanderbilt Law Research Paper 17-10 (MacArthur Foundation Research Network on Law and Neuroscience, 2016).

16. "No Lie MRI," accessed July 27, 2018, http://www.noliemri.com/.

17. Daniel D. Langleben and Jane Campbell Moriarty, "Using Brain Imaging for Lie Detection: Where Science, Law, and Research Policy Collide," *Psychology, Public Policy and Law* 19(2) (2013): 222–34.

18. For examples of cases where courts excluded fMRI results for lie detection purposes, see *United States v. Semrau,* 693 F.3d 510 (6th Cir. 2012); *Harrington v. State,* 659 N.W.2d 509 (Iowa 2003); *Wilson v. Corestaff Servs. L.P.,* 900 N.Y.S.2d 639 (Sup. Ct. 2010); and *Smith v. State,* 32 A.3d 59 (Md. 2011).

19. Martha J. Farah et al., "Functional MRI–Based Lie Detection: Scientific and Societal Challenges," *Nature Review of Neuroscience* 15 (2014) 123, 125; Teneille R. Brown and Emily R. Murphy, "Through a Scanner Darkly: Functional Neuroimaging as Evidence of a Criminal Defendant's Past Mental States," *Stanford Law Review* 62(4) (2010): 1119–208; Henry T. Greeley and Judy Illes, "Neuroscience-Based Lie Detection: The Urgent Need for Regulation," *American Journal of Law and Medicine* 33 (2007): 377.

20. Vrij, *Detecting Lies,* 164–66, 183–84.

21. Maureen O'Sullivan, "The Fundamental Attribution Error in Detecting Deception: The Boy Who-Cried-Wolf Effect," *Personality and Social Psychology Bulletin* 29(10) (2003): 1316–27.

22. Maurice Possley, "Mark Weiner" (kidnapping), *NRE,* last updated January 30, 2018, http://www.law.umich.edu/special/exoneration/Pages/casedetail.aspx?caseid =4715; Maurice Possley, "Bradley Cooper" (stalking), *NRE,* November 4, 2013, https://www.law.umich.edu/special/exoneration/Pages/casedetail.aspx?caseid=4293; Dan Bilefsky, "A Revenge Plot So Intricate, the Prosecutors Were Pawns" (robbery), *New York Times,* July 7, 2011, https://www.nytimes.com/2011/07/26/nyregion /a-revenge-plot-so-intricate-the-prosecutors-were-pawns.html; Maurice Possley,

"Michael Waithe" (burglary), *NRE,* updated April 7, 2018, https://www.law.umich
.edu/special/exoneration/Pages/casedetail.aspx?caseid=4631.

23. "Sexual Violence Prevention," Centers for Disease Control and Prevention,
updated April 5, 2018, https://www.cdc.gov/features/sexualviolence/index.html.

24. Department of Justice, Office of Justice Programs, Bureau of Justice Statistics, *National Crime Victimization Survey,* 2010–2014 (Washington, DC, 2015).

25. Department of Justice, Office of Justice Programs, Bureau of Justice Statistics, *Female Victims of Sexual Violence,* 1994–2010 (Washington, DC, 2013).

26. Ken Armstrong and T. Christian Miller, "For Some Victims, Reporting a
Rape Can Bring Doubt, Abuse—and Even Prosecution, *ProPublica* (copublished
with the *New York Times*), November 24, 2017, https://www.propublica.org/article
/for-some-victims-reporting-a-rape-can-bring-doubt-abuse-and-even-prosecution;
Maurice Possley, "Fancy Figueroa," *NRE,* July 26, 2014, http://www.law.umich
.edu/special/exoneration/Pages/casedetail.aspx?caseid=4474.

27. T. Christian Miller and Ken Armstrong, *A False Report: A True Story of
Rape in America* (New York: Penguin, 2018).

28. "False Reporting: Overview," *NSVRC* (National Sexual Violence Resource
Center), 2012, https://www.nsvrc.org/sites/default/files/2012-03/Publications_
NSVRC_Overview_False-Reporting.pdf.

29. Richmond Lattimore, "Phaedra and Hippolytus," Arion: A Journal of
Humanities and the Classics 1(3) (autumn 1962): 5.

30. Maurice Possley, "Casey Ehrlick," *NRE,* updated June 23, 2016, http://www
.law.umich.edu/special/exoneration/Pages/casedetail.aspx?caseid=4925.

31. Stephanie Denzel, "William McCaffrey," *NRE,* updated November 3, 2015,
http://www.law.umich.edu/special/exoneration/Pages/casedetail.aspx?caseid=
3417.

32. Ashley Powers, "A 10-year Nightmare over Rape Conviction Is Over," *Los
Angeles Times,* May 25, 2012, http://articles.latimes.com/2012/may/25/local/la-me-
rape-dismiss-20120525; Phil Willon and Patrick McGreevy, "Payday for Football
Star and Other Wrongly Convicted Californians," *Los Angeles Times,* June 17, 2015,
http://www.latimes.com/local/political/la-me-ln-wrongly-convicted-californians-
20150617-story.html.

33. Jean Merl, "Long Beach Unified Wins $2.6 million over False Rape Accusation,"
Los Angeles Times, June 22, 2013, http://articles.latimes.com/2013/jun/22/local/la-me-
adv-brian-banks-20130623; Willon and McGreevy, "Payday for Football Star."

34. Upon his exoneration in 2012, Banks was finally given a chance to play professional football with the Atlanta Falcons, but he was released without a contract
in the preseason. Banks wrote a memoir (with Mark Dagostino) about his ordeal,
*What Set Me Free: A True Story of a Wrongful Conviction, a Dream Deferred, and a
Man Redeemed* (New York: Atria Books, 2019)

35. *Brian Banks,* Bleecker Street, accessed November 22, 2019, https://bleecker-
streetmedia.com/brianbanks.

36. Victoria Ward, "Lesbian Fantasist Invented 15 Rapes and Sexual Assaults
Which Saw Man Jailed to Get Sympathy from Girlfriends, Court Hears," *London*

Telegraph, August 24, 2017, retrieved from https://www. elegraph.co.uk/news/2017 /08/24/woman-falsely-accused-15-men-rape-sexual-assault-jailed-ten/.

37. "Jemma Beale Case: Mahad Cassim's Reputation 'Ruined,'" *BBC News,* August 26, 2017, https://www.bbc.com/news/uk-england-london-41060237.

38. Maurice Possley, "Dan Lackey," *NRE,* posted before June 2012, http://www .law.umich.edu/special/exoneration/Pages/casedetail.aspx?caseid=3369.

39. John O'Brien, "Sins and Confessions: Dan Lackey Case Shows That in a Court of Law, Things Are Not Always as They Seem," *Syracuse.com,* April 19, 2009, https://www.syracuse.com/news/index.ssf/2009/04/steve_lackey_brought_bad_ news.html.

40. Maurice Possley, "Anthony Cooper," *NRE,* September 22, 2015, https:// www.law.umich.edu/special/exoneration/Pages/casedetail.aspx?caseid=4757.

41. Maurice Possley, "Joe Elizondo," *NRE,* October 14, 2012, https://www.law .umich.edu/special/exoneration/Pages/casedetail.aspx?caseid=4018; "Mary Ann Elizondo," *NRE,* updated June 27, 2016, https://www.law.umich.edu/special /exoneration/Pages/casedetail.aspx?caseid=4019.

42. Andrew Selsky, "A Man Serving a 50-Year Sentence for a Sex Crime Conviction Has Been Exonerated after the Discovery of a Missing Dog," *Time,* September 11, 2018, http://time.com/5392256/oregon-joshua-horner-exonerated/.

43. Maurice Possley, "Ricky Dale Harmon," *NRE,* October 19, 2012, http:// www.umich.edu/special/exoneration/Pages/casedetail.aspx?caseid=4028.

44. Maurice Possley, "Barry Byars," *NRE,* May 8, 2013, http://www.law.umich .edu/special/exoneration/Pages/casedetail.aspx?caseid=4162.

45. For a general discussion, see George Malcolm Yool, *1692 Witch Hunt: The Layman's Guide to the Salem Witchcraft Trials* (Westminster, MD: Heritage Books, 2007).

46. For more on this child sexual abuse scare, see Hon. Dan Stidham et al., "Satanic Panic and Defending the West Memphis Three: How Cultural Differences Can Play a Major Role in Criminal Cases," *University of Memphis Law Review* 42 (2012): 1061; Tonya Brito, "Paranoid Parents, Phantom Menaces, and the Culture of Fear," *Wisconsin Law Review* 2000 (2000): 519.

47. Linda Rodriguez McRobbie, "The Real Victims of Satanic Ritual Abuse," *Slate,* January 7, 2014, https://slate.com/technology/2014/01/fran-and-dan-keller-freed-two-of-the-last-victims-of-satanic-ritual-abuse-panic.html.

48. For an in-depth discussion of the Keller case specifically, and the national hysteria over allegations of satanic ritual abuse in the early 1990s, see Gary Cartwright, "The Innocent and the Damned," *Texas Monthly,* April 2014, https://www .texasmonthly.com/articles/the-innocent-and-the-damned/.

49. Alexandra Gross, "Richard Cox," *NRE,* posted before June 2012, http:// www.law.umich.edu/special/exoneration/Pages/casedetail.aspx?caseid=3129.

50. Lona Manning, "Nightmare at the Day Care: The Wee Care Case," *Crime Magazine,* October 13, 2009, http://www.crimemagazine.com/nightmare-day-care-wee-care-case.

51. Simon, *In Doubt,* 99–106.

52. Elizabeth F. Loftus and Deborah Davis, "Recovered Memories," *Annual Review of Clinical Psychology* 469 (2006): 476.

53. Elizabeth F. Loftus, "Leading Questions and the Eyewitness Report," *Cognitive Psychology* 7 (1975): 560–72.

54. Hans Crombag et al., "Crashing Memories and the Problem of 'Source Monitoring,'" *Applied Cognitive Psychology* 10 (1996): 95–104.

55. Jordan Smith, "Believing the Children," *Austin Chronicle,* March 27, 2009, https://www.austinchronicle.com/news/2009-03-27/believing-the-children/.

56. Cartwright, "The Innocent and the Damned."

57. *Ex Parte Daniel Keller,* No. WR-36, 232-02, Texas Court of Criminal Appeals, May 20, 2015 (unpublished decision), available at 2015 WL 3462703; *Ex Parte Frances Keller,* No. WR-36, 864-02, Texas Court of Criminal Appeals, May 20, 2015 (unpublished decision), available at 2015 WL 3462646.

58. Cartwright, "The Innocent and the Damned."

59. *Ex Parte Daniel Keller,* No. WR-36, 232-02 (Johnson, J., concurring opinion).

CHAPTER 3. POLICE

1. Lisa Demer, "Former Bethel Cop Must Serve Time for Violent 2014 Arrest Caught on Video," *Anchorage Daily News,* August 25, 2016, https://www.adn.com /alaska-news/rural-alaska/2016/08/24/ex-bethel-cop-must-serve-time-for-violent-2014-arrest-caught-on-video/; Maurice Possley, "Wassillie Gregory," *NRE,* updated June 1, 2015, at http://www.law.umich.edu/special/exoneration/Pages/casedetail .aspx?caseid=4696.

2. Jerome H. Skolnick and James J. Fyfe, *Above the Law* (New York: Simon and Shuster, 1993), 92.

3. City of New York, Commission to Investigate Allegations of Police Corruption and the Anti-Corruption Procedures of the Police Department, "Commission Report" (hereafter cited as the Mollen Commission Report), July 7, 1994, available at *Internet Archive,* https://archive.org/details/MollenCommissionNYPD.

4. Mollen Commission Report, 1.

5. Sewell Chan, "The Abner Louima Case: 10 Years Later," *New York Times,* August 8, 2007, https://cityroom.blogs.nytimes.com/2007/08/09/the-abner-louima-case-10-years-later/.

6. Chan, "The Abner Louima Case."

7. The following portion of this account is based on *Louima v. City of New York,* Third Amended Complaint and Demand for a Jury Trial, October 2000, at 4, 6, 42, 63, available at Civil Rights Litigation Clearinghouse, University of Michigan Law School, https://www.clearinghouse.net/chDocs/public/PN-NY-0001-0001.pdf.

8. Gabriel J. Chin and Scott C. Wells, "The Blue Wall of Silence as Evidence of Bias and Motive to Lie: A New Approach to Police Perjury," *University of Pittsburgh Law Review* 59 (1998): 233, 243–44. An editorial at the time observed, "Turetzky

[one of the officers who came forward in the *Louima* case] is under police protection, which says two things quite clearly. 1) When it comes to certain cops, a man with a conscience can be in danger, and, 2) Obviously, there are enough decent sorts in the NYPD to afford Turetzky the protection he deserves. And needs." "Know Them by Their Silence," *(New York) Daily News,* August 20, 1997, p. 32.

9. David Weisburd and Rosann Greenspan, "Police Attitudes toward Abuse of Authority: Findings from a National Survey (Research in Brief)," *National Institute of Justice,* May 2000, https://www.ncjrs.gov/pdffiles1/nij/181312.pdf. In response to this survey of police officer attitudes about the abuse of authority, a majority of police officers agreed that "it was not unusual for a police officer to turn a blind eye to improper conduct by other officers"; and 61 percent of police officers believed that "police do not always report even serious criminal violations that involve the abuse of authority by fellow officers."

10. *Floyd v. City of New York,* 959 F.Supp.2d 540, 596, 600 (S.D.N.Y. 2013).

11. *Floyd,* 959 F.Supp.2d at 597.

12. *Floyd,* 959 F.Supp.2d at 600.

13. *Floyd,* 959 F.Supp.2d at 600.

14. *Matthews v. City of New York et al.,* Complaint, 12 Civ. 1354, p. 28.

15. *Matthews,* Complaint, at 21.

16. Victoria Bekiempis, "NYPD Whistleblower Getting $280K After He Was Harassed for Exposing Quotas," *New York Daily News,* December 7, 2015, https://www.nydailynews.com/new-york/nypd-whistleblower-280k-settlement-article-1.2457687.

17. Saki Knafo, "A Black Police Officer's Fight against the NYPD," *New York Times Magazine,* February 21, 2016, https://www.nytimes.com/2016/02/21/magazine/a-black-police-officers-fight-against-the-nypd.html.

18. The 2018 award-winning documentary film *Crime + Punishment,* directed by Stephen Maing, depicts the efforts of the NYPD 12, who challenged the quota system and its impact on young minorities in New York City.

19. The following account of the Stinson case is based on Benjamin Weiser, "New York City to Pay up to $75 Million over Dismissed Summonses," *New York Times,* January 23, 2017, https://www.nytimes.com/2017/01/23/nyregion/new-york-city-agrees-to-settlement-over-summonses-that-were-dismissed.html; Benjamin Weiser, "Class Action Lawsuit, Blaming Police Quotas, Takes on Criminal Summonses," May 5, 2015, https://www.nytimes.com/2015/05/18/nyregion/class-action-lawsuit-blaming-police-quotas-takes-on-criminal-summonses.html.

20. *Stinson v. City of New York,* 10 Civ. 4228 (RWS), "Stipulation and Proposed Preliminary Approval Order," Appendix A, Filed January 23, 2017, available at *Courthouse News Service,* https://www.courthousenews.com/wp-content/uploads/2017/01/Stinson-deal.pdf.

21. Hailey Branson Potts and Emily Alpert Reyes, "City Will Pay LAPD Officer Nearly $1 Million to End Lawsuit over Ticket Quotas," *Los Angeles Times,* January 13, 2016, https://www.latimes.com/local/cityhall/la-me-0114-lapd-settlement-20160114-story.html.

22. Shaun Ossei-Owusu, "Race and the Tragedy of Quota-Based Policing," *American Prospect,* November 3, 2016, http://prospect.org/article/race-and-tragedy-quota-based-policing-0.

23. Ossei-Owusu, "Race and the Tragedy of Quota-Based Policing."

24. Ossei-Owusu, "Race and the Tragedy of Quota-Based Policing."

25. Alice Brennan and Dan Lieberman, "Florida City's 'Stop and Frisk' Nabs Thousands of Kids, Finds 5-Year-Olds 'Suspicious,'" *Fusion.TV,* May 9, 2015, https://fusion.tv/story/5568/florida-citys-stop-frisk-nabs-thousands-of-kids-finds-5-year-olds-suspicious/.

26. "Texas Officer Accuses Unit of Having Arrest Quotas," *PoliceOne.com,* June 29, 2018, https://www.policeone.com/patrol-issues/articles/477145006-Texas-officer-accuses-unit-of-having-arrest-quotas/.

27. Chris Baynes, "Baltimore Police Officers 'Carried BB Guns to Plant on Unarmed Suspects They Shot,' Court Hears," *Independent,* February 1, 2018, https://www.independent.co.uk/news/world/americas/baltimore-police-carried-bb-guns-plant-unarmed-suspects-shooting-victims-corruption-maurice-ward-a8189731.html.

28. Robert Lewis and Noah Veltman, "Can the NYPD Spot the Abusive Cop?" *WNYC,* December 5, 2014, https://www.wnyc.org/story/can-the-nypd-spot-the-abusive-cop/.

29. The following account of Edward Williams's experience is based on Phil Trexler, "Akron Man Says Withheld Video Proves His Innocence," *Akron Beacon Journal,* May 5, 2014, https://www.ohio.com/akron/news/akron-man-says-withheld-police-video-proves-his-innocence; Maurice Possley, "Edward Williams," *NRE,* updated February 2, 2018, https://www.law.umich.edu/special/exoneration/Pages/casedetail.aspx?caseid=4668; Brian Grosh, "Firm Says Akron Didn't Pay for Work on Cops Secret Recordings," *Courthouse News Service,* November 28, 2016, https://www.courthousenews.com/firm-says-akron-didnt-pay-for-work-on-cops-secret-recordings/.

30. Phil Trexler, "Former Akron Police Officer Schismenos Recorded out of Fear of Retaliation," *Akron Beacon Journal,* January 2, 2015, https://www.ohio.com/article/20150102/NEWS/301029255.

31. Trexler, "Akron Man Says Withheld Video Proves His Innocence."

32. Possley, "Edward Williams."

33. Since 2015, the *Washington Post* has maintained a database, "Fatal Force," cataloging fatal police shootings: https://www.washingtonpost.com/graphics/2018/national/police-shootings-2018/?noredirect=on&utm_term=.fc0c85cdf117.

34. Jose A. Del Real, "No Charges in Sacramento Police Shooting," *New York Times,* March 2, 2019, https://www.nytimes.com/2019/03/02/us/stephon-clark-police-shooting-sacramento.html.

35. Mitch Smith, "Four Chicago Police Officers Fired for Cover-Up of Laquan McDonald Shooting," *New York Times,* July 19, 2019, https://www.nytimes.com/2019/07/19/us/chicago-police-fired-laquan-mcdonald.html.

36. Nikelle Murphy, "Ten States That Pay Police Officers the Highest (and Lowest) Salaries," *Culture Cheat Sheet,* June 7, 2018, https://www.cheatsheet.com/culture/states-pay-police-officers-highest-lowest-salaries.html/.

37. Jason Meisner and Megan Crepeau, "Charges to Be Thrown Out against 18 More Men Whose Convictions Linked to Corrupt Chicago Cop," *Chicago Tribune,* September 21, 2018, https://www.chicagotribune.com/news/local/breaking/ct-met-corrupt-ex-chicago-cop-charges-dropped-20180921-story.html.

38. Maurice Possley, "Leonard Gipson," *NRE,* updated March 30, 2019, https://www.law.umich.edu/special/exoneration/Pages/casedetail.aspx?caseid=5412. Multiple news accounts incorrectly misspell Gipson's last name as "Gibson."

39. Don Babwin, "15 Convictions Linked to Corrupt Chicago Cop Are Thrown Out," *Washington Post,* November 16, 2017, https://www.washingtontimesreporter.com/news/20171116/15-convictions-linked-to-corrupt-chicago-cop-are-thrown-out.

40. Maurice Possley, "Lionel White, Sr.," *NRE,* updated December 7, 2017, https://www.law.umich.edu/special/exoneration/Pages/casedetail.aspx?caseid=5053.

41. Possley, "Lionel White, Sr."

42. Jason Meisner, "Former Chicago Cop Gets 22 Months for Stealing from FBI Informant," *Chicago Tribune,* October 9, 2013, https://www.chicagotribune.com/news/breaking/chi-former-chicago-cop-gets-22-months-for-stealing-from-fbi-informant-20131009-story.html.

43. Jamie Kalven, "In the Chicago Police Department, If the Bosses Say It Didn't Happen, It Didn't Happen," *Intercept,* October 6, 2016, https://theintercept.com/2016/10/06/in-the-chicago-police-department-if-the-bosses-say-it-didnt-happen-it-didnt-happen/.

44. Maurice Possley, "Claudia Salcedo," *NRE,* March 9, 2015, https://www.law.umich.edu/special/exoneration/Pages/casedetail.aspx?caseid=4653.

45. Possley, "Claudia Salcedo."

46. Matt Gelb, "Former Philly Narcotics Cop Jeffrey Walker Sentenced to 3 1/2 Years in Prison," *Philadelphia Inquirer,* July 29, 2015, http://www.philly.com/philly/news/20150730_Former_Philly_narcotics_cop_Jeffrey_Walker_sentenced_to_31_2_years_in_prison.html.

47. Mark Fazlollah, Craig R. McCoy, and Jeremy Roebuck, "Philadelphia's DA Office Keeps Secret List of Suspect Police," *Philadelphia Inquirer,* February 13, 2018, http://www.philly.com/philly/news/philadelphia-police-misconduct-list-larry-krasner-seth-williams-meek-mill-20180213.html?mobi=true.

48. Justin Fenton, "2 Baltimore Police Gun Trace Task Force Officers Sentenced: Jenkins Receives 25 Years, Taylor Gets 18," *Baltimore Sun,* June 7, 2018, https://www.baltimoresun.com/news/maryland/crime/bs-md-ci-gttf-jenkins-taylor-sentencing-20180606-story.html.

49. Maurice Possley, "Umar Burley," *NRE,* June 6, 2019, https://www.law.umich.edu/special/exoneration/Pages/casedetail.aspx?caseid=5568; Angela Roberts et al. (Capitol News Service), "Plea Deals Punish the Innocent, Hide the Guilty in Baltimore Police Scandal," *Injustice Watch,* May 30, 2018, https://www.injusticewatch.org/interactives/2018/plea-bargain/baltimore.html.

50. Jessica Lussenhop, "Rogue Baltimore Police Unit Ringleader Wayne Jenkins Sentenced," *BBC News*, June 7, 2018, https://www.bbc.com/news/world-us-canada-44402948.

51. Richard Covey, "Police Misconduct as a Cause of Wrongful Convictions," *Washington University Law Review* 90(4) (2013), 1137–38.

52. Covey, "Police Misconduct as a Cause of Wrongful Convictions," 1138.

53. Blakeslee, *Tulia*.

54. Nkechi Taifa, *Tulia: Tip of the Drug War Iceberg* (New York: Open Society Policy Center, 2005), 7, https://www.opensocietyfoundations.org/sites/default/files/tulia.pdf.

55. Alan Bean, *Taking Out the Trash in Tulia, Texas* (DeSoto, TX: Advanced Concept Design Books, 2010).

56. Bean, *Taking Out the Trash,* 8.

57. Rob Warden, "Town of Tulia, Center for Wrongful Convictions, Northwestern University, accessed January 5, 2020, http://www.law.northwestern.edu/legalclinic/wrongfulconvictions/exonerations/tx/town-of-tulia.html.

58. Bean, *Taking Out the Trash,* 5.

59. "Tulia Defendants Disappointed at Coleman's Verdict," KCBD, updated July 3, 2005, http://www.kcbd.com/story/2813548/tulia-defendants-disappointed-at-colemans-verdict/.

60. "Erma Faye Stewart and Regina Kelly, Hearne, Texas," *Frontline,* pbs.org, accessed November 23, 2019, https://www.pbs.org/wgbh/pages/frontline/shows/plea/four/stewart.html.

61. Michele Alexander, "Go to Trial: Crash the System," *New York Times,* March 10, 2012, https://www.nytimes.com/2012/03/11/opinion/sunday/go-to-trial-crash-the-justice-system.html?fbclid=IwAR3sC4UWCfBbLopCEn-md6UbL4zI7d5n_KRTnb2uXUrIq_HMVfihnsdzwHk.

62. John P. Crank and Michael A. Caldero, *Police Ethics: The Corruption of Noble Cause,* 3rd ed. (New York: Routledge, 2011), 31.

63. Crank and Caldero, *Police Ethics,* 22.

64. Anthony Bottoms and Justice Tankebe, "Beyond Procedural Justice: A Dialogic Approach to Legitimacy in Criminal Justice," *Journal of Criminal Law and Criminology* 102 (2012): 119, 154.

65. Associated Press, "Wrongful Jailing to Cost Philadelphia $1 Million," *New York Times,* August 17, 1996, https://www.nytimes.com/1996/08/17/us/wrongful-jailing-to-cost-philadelphia-1-million.html.

66. Associated Press, "Wrongful Jailing to Cost Philadelphia $1 Million"; Don Terry, "Philadelphia Shaken by Criminal Police Officers," *New York Times,* August 28, 1995, https://www.nytimes.com/1995/08/28/us/philadelphia-shaken-by-criminal-police-officers.html.

67. Megan Blarr, "More Cases Involving Suspended Auburn Corrections Officer Dismissed," *Auburn Citizen,* January 20, 2017, https://auburnpub.com/news/local/more-cases-involving-suspended-auburn-corrections-officer-dismissed/article_c6b91ce0-77f7-5aff-a193-5cdf0f29fec1.html.

68. Maurice Possley, "Thomas Ozzborn," *NRE,* updated September 14, 2018, http://www.law.umich.edu/special/exoneration/pages/casedetail.aspx?caseid=5163.

69. Possley, "Thomas Ozzborn"; Maurice Possley, "Donessia Brown," *NRE,* updated September 14, 2018, http://www.law.umich.edu/special/exoneration/pages /casedetail.aspx?caseid=5174; Maurice Possley, "Sean Gaines," *NRE,* July 3, 2017, http://www.law.umich.edu/special/exoneration/pages/casedetail.aspx?caseid=5162; Maurice Possley, "Naythen Aubain," *NRE,* July 17, 2017, http://www.law.umich.edu /special/exoneration/Pages/casedetail.aspx?caseid=5171; Maurice Possley, "Jose Muniz," *NRE,* July 17, 2017, http://www.law.umich.edu/special/exoneration/Pages /casedetail.aspx?caseid=5172.

70. For more on the impact of confessions in court, see Sara C. Appleby and Saul M. Kassin, "When Self-Report Trumps Science: Effects of Confessions, DNA, and Prosecutorial Theories on Perceptions of Guilt," *Psychology, Public Policy, and Law* 22(2) (2016): 127–40; Saul Kassin et al., "Confessions That Corrupt: Evidence from the DNA Exoneration Case Files," *Psychological Science* 23 (2012): 1–5; Iris Blandon-Gitlin et al., "Jurors Believe Interrogation Tactics Are Not Likely to Elicit False Confessions: Will Expert Witness Testimony Inform Them Otherwise?" *Psychology, Crime, and Law* 17 (2011): 239–60; Saul Kassin and Holly Sukel, "Coerced Confessions and the Jury: An Experimental Test of the 'Harmless Error' Rule," *Law and Human Behavior* 21(1) (February 1997): 27–46.

71. Saul M. Kassin, "Why Confessions Trump Innocence," *American Psychology* 67(6) (September 2012): 431, 433.

72. Appleby and Kassin, "When Self-Report Trumps Science."

73. The facts about Nicole Harris's conviction and exoneration are based on *Harris v. Thompson,* 698 F.3d 609, 613–621 (7th Cir. 2012); Maurice Possley, "Nicole Harris," *NRE,* updated November 17, 2017, https://www.law.umich.edu/special/exoneration /Pages/casedetail.aspx?caseid=4202; Jason Meisner, "Jury Sides with Chicago Police, Awards No Damages to Woman Who Alleged Coerced Confession in Son's Death, *Chicago Tribune,* November 17, 2017, http://www.chicagotribune.com/news/local /breaking/ct-met-chicago-police-trial-nicole-harris-20171117-story.html.

74. Saul M. Kassin et al., "Police-Induced Confessions: Risk Factors and Recommendations," *Law and Human Behavior* 34 (2010): 3, 16

75. Brandon L. Garrett observes, "The vast majority of these exonerees made statements in their interrogations that were contradicted by crime scene evidence, victim accounts, or other evidence known to police during their investigation." Garrett, "The Substance of False Confessions," *Stanford Law Review* 62 (2010): 1051, 1087.

76. *Harris v. Thompson,* 698 F.3d 609.

77. *Harris v. Thompson,* 698 F.3d 698 F.3d at 612, 638.

CHAPTER 4. PROSECUTORS

1. *Carter v. Burch,* Appellant Petition for a Writ of Certiorari, 1994 WL 16042475; *Carter v. Burch,* 34 F.3d 257 n. 2 (4th Cir. 1994); Maurice Possley,

"William Douglas Carter," *NRE,* updated November 21, 2016, https://www.law
.umich.edu/special/exoneration/Pages/casedetail.aspx?caseid=4111.

2. Robert O'Harrow Jr., "Witness in VA Retrial Says She Was 'Briefed' First
Time," *Washington Post,* July 17, 1997, https://www.washingtonpost.com/archive
/local/1992/07/17/witness-in-va-retrial-says-she-was-briefed-first-time/8e3d3c5d-
66d9-470b-9388-5880d1b9cc54/?utm_term=.bea74b02ec3f.

3. Robert O'Harrow, Jr., "Businessman to Be Freed in Shooting," *Washington
Post,* February 11, 1992, https://www.washingtonpost.com/archive/local/1992/02
/11/businessman-to-be-freed-in-shooting/599f1946-2009-4e15-82aa-d26cd0f41f65
/?utm_term=.2fc9c6c4fc80.

4. *Carter,* 34 F.3d at 260.

5. *Carter,* 34 F.3d at 260.

6. Robert O'Harrow Jr., "Retrial Reverses Fortune for Carter," *Washington Post,*
July 29, 1992, https://www.washingtonpost.com/archive/local/1992/07/29/retrial-
reverses-fortune-for-carter/dc1c55e0-8607-4ae7-8a7d-d629dd3c6dd4/?utm_term=
.2789e3bea217.

7. Debbi Wilgoren, "Bar Clears Prosecutor in '87 Shooting Probe," *Washington
Post,* September 24, 1994, https://www.washingtonpost.com/archive/local
/1994/09/24/bar-clears-prosecutor-in-87-shooting-probe/3f55a356-332a-416a-b90c-
b5d8f6c66329/.

8. See Jocelyn Simonson, "The Place of 'The People' in Criminal Procedure,"
Columbia Law Review 199(1) (2019): 249–307.

9. *Berger v. United States,* 295 U.S. 78, 88 (1935).

10. Model Rules of Professional Conduct, Rule 3.8: Special Responsibilities of a
Prosecutor, *American Bar Association,* 2016, accessed July 30, 2019, https://www
.americanbar.org/groups/professional_responsibility/publications/model_rules_
of_professional_conduct/rule_3_8_special_responsibilities_of_a_prosecutor/.

11. William Blackstone, *Commentaries on the Laws of England,* 21st ed. (1765;
London: Sweet, Maxwell, Stevens & Norton, 1844), bk. IV, ch. 27, p. 358.

12. *Berger,* 295 U.S. at 78.

13. Angela Davis, "Prosecutors Who Intentionally Break the Law," *American
Criminal Law Brief* 1(2) (2006), available at *Digital Commons,* https://digitalcom-
mons.wcl.american.edu/cgi/viewcontent.cgi?referer=&httpsredir=1&article=1001
&context=clb.

14. For a general discussion of what cognitive science shows about prosecutor
thinking, see Alafair D. Burke, "Improving Prosecutorial Decision Making: Some
Lessons of Cognitive Science," *William and Mary Law Review,* 47 (2006) 1587,
1590–1601.

15. Burke, "Improving Prosecutorial Decision Making," 1599.

16. Daniel S. Medwed, "The Zeal Deal: Prosecutorial Resistance to Post-conviction Claims of Innocence," *Boston University Law Review,* 84: 125 (2004): 125–83.

17. Kenneth Bresler, "I Never Lost a Trial: When Prosecutors Keep Score
of Criminal Convictions," *Georgetown Journal of Legal Ethics* 9 (1996): 537,
541–42.

18. Peter Joy and Kevin McMunigal, "Contingent Rewards for Prosecutors?" *Criminal Justice* 26(3) (Fall 2011), available at https://www.americanbar.org /content/dam/aba/publications/criminal_justice_magazine/fa11_Ethics.pdf.

19. Jeff Burlew, "Prosecutor Who Sparked Jackson County Drug-Planting Probe Resigns as Whistleblower," *Tallahassee Democrat,* September 29, 2018, https:// www.tallahassee.com/story/news/2018/09/29/prosecutor-who-sparked-jackson-drug-planting-probe-resigns-whistleblower/1441015002/; Jeff Burlew, "119 Cases Dropped Involving Fired Jackson County Deputy Zachary Wester," Tallahassee Democrat, September 27, 2018, https://www.tallahassee.com/story/news/2018 /09/25/119-cases-dropped-involving-fired-deputy/1423190002/.

20. Burlew, "Prosecutor Who Sparked Jackson County Drug-Planting Probe Resigns."

21. Evan Hughes, "America's Prosecutors Were Supposed to Be Accountable to Voters; What Went Wrong?" *Politico Magazine,* November 5, 2017, https://www .politico.com/magazine/story/2017/11/05/cyrus-vance-jr-americas-prosecutor-problem-215786.

22. "America's Prosecutor Problem," *Fusion,* http://interactive.fusion.net/how-to-rig-an-election/district-attorney-race.html.

23. Robert P. Mosteller, "The Duke Lacrosse Case, Innocence, and False Identifications: A Fundamental Failure to Do Justice," *Fordham Law Review,* 76 (2007): 1337, 1350.

24. Mosteller, "The Duke Lacrosse Case," 1337.

25. "An Epidemic of Prosecutor Misconduct," White Paper, *Center for Prosecutor Integrity,* 2013, p. 8, http://www.prosecutorintegrity.org/wp-content/uploads /EpidemicofProsecutorMisconduct.pdf.

26. "An Epidemic of Prosecutor Misconduct," 10.

27. For instance, in *Miranda v. Arizona,* 384 U.S. 436 (1966), the Supreme Court created a "prophylactic rule" requiring the suppression of statements obtained by police who fail to properly advise defendants of their rights.

28. "Harmless Error: The Methodology," *Center for Public Integrity,* June 26, 2003, https://publicintegrity.org/state-politics/harmful-error/methodology-the-team-for-harmful-error/.

29. *Imbler v. Pachtman,* 424 U.S. 409 (1976).

30. *Imbler,* 424 U.S. at 421–24.

31. *Imbler,* 424 U.S. at 429.

32. Shawn Musgrave, "Scant Discipline Follows Prosecutor's Impropriety in Massachusetts," *New England Center for Investigative Reporting,* March 6, 2017, https://www.necir.org/2017/03/06/scant-discipline-follows-prosecutors-impropriety-massachusetts/.

33. Shawn Musgrave, "Three Former Prosecutors Accused of Misconduct in Amherst Drug-Scandal," *Boston Globe,* July 9, 2019, https://www.bostonglobe.com /metro/2019/07/09/three-former-state-prosecutors-accused-misconduct/YZGwO-QACD9KumldJbknJ4J/story.html.

34. Musgrave, "Three Former Prosecutors Accused of Misconduct."

35. *Bordenkircher v. Hayes,* 434 U.S. 357, 364 (1978).

36. *United States v. Jackson,* 390 U.S. 570 (1968).

37. *Jackson,* 390 U.S. at 583.

38. *Bordenkircher,* 434 U.S. at 357.

39. *Bordenkircher,* 434 U.S. at 364–65.

40. Possley, "Medell Banks."

41. Alexandra Gross, "John Peel," *NRE,* http://www.law.umich.edu/special/exoneration/Pages/casedetail.aspx?caseid=3813.

42. The following account of Hodges's story is drawn from Maurice Possley, "Devron Hodges," *NRE,* https://www.law.umich.edu/special/exoneration/Pages/casedetail.aspx?caseid=4645.

43. Covey, "Police Misconduct as a Cause of Wrongful Convictions," 1133, 1159.

44. Lucian E. Dervan, "Bargained Justice: Plea Bargaining's Innocence Problem and the *Brady* Safety Valve," *Utah Law Review* 51 (2012): 85; Donald A. Dripps, "Guilt, Innocence, and Due Process of Plea Bargaining," *William and Mary Law Review* 57 (2016): 1343, 1360–63.

45. *U.S. v. Golding,* 168 F.3d 700 (4th Cir. 1999).

46. *Golding,* 168 F.3d 700.

47. In referencing Mrs. Golding's absence from the stand, the prosecution also ran afoul of the protection afforded by spousal privilege.

48. Joseph Goldstein, "'Testilying' by Police: A Stubborn Problem," *New York Times* March 18, 2018, https://www.nytimes.com/2018/03/18/nyregion/testilying-police-perjury-new-york.html

49. Jim Dwyer, "The Drugs? They Came from the Police," *New York Times,* October 14, 2011, https://www.nytimes.com/2011/10/14/nyregion/those-drugs-they-came-from-the-police.html?ref=nyregion&module=inline.

50. Daniel S. Medwed, *Prosecution's Complex: America's Race to Convict and Its Impact on the Innocent* (New York: New York University Press 2012), 97–98, 85–87.

51. Standard 3-1.4, The Prosecutor's Heightened Duty of Candor, *American Bar Association,* https://www.americanbar.org/groups/criminal_justice/standards/ProsecutionFunctionFourthEdition/.

52. *Brady v. Maryland,* 373 U.S. 83 (1963).

53. *United States v. Olsen,* 737 F.3d 625, 632 (9th Cir. 2013) (Kozinski, C.J., dissenting).

54. *Turner v. Schriver,* 327 F.Supp.2d 174 (S.D.N.Y. 2004).

55. *Turner,* 327 F.Supp.2d at 178–79.

56. *Turner,* 327 F.Supp.2d at 181.

57. *Turner,* 327 F.Supp.2d at 184–85.

58. *Olsen,* 737 F.3d at 633.

59. Ronald Smothers, "Mississippi Governor Bans Same-Sex Marriage," *New York Times,* August 24, 1996, https://www.nytimes.com/1996/08/24/us/mississippi-governor-bans-same-sex-marriage.html.

60. *Lawrence v. Texas,* 539 U.S. 558 (2003).

61. Joel Roberts, 11 States Ban Same-Sex Marriages, *CBS News,* September 30, 2004, retrieved from https://www.cbsnews.com/news/11-states-ban-same-sex-marriage/; *Obergefell v. Hodges,* 576 U.S. __ (2015).

62. Maurice Possley, "Leigh Stubbs," *NRE,* October 25, 2018, https://www.law.umich.edu/special/exoneration/Pages/casedetail.aspx?caseid=5398; Maurice Possley, "Tammy Vance," *NRE,* October 25, 2018, https://www.law.umich.edu/special/exoneration/pages/casedetail.aspx?caseid=5399.

63. Possley, "Leigh Stubbs"; Possley, "Tammy Vance."

64. Maurice Possley, "Dewey Davis," *NRE,* updated February 5, 2018, https://www.law.umich.edu/special/exoneration/Pages/casedetail.aspx?caseid=3156

65. Jacqueline McMurtrie, "The Unindicted Co-Ejaculator and Necrophilia: Addressing Prosecutors' Logic Defying Responses to Exculpatory DNA Results," *Journal of Criminal Law and Criminology,* 105 (2015): 853.

66. Medwed, "The Zeal Deal," 129.

67. Lara Bazelon, "The Innocence Deniers," *Slate,* January 18, 2018, https://slate.com/news-and-politics/2018/01/innocence-deniers-prosecutors-who-have-refused-to-admit-wrongful-convictions.html.

68. Michael Kiefer, "The Long Journey from Death Row to Freedom: Arizona Lawyer's Sleuthing Frees Murder Convict," *AZ Central,* June 15, 2017, https://www.azcentral.com/story/news/local/arizona-investigations/2017/06/15/nevada-death-row-inmate-ser-free-arizona-lawyer/394809001/.

69. Brad Heath and Kevin McCoy, "Prosecutors Conduct Can Tip Justice Scales," *USA Today,* September 23, 2010.

70. The Central Park 5 case continues to provoke important discussions about race and wrongful convictions. See, for example, the Netflix series based on the case, Ava DuVernay (dir.), *When They See Us* (2019), https://www.netflix.com/title/80200549. For an excellent documentary about the Central Park 5, case see Ken Burns, Sarah Burns, and David McMahon, *Central Park 5* (2012), Sundance Selects, http://kenburns.com/films/central-park-five/.

71. Sam Asch, "Effects of Group Pressure upon the Modification and Distortion of Judgment," in H. Guetzkow, ed., *Groups, Leadership, and Men* (Pittsburgh: Carnegie Press, 1951).

72. Nina Morrison, "What Happens When Prosecutors Break the Law?" *New York Times,* June 18, 2018, https://www.nytimes.com/2018/06/18/opinion/kurtzrock-suffolk-county-prosecutor.html.

73. Christopher Goffard, "Prosecutors Who Withhold or Tamper with Evidence Now Face Felony Charges," *Los Angeles Times,* October 3, 2016, https://www.latimes.com/local/lanow/la-me-prosecutor-misconduct-20161003-snap-story.html.

CHAPTER 5. DEFENSE LAWYERS

1. Although Charles Robins changed his name to Ha'im Al Matin Sharif while on death row, I use the name Robins throughout this description because court

documents refer to him as such. The following facts come from *Charles Robins, aka Ha'Im al Matin Sharif v. Baker,* Appellant's Opening Brief to the Nevada Supreme Court, Appeal from Order Dismissing Petition for Writ of Habeas Corpus (Post-conviction), No. 65063, August 11, 2014 (in author's possession); and Michael Kiefer, "Arizona Lawyers Sleuthing Frees Nevada Death Row Inmate," *Reno Gazette Journal,* June 15, 2017, https://www.rgj.com/story/news/crime/2017/06/15/arizona-lawyers-sleuthing-frees-nevada-death-row-inmate/400528001/.

2. *Charles Lamont Robins a/k/a Ha'im Al Matin Sharif v. The State of Nevada,* No. 65063, 2016 WL 5801204 (Nev., September 22, 2016).

3. "Partial Innocence, Conviction Reduced: Ha'im Al Matin Sharif (AKA Charles Robins)," *Death Penalty Information Center,* accessed November 30, 2019, https://deathpenaltyinfo.org/additional-innocence-information.

4. Michael Kiefer, "Arizona Lawyers Sleuthing Frees Nevada Death Row Inmate," *Reno Gazette Journal,* June 15, 2017, https://www.rgj.com/story/news/crime/2017/06/15/arizona-lawyers-sleuthing-frees-nevada-death-row-inmate/400528001/.

5. "Partial Innocence, Conviction Reduced."

6. Equal Justice Initiative, *Lynching in America: Confronting the Legacy of Racial Terror,* 3d ed. (Montgomery, AL, 2017), https://lynchinginamerica.eji.org/report/.

7. Equal Justice Initiative, *Lynching in America.*

8. Michael J. Klarman, "Scottsboro," *Marquette Law Review* 93 (2009): 379, 381–382.

9. Klarman, "Scottsboro," 383.

10. Klarman, "Scottsboro."

11. Klarman, "Scottsboro," 397.

12. Bryan Lymon, "Alabama Grants Posthumous Pardons to Scottsboro Boys," *USA Today,* November 21, 2013, https://www.usatoday.com/story/news/nation/2013/11/21/scottsboro-boys-pardoned/3662205/.

13. *Powell v. Alabama,* 287 U.S. 45, 69–70 (1932).

14. *Gideon v. Wainwright,* 372 U.S. 335 (1963).

15. Richard A. Oppel Jr. and Judgal K. Patel, "One Lawyer, 194 Felony Cases, and No Time," *New York Times,* January 31, 2019, https://www.nytimes.com/interactive/2019/01/31/us/public-defender-case-loads.html.

16. Mary Sue Backus and Pail Marcus, "The Right to Counsel in Criminal Cases: Still a National Crisis," *George Washington Law Review* 86 (November 2018): 1546, 1580; Stephen D. Owens et al., "Indigent Defense Services in the United States, FY 2008–2012," U.S. Department of Justice, Bureau of Justice Statistics, NCJ 246683, updated April 21, 2015, https://www.bjs.gov/content/pub/pdf/idsus0812.pdf; The Constitution Project, *Justice Denied: America's Continuing Neglect of our Constitutional Right to Counsel* (2009), 53, https://constitutionproject.org/wp-content/uploads/2012/10/139.pdf.

17. John P. Gross, *Gideon at 50,* Part 1: *Rationing Justice: The Underfunding of Assigned Counsel Systems* (Washington, DC: National Association of Criminal

Defense Lawyers, 2013), 12, 15, https://www.nacdl.org/reports/gideonat50/rationingjustice/.

18. "In Your State," *Gideon at 50,* accessed November 30, 2019, http://gideonat50.org/in-your-state/#state-funding-level; Owens et al., "Indigent Defense."

19. Stephen Hale, "Buried under Workload, Public Defender's Office Pushes Back," *Nashville Scene,* February 2, 2017, https://www.nashvillescene.com/news/cover-story/article/20850716/facing-an-unmanageable-workload-the-public-defenders-office-is-now-limiting-the-cases-it-takes.

20. Dylan Walsh, "On the Defensive," *Atlantic,* June 2, 2016, https://www.theatlantic.com/politics/archive/2016/06/on-the-defensive/485165/.

21. Robert C. Boruchowitz et al., "Minor Crimes, Massive Waste: The Terrible Toll of America's Broken Misdemeanor Courts," *National Association of Criminal Defense Law,* (2009), 21, https://www.nacdl.org/reports/misdemeanor/.

22. Oppel and Patel, "One Lawyer, 194 Felony Cases, and No Time."

23. Doug Mataconis, "There's a Criminal Defense Crisis in New Mexico, and Nobody Seems to Care," *Outside the Beltway,* December 30, 2016, https://www.outsidethebeltway.com/theres-a-criminal-defense-crisis-in-new-mexico-and-nobody-seems-to-care/.

24. Mataconis, "There's a Criminal Defense Crisis in New Mexico."

25. Dottie Carmichael et al., *Guidelines for Indigent Defense Caseloads: A Report to the Texas Indigent Defense Commission* (College Station: Public Policy Research Group, Texas A&M University, January 2015), http://www.tidc.texas.gov/media/31818/150122_weightedcl_final.pdf.

26. Carmichael et al., "Guidelines for Indigent Defense Caseloads," 5.

27. Carmichael et al., "Guidelines for Indigent Defense Caseloads," appendix D; Oppel and Patel, "One Lawyer, 194 Felony Cases, No Time."

28. Jonathan Rapping, "National Crisis, National Neglect: Realizing Justice Through Transformative Change," *University of Pennsylvania Journal of Law and Social Change* 13 (2010): 331, 338–39.

29. Rapping, "National Crisis, National Neglect."

30. Emily Lane, "Orleans Public Defenders on '60 Minutes': Innocent Imprisoned Because We're Overworked," *nola.com,* April 17, 2017, https://perma.cc/Z4RT-KN3T.

31. The story of "Mary" comes from a report by the National Legal Aid and Defender Association, "A Strategic Plan to Ensure Accountability and Protect Fairness in Louisiana's Criminal Courts," September 22, 2006, pp, 36–38, http://www.nlada.net/sites/default/files/la_orleansevalncej09-2006_report.pdf.

32. *Strickland v. Washington,* 466 U.S. 668 (1984).

33. *Fields v. White,* Civil No. 15-38-ART (E.D. Kentucky, June 23, 2016).

34. Mary Sue Backus and Paul Marcus, "The Right to Counsel in Criminal Cases: A National Crisis," *Hastings Law Journal* 57 (2006): 1031, 1088.

35. The following facts are taken from copies of the record and applicable motions, made available by the North Carolina Innocence Inquiry Commission,

State v. Israel Grant, (Mecklenburg—05 CRS 244094; 05 CRS 076342), http://innocencecommission-nc.gov/wp-content/uploads/state-v-grant/state-v-grant-brief.pdf.

36. "Three Judge Panel Decision for Grant," North Carolina Innocence Inquiry Commission, accessed December 1, 2019, http://innocencecommission-nc.gov/three-judge-panel-decision-for-israel-grant/; Ken Otterbourg, "Israel Grant," *NRE,* updated August 27, 2019, http://www.law.umich.edu/special/exoneration/pages/casedetail.aspx?caseid=5483.

37. Maurice Possley, "Herbert Landry," *NRE,* January 30, 2017, https://www.law.umich.edu/special/exoneration/Pages/casedetail.aspx?caseid=5078.

38. Maurice Possley, "Nick Rhoades," *NRE,* July 11, 2016, https://www.law.umich.edu/special/exoneration/Pages/casedetail.aspx?caseid=4514.

39. Jonathan A. Rapping, "You Can't Build on Shaky Ground: Laying the Foundation for Indigent Defense Reform Through Values-Based Recruitment, Training and Mentoring," *Harvard Law and Policy Review* 3 (2009): 161, 174.

40. *Rhoades v. State of Iowa,* 848 N.W.2d 22, 33 (Iowa 2014).

41. "Compensation Statutes: A National Overview," University of Michigan Law School, updated May 21, 2018, https://www.law.umich.edu/special/exoneration/Documents/CompensationByState_InnocenceProject.pdf.

42. U.S. Department of Justice, Office of Sex Offender Sentencing, Monitoring, Apprehending, Registering, and Tracking, *Smart Summary: Global Survey of Sex Offender Registration and Notification Systems, smart.gov* (2016), 2, https://www.smart.gov/pdfs/global-survey-2016-final.pdf.

43. *Missouri Revised Statutes,* Sec. 589.426 (2019).

44. Kelly Rossman-McKinney, "Press Release: Attorney General Nessel Weighs In on Sex Offender Registration Cases before MI Supreme Court," *Michigan.gov,* February 8, 2019, https://www.michigan.gov/som/0,4669,7-192-47796-489212--,00.html.

45. *People v. David Allen Snyder,* Amicus Curiae, Michigan Attorney General Dana Nessel, February 8, 2019, *Michigan.gov,* https://www.michigan.gov/documents/ag/REcd.153696_Snyder_SORA_br_MSC-FINAL_marked_645821_7.pdf.

46. Frederic N. Tulsky and Sean Webby, "Error Left Man with Label of Molester: Mistake Took Decades for Officials to Fix," *San Jose Mercury News,* April 9, 2006.

47. Tulsky and Sean Webby, "Error Left Man with Label of Molester."

48. Maurice Possley, "Darian Contee," *NRE,* updated November 18, 2014, https://www.law.umich.edu/special/exoneration/Pages/casedetail.aspx?caseid=4023.

49. Stephani Bibas, "Plea Bargaining outside the Shadow of Trial," *Harvard Law Review,* 117 (June 2004): 2463, 2479–89; Margareth Etienne, "Remorse, Responsibility, and Regulating Advocacy: Making Defendants Pay for the Sins of Their Lawyers," *N.Y.U. Law Review* 78 (2003): 2103, 2171–73.

50. Eve Brensike Primus, "Culture as a Structural Problem in Indigent Defense," *Minnesota Law Review* 100 (2016): 1769.

51. Lydia DePillis, "Harris County's System for Defending the Poor Is Still Woefully Inadequate, State Audit Finds," *Houston Chronicle*, October 12, 2016, https://www.houstonchronicle.com/houston/article/Harris-County-s-system-for-defending-the-poor-9966511.php.

52. Lise Olsen, "Hundreds of Indigent Inmates Jailed for Months Pretrial," *Houston Chronicle*, October 3, 2009, https://www.chron.com/news/houston-texas/article/Hundreds-of-indigent-inmates-jailed-for-months-1566415.php; Lise Olson, "Attorneys Overworked in Harris County Death-Row Cases," *Houston Chronicle*, May 25, 2009, https://www.chron.com/news/houston-texas/article/Attorneys-overworked-in-Harris-County-death-row-1727249.php.

53. DePillis, "Harris County's System."

54. Anderson Cooper, "Interview with David Martin," *CNN AC360*, October 16, 2009, available on YouTube, https://www.youtube.com/watch?time_continue=99&v=L5cFKpjRnXE.

55. Grann, "Trial by Fire."

56. Grann, "Trial by Fire"; Cooper, "Interview with David Martin."

57. Cooper, "Interview with David Martin."

58. Janet Jacobs, "Those Closest to the Case Shed No Tears for Willingham," *Corsicana Daily Sun*, September 6, 2009, p. 8A.

59. Cooper, "Interview with David Martin."

60. Maurice Possley, "Timothy Britt," *NRE*, December 3, 2017, https://www.law.umich.edu/special/exoneration/Pages/casedetail.aspx?caseid=5238.

61. Tomeka Sinclair, "Man Freed after Rape Conviction Dismisses," *(Lumberton, NC) Robesonian*, November 21, 2017, https://www.robesonian.com/news/104968/man-freed-after-rape-conviction-dismisses; Tonya Brown, "Conviction Dismissed, Robeson County Man Freed from Prison after More than 4 Years," *ABC15 News*, November 28, 2017, https://wpde.com/news/local/robeson-county-man-freed-from-prison-after-conviction-dismissed.

CHAPTER 6. JUDGES

1. A defendant may opt for a bench trial for any number of reasons. They may believe a judge will be more impartial than a jury because of the nature of the charges or the parties, or that a judge may better understand the law than a jury. Or they may simply seek to expedite the proceedings.

2. The following case details in this paragraph are found in *Tucker v. Palmer*, 541 F.3d 652, 663, 664, 667 n. 6 (6th Cir. 2008).

3. *Tucker*, 541 F.3d at 664.

4. *Tucker v. Palmer*, 2007 WL 869164 (E.D. Mich. 2007).

5. *Tucker*, 541 F.3d at 654.

6. *Tucker*, 541 F.3d at 661.

7. *Tucker*, 541 F.3d at 662.

8. *Tucker*, 541 F.3d at 668; see also id. at 667 n. 6.

9. *Tucker,* 541 F.3d at 668–69.

10. *Tucker,* 541 F.3d at 670–71.

11. In capital cases, juries decide on the sentence of death.

12. In a 2004 law review article entitled "Bad Judges," Geoffrey P. Miller grouped "bad judging" into twelve categories: "(1) corrupt influence on judicial action; (2) questionable fiduciary appointments; (3) abuse of office for personal gain; (4) incompetence and neglect of duties; (5) overstepping of authority; (6) interpersonal abuse; (7) bias, prejudice, and insensitivity; (8) personal misconduct reflecting adversely on fitness for office; (9) conflict of interest; (10) inappropriate behavior in a judicial capacity; (11) lack of candor; and (12) electioneering and purchase of office." *Texas Law Review* 83 (2004): 431, 432–33.

13. American Bar Association, Special Functions of the Trial Judge, Standard 6-1.6 (d), https://www.americanbar.org/groups/criminal_justice/publications /criminal_justice_section_archive/crimjust_standards_trialjudge/.

14. Jeffrey J. Rachlinski et al., "Does Unconscious Racial Bias Affect Trial Judges?" *Notre Dame Law Review* 84 (2009): 1195; Gregory S. Parks, "Judging Racism," *Cardozo Law Review de novo* (2012): 238, 246–47.

15. See (and take, if you wish) the IAT at https://implicit.harvard.edu/implicit /takeatest.html.

16. Rachlinski, "Does Unconscious Racial Bias Affect Trial Judges?" 1206.

17. Rachlinski, "Does Unconscious Racial Bias Affect Trial Judges?" 1210, 1218, 1221.

18. Bryan Stevenson, *Just Mercy* (New York: Penguin Books, 2014).

19. "One Lawyer's Fight for Young Blacks and 'Just Mercy,'" *Fresh Air,* August 21, 2015, available at National Public Radio, https://www.npr.org/2015/08/21 /433478728/one-lawyers-fight-for-young-blacks-and-just-mercy. Stevenson tells various versions of this story frequently in his appearances.

20. Nazgol Ghandnoosh, "Black Lives Matter: Eliminating Racial Inequity in the Criminal Justice System," *The Sentencing Project,* February 3, 2015, https://bit .ly/2Ngeagy.

21. The following account is based on Joe Kemp, "Sikh Driver Labeled 'Terrorist' by Mississippi Traffic Cops before Judge Calls Turban 'That Rag': ACLU," *New York Daily News,* September 28, 2013, https://www.nydailynews.com/news /national/sikh-truck-driver-labeled-terrorist-mississippi-traffic-cops-judge-calls-man-turban-rag-aclu-article-1.1470362.

22. ACLU of Mississippi, complaint to Mississippi Department of Transportation, American Civil Liberties Union, September 25, 2013, https://www.aclu.org /sites/default/files/assets/letter_to_dot.pdf.

23. "Justice Court," *Pike County, Mississippi, Website,* accessed December 1, 2019, http://co.pike.ms.us/departments/justice_court.

24. Yarimi Farima, "Judge Abruptly Retires after Reportedly Calling Black Defense Attorney a Gorilla,"*12 News* (CBS), August 24, 2018, https://cbs12.com/news /local/judge-abruptly-retires-after-reportedly-calling-black-defense-attorney-a-gorilla.

25. David Ovalle, "Miami Judge Who Called Black Defendant 'Moolie' Faces Suspension for Using Slurs," *Miami Herald,* May 21, 2018, https://www.miamiherald.com/news/local/crime/article211618154.html.

26. Associated Press, "Judge in Charleston Case Once Used Racial Slur," *Indy Star,* June 20, 2015, https://www.indystar.com/story/news/crime/2015/06/20/charleston-judge-james-gosnell-racial-slur-on-bench/29025559/.

27. Barry Paddock and Rich Shapiro, "S.C. Judge Urges Support for Accused Murderer Dylann Roof's Family in Bizarre Court Speech," *New York Daily News,* June 19, 2015, https://www.nydailynews.com/news/crime/s-judge-urges-support-dylann-roof-family-article-1.2264319.

28. Nazgol Ghandnoosh, "Race and Punishment: Racial Perceptions of Crime and Support for Punitive Policies," *The Sentencing Project* (September 2014), 26, https://bit.ly/2Hcxg3D.

29. Maurice Possley, "Raynella Dossett Leath," *NRE,* June 2, 2017, https://www.law.umich.edu/special/exoneration/Pages/casedetail.aspx?caseid=5146.

30. Possley, "Raynella Dossett Leath."

31. *Leath v. Tennessee,* Post-conviction No. 104426, In the Criminal Court of Knox County, Tennessee, Findings of Fact and Conclusions of Law: Final Judgment Order (May 11, 2016), at 18–19, available at DocumentCloud, https://www.documentcloud.org/documents/2831107-Senior-Judge-Paul-Summers-opinion-granting.html.

32. *Leath,* Final Judgment Order, at 22, 27.

33. Baumgartner fed his addiction through various acts of misconduct. He engaged in "doctor shopping," enabling him to obtain numerous opioid prescriptions from multiple doctors, forced court staff and convicted defendants to obtain pills for him, bought drugs from convicted felons, and had an extramarital affair with a woman who had graduated from his own drug court and who supplied him with sex and drugs. *Leath,* Final Judgment Order, at 24–27.

34. *Leath,* Final Judgment Order; Jamie Satterfield, "Court of Secrecy: How Richard Baumgartner, a Drug-Addicted Judge, Stayed on the Bench Despite Warning," *Knoxville News Sentinel,* February 12, 2012, http://archive.knoxnews.com/news/local/court-of-secrecy-how-richard-baumgartner-a-drug-addicted-judge-stayed-on-the-bench-despite-warnin-ep-357208631.html/.

35. Possley, "Raynella Dossett Leath."

36. *Leath,* Final Judgment Order.

37. A Philadelphia judge, Paul Michael Pozonsky, was disbarred after pleading guilty to stealing cocaine from an evidence locker in his courtroom. Ironically (or perhaps not), Pozonsky had founded the Washington County drug court in 2005, designed to provide treatment and hold noncompliant drug offenders criminally accountable for their actions.

38. Patrick R. Krill and R. Johnson, "The Prevalence of Substance Use and Other Mental Health Concerns among American Attorneys," *Journal of Addiction Medicine* 10(1) (2016): 46–52.

39. Alicia Bannon, *Rethinking Judicial Selection in State Courts* (New York: Brennan Center for Justice, 2016), 1, 7, https://www.brennancenter.org/sites/default/files/publications/Rethinking_Judicial_Selection_State_Courts.pdf.

40. Juvenile Law Center, "Luzerne 'Kids for Cash' Scandal," accessed December 1, 2019, https://jlc.org/luzerne-kids-cash-scandal.

41. Robert May (dir.), *Kids for Cash* (2013), available at https://kidsforcashthe-movie.com/character-stories/.

42. Clark Neily, *Are a Disproportionate Number of Federal Judges Former Government Advocates?* (Washington, DC: Cato Institute, September 18, 2019), https://www.cato.org/publications/studies/are-disproportionate-number-federal-judges-former-government-advocates#null.

43. Lefstein, quoted in Bill Whitehurst, Gideon's Broken Promise*: America's Continuing Quest for Equal Justice A Report on the American Bar Association's Hearings on the Right to Counsel in Criminal Proceedings.* (Chicago: American Bar Association, 2004), 21, https://www.americanbar.org/content/dam/aba/administrative/legal_aid_indigent_defendants/ls_sclaid_def_bp_right_to_counsel_in_criminal_proceedings.authcheckdam.pdf.

44. Ernie Lewis and Dan Goyette, "Report on the Evaluation of the Office of the Orleans Public Defenders," Louisiana Public Defender Board, July 2012, https://bit.ly/2Z7DA6C.

45. Committee on Identifying the Needs of the Forensic Sciences Community, National Research Council, *Strengthening Forensic Science in the United States: A Path Forward* (Washington, DC: National Academy of Sciences, 2009), 29 (hereafter cited as NAS Report), available at National Criminal Justice Reference Service, https://www.ncjrs.gov/pdffiles1/nij/grants/228091.pdf.

46. *Frye v. United States,* 293 F. 1013 (D.C. Cir. 1923).

47. *Daubert v. Merrell Dow Pharm., Inc.,* 509 U.S. 579, 590 (1993).

48. Editorial, "Junk Science at the F.B.I.," *New York Times,* April 27, 2015, https://www.nytimes.com/2015/04/27/opinion/junk-science-at-the-fbi.html.

49. Possley, "Leigh Stubbs"; Possley, "Tammy Vance."

50. Radley Balko, "Leigh Stubbs, Mississippi Woman, Serving 44-Year Sentence Despite Discredited Testimony," *Huffington Post,* updated December 6, 2017, https://www.huffpost.com/entry/leigh-stubbs-michael-west-forensics-discredited-testimony_n_922219.

51. Michael J. Saks et al., "Forensic Bitemark Identification: Weak Foundations, Exaggerated Claims," *Journal of Law and the Biosciences* 3(3) (2016): 538–75.

52. The following account of the trial and its outcome is based on Balko, "Leigh Stubbs."

53. "2 Convictions Overturned in 2001 Attack on Vicksburg Women," *Vicksburg Post,* July 3, 2012, https://www.vicksburgpost.com/2012/07/03/2-convictions-overturned-in-2001-attack-on-vicksburg-woman/.

54. Jon Schuppe, "We Are Going Backward: How the Justice System Ignores Science in the Pursuit of Convictions," *NBC News,* January 23, 2019, https://www

.nbcnews.com/news/us-news/we-are-going-backward-how-justice-system-ignores-science-pursuit-n961256.

55. Jay William Burnett and Catherine Greene Burnett, "Ethical Dilemmas Confronting a Felony Trial Judge: To Remove or Not to Remove Deficient Counsel," *Southern Texas Law Review* 41 (2000): 1315, 1316.

56. Denis Slattery, "Bronx Prosecutor Bashed and Barred from Courtroom for Misconduct," *New York Daily News,* April 6, 2014, https://www.nydailynews.com/new-york/bronx/bronx-prosecutor-barred-courtroom-article-1.1746238.

57. Denis Slattery, "Bronx Judge Investigated for Barring Prosecutor from Courtroom," *New York Daily News,* August 7, 2014, https://www.nydailynews.com/new-york/bronx/bronx-judge-investigated-barring-prosecutor-courtroom-article-1.1896016.

58. Slattery, "Bronx Judge Investigated."

59. Thompson P. Sullivan and Maurice Possley, "The Chronic Failure to Discipline Prosecutors for Misconduct: Proposal for Reform," *Journal of Criminal Law and Criminology,* 105 (2016) 881.

60. ABA Standards Relating to Pleas of Guilty, Standard 14 §3.3 ("A judge should not ordinarily participate in plea negotiation discussions among the parties"); Federal Rules of Criminal Procedure, 11(c)(1). Rishi Raj Batra has collected comprehensive data about the different jurisdictional approaches to judicial participation in plea bargains. See Rishi Raj Batra, "Judicial Participation in Plea Bargaining: A Dispute Resolution Perspective," *Ohio State Law Journal* 76 (2015): 565, 574.

61. "Criminal Law—Plea Bargains—District Court Denies Plea Bargain Due to the Public Interest in Understanding the Opioid Epidemic—*U.S. v. Walker,* No. 2:17-cr-0010, 2017 WL 2766452 (S.W. Va. June 26, 2017)," *Harvard Law Review* 131 (2018): 2073, 2079–80.

62. Malvina Halbertstam, "Criminal Law: Towards Neutral Principles in the Administration of Criminal Justice: A Critique of Supreme Court Decisions Sanctioning the Plea Bargaining Process," *Journal of Criminal Law and Criminology* 73 (1982): 1, 36.

63. Transactional Records Access Clearinghouse Reports (2014), cited in Brian A. Jackson et al., *Fostering Innovation in the U.S. Court System: Identifying High-Priority Technology and Other Needs for Improving Court Operations and Outcomes* (Santa Monica, CA: RAND Corporation, 2016), 10.

64. Stephanos Bibas, "Designing Plea Bargaining from the Ground Up: Accuracy and Fairness without Trials as Backstops," *William and Mary Law Review* 57 (2016): 1055, 1065 n. 41 (collecting cases).

65. Riley Yates, "Defense Attorney Files Motion Criticizing County Judge, Asks for His Recusal," *(Allentown, PA) Morning Call,* October 22, 2018, https://www.mcall.com/news/police/mc-nws-northampton-county-judge-criticized-for-pressuring-guilty-pleas-20181022-story.html.

66. Batra, "Judicial Participation in Plea Bargaining."

67. Riley Yates, "Take This Plea or Else," *Morning Call,* June 30, 2012, https://www.mcall.com/news/local/mc-xpm-2012-06-30-mc-northampton-county-court-arraignments-guilty-pl-20120630-story.html.

68. Issa Kohler-Hausmann, "Misdemeanor Justice: Control without Conviction," *American Journal of Sociology* 119 (2013): 351, 370–71.

69. Yates, "Defense Attorney Files Motion Criticizing County Judge."

70. Riley Yates, "Northampton Judge Reversed on DUI Conviction," *Morning Call,* January 9, 2019.

71. Riley Yates, "Policy of Taking Driver's Licenses before a DUI Conviction Draws Critics," *Morning Call,* https://www.mcall.com/news/local/mc-xpm-2012-01-28-mc-northampton-county-license-judge-dui-20120128-story.html.

72. Riley Yates, "DUI Defendant Acquitted by Jury, Convicted by Judge," *Morning Call,* February 8, 2012; Riley Yates, "Northampton County Judge Bashed for About-Face on Jury Ruling," *Morning Call,* February 10, 2012.

73. National Association of Criminal Defense Lawyers, *The Trial Penalty: The Sixth Amendment Right to Trial on the Verge of Extinction and How to Save It* (Washington, DC, 2018), 6, www.nacdl.org/trialpenaltyreport.

74. Slattery, "Bronx Judge Investigated."

75. Rob Warden, "Town of Tulia: Texas 'Officer of the Year' Chalked Up 38 Wrongful Convictions," Center on Wrongful Convictions, Northwestern University, http://www.law.northwestern.edu/legalclinic/wrongfulconvictions/exonerations/tx/town-of-tulia.html.

76. Doron Teichman, "The Hindsight Bias and the Law in Hindsight," in Doron Teichman and Eyal Zamir, eds., *The Oxford Handbook of Behavioral Economics and the Law* (New York: Oxford University Press, 2014), 354.

77. Daniel Kahneman, *Thinking, Fast and Slow* (New York: Farrar, Straus & Giroux, 2011), 202; Keith A. Findley and Michael S. Scott, "The Multiple Dimensions of Tunnel Vision," *Wisconsin Law Review* 2 (2006): 291, 292.

78. Keith A. Findley, "Innocence Protection in the Appellate Process," *Marquette Law Review* 93 (2009): 591, 605.

79. Brandon L. Garrett, "Judging Innocence," *Columbia Law Review* 108 (2008): 55.

80. Garrett, "Judging Innocence," 107–8.

81. The facts of Agnew's case are taken from *Agnew v. Leibach,* 250 F.3d 1123 (7th Cir. 2011); Maurice Possley, "Gregory Agnew," *NRE,* January 18, 2018, http://www.law.umich.edu/special/exoneration/Pages/casedetail.aspx?caseid=5262.

82. *Agnew,* 250 F.3d at 1135.

83. Possley, "Gregory Agnew."

84. *Strickland v. Washington,* 466 U.S. 668 (1984).

85. Stephen B. Bright, "Counsel for the Poor: The Death Sentence Not for the Worst Crime but for the Worst Lawyer," *Yale Law Journal* 103 (1994): 1835, 1852. Bright notes: "The vice president of the Georgia Trial Lawyers Association once described the simple test used in that state to determine whether a defendant receives adequate counsel as 'the mirror test.' 'You put a mirror under the

court-appointed lawyer's nose, and if the mirror clouds up, that's adequate counsel.'"

86. *United States v. Olsen,* 737 F.3d 625, 633 (9th Cir. 2013).

CHAPTER 7. MISDEMEANORS

1. For a vivid description of New York's pre-arraignment holding cells, see William Glaberson, "Trapped in the Terror of New York's Holding Pens," *New York Times,* March 23, 1990, https://www.nytimes.com/1990/03/23/nyregion/trapped-in-the-terror-of-new-york-s-holding-pens.html.

2. New York Penal Law, sec. 140 et seq.

3. Megan Stevenson and Sandra Mayson, "The Scale of Misdemeanor Justice," *Boston University Law Review* 98 (2018): 731, 737.

4. *NRE,* data sorted by "Misdemeanors," from June 30, 2019.

5. *Maryland NAACP, et al. v. Baltimore City Police Department, et al.,* Civil Case No. 24-C-06-005088, Complaint, paras. 45–59 (Baltimore, City Circuit Court 2006), https://www.aclu-md.org/sites/default/files/field_documents/bcpd_complaint.pdf.

6. *Maryland NAACP, et al.,* paras. 45–59.

7. *Maryland NAACP, et al.,* para. 51.

8. *Maryland NAACP, et al.,* para. 54, 56.

9. *Argersinger v. Hamlin,* 407 U.S. 25 (1972).

10. Insha Rahman, "Chipping Away at New York City's Unjust and Misguided Bail System," *Think Justice Blog,* April 29, 2016, Vera Institute of Justice, https://www.vera.org/blog/chipping-away-at-new-york-citys-unjust-and-misguided-bail-system.

11. John H. Blume and Rebecca K. Helm, "The Unexonerated: Factually Innocent Defendants Who Plead Guilty," *Cornell Law Review* 100 (2014): 157, 158–61.

12. Samuel R. Gross, "Errors in Misdemeanor Adjudications," *Boston University Law Review* 98 (2018): 999.

13. Dean Balsamini, "This Judge Is Cleaning House of Jurists Who Can't Manage Huge Case Backlogs," *New York Post,* December 4, 2016, https://nypost.com/2016/12/04/this-judge-is-cleaning-house-of-jurists-who-cant-manage-huge-case-backlogs/.

14. Jenny M. Roberts, "The Innocence Movement and Misdemeanors," *Boston University Law Review* 98 (2018): 779, 810–14.

15. For instance, the Connecticut Innocence Project limits assistance to cases where a person is serving a minimum ten-year sentence and has five or more years left to serve. Connecticut Innocence Project, Post-conviction Unit, accessed August 17, 2019, https://portal.ct.gov/OCPD/Innocence-Project/What-is-the-Connecticut-Innocence-Project.

16. Jenny M. Roberts. "Why Misdemeanors Matter: Defining Effective Advocacy in the Lower Criminal Courts," *U.C. Davis Law Review* 45 (2011): 277.

17. Roberts, "Why Misdemeanors Matter"; see also Michael Pinard, "Collateral Consequences of Criminal Convictions: Confronting Issues of Race and Dignity," *N.Y.U. Law Review* 85 (2010): 457, 489–95, 514 n. 331.

18. *Nichols v. United States,* 511 U.S. 738 (1994).

19. Maurice Possley, "Corey Anthony Love," *NRE,* December 12, 2015, https://www.law.umich.edu/special/exoneration/Pages/casedetail.aspx?caseid=4192.

20. *Ex Parte Corey Anthony Love,* Applicant, No. WR-79,492-01, June 5, 2013, 2013 WL 2446511.

21. Lise Olsen and Anita Hassan, "298 Wrongful Drug Convictions Identified in Ongoing Audit," *Houston Chronical,* July 16, 2016, https://www.houstonchronicle.com/news/houston-texas/houston/article/298-wrongful-drug-convictions-identified-in-8382474.php.

22. Ryan Gabrielson and Topher Sanders, "Busted," *ProPublica,* July 7, 2016, https://www.propublica.org/article/common-roadside-drug-test-routinely-produces-false-positives.

23. *NRE,* data filtered by "Harris County," "CIU," "Drug Possession or Sale," from June 30, 2019.

24. Randy Balko, March 13, 2018, "Why Are Police Departments Still Using Drug Field Tests?" *Washington Post,* March 13, 2018, https://www.washingtonpost.com/news/the-watch/wp/2018/03/13/why-are-police-departments-still-using-drug-field-tests/?utm_term=.b652e865fd25.

25. Ryan Gabrielson, "Unreliable and Unchallenged," *ProPublica,* October 28, 2016, https://www.propublica.org/article/unreliable-and-unchallenged.

26. Gabrielson, "Unreliable and Unchallenged."

27. Howard Cohen, "She Told Cops They Were Vitamins, But Botched Field Test Kept Florida Mom in Jail for Months," *Miami Herald,* March 10, 2018, https://www.miamiherald.com/news/state/florida/article204511844.html.

28. *Ligon v. City of New York,* Complaint, at 1 (S.D.N.Y. March 28, 2012), retrieved from https://www.bronxdefenders.org/wp-content/uploads/2016/06/Ligon-v.-City-of-New-York-Complaint-3-28-12.pdf.

29. *Ligon v. City of New York,* Complaint, at 34.

30. *Ligon v. City of New York*, 925 F.Supp.2d 478, 496 (S.D.N.Y. 2013).

31. New York Lawyers for the Public Interest, *No Place like Home: A Preliminary Report on Police Interactions with Public Housing Residents in New York City* (New York, September 2008), 2.

32. *Ligon v. City of New York,* Complaint, para. 149.

33. *Ligon v. City of New York,* Complaint, para. 150.

34. *Ligon v. City of New York,* Complaint, paras. 149, 193.

35. George L. Kelling and James Q. Wilson, "Broken Windows: The Police and Neighborhood Safety," *Atlantic,* March 1982, https://www.theatlantic.com/magazine/archive/1982/03/broken-windows/304465/.

36. "Broken Windows: How a Theory of Crime and Policing Was Born and Went Terribly Wrong," *Hidden Brain,* National Public Radio, November 1, 2011, https://

www.npr.org/2016/11/01/500104506/broken-windows-policing-and-the-origins-of-stop-and-frisk-and-how-it-went-wrong.

37. Amy Lamoureux, "This Might Be the Most Absurd Case of Police Harassment Ever," *All That's Interesting,* April 18, 2018, https://allthatsinteresting.com/earl-sampson; Conor Friedersdorf, "Asking America's Police Officers to Explain Abusive Cops," *Atlantic,* February 2, 2015, https://www.theatlantic.com/politics/archive/2015/02/This-american-life-cops-see-it-differently/385874/.

38. Rachel Siegel, "They Can't Be Here for Us: Black Men Arrested at Starbucks Tell Their Story for the First Time," *Washington Post,* April 19, 2018, https://www.washingtonpost.com/news/business/wp/2018/04/19/they-cant-be-here-for-us-black-men-arrested-at-starbucks-tell-their-story-for-the-first-time/?utm_term=.641e4ee31d1f.

39. Rachel Krishna and Brianna Sacks, "The LA Fitness Employees Who Called the Police on 2 Black Men Working Out Are No Longer at the Company," *Buzz-Feed,* April 19, 2018, https://www.buzzfeednews.com/article/krishrach/two-black-men-had-the-cops-called-on-them-after-their-gym.

40. *Thompson v. City of Louisville,* 362 U.S. 199 (1960).

41. *Papachristou v. Jacksonville,* 405 U.S. 156 (1972).

42. *Papachristou,* at 156 n. 1.

43. *Williams v. State of Maryland* (Court of Special Appeals 2000), available at *Justia: US Law,* https://cases.justia.com/maryland/court-of-special-appeals/2054800-0.pdf?ts=1462360286.

44. "Investigation of the Baltimore City Police Department Report," U.S. Department of Justice, Civil Rights Division, August 10, 2016, https://www.justice.gov/crt/filc/883296/download.

45. Consent Decree, Department of Justice and the Police Department of Baltimore, Case 1:17-cv-00099-JKB, U.S. Department of Justice, Civil Rights Division, January 12, 2017, https://www.justice.gov/crt/case-document/file/925036/download.

46. Josh Bowers, "Legal Guilt, Normative Innocence, and the Equitable Decision Not to Prosecute," *Columbia Law Review* 110(7) (November 2010): 1655, 1657–58, 1716–20.

47. Michael Tonry, *Malign Neglect: Race, Crime, and Punishment in America* (New York: Oxford University Press, 1995).

CONCLUSION

1. Jessica S. Henry, "How Corruption in Forensic Science Is Harming the Criminal Justice System," *The Conversation,* January 25, 2019, http://jessicahenryjustice.com/how-corruption-in-forensic-science-is-harming-the-criminal-justice-system/.

2. NAS Report, 100.

3. Executive summary, in NAS Report, 7.

4. President's Council of Advisors on Science and Technology, *Report to the President: Forensic Science in Criminal Courts; Ensuring Scientific Validity of Feature-Comparison Methods* (Washington, DC: Executive Office of the President, 2016), archived at https://obamawhitehouse.archives.gov/sites/default/files/microsites/ostp /PCAST/pcast_forensic_science_report_final.pdf (hereafter cited as PCAST Report).

5. PCAST Report, 9.

6. Seth Augenstein, "Bite Mark Evidence Should Be Deceased, Says Dentist," *Forensic Magazine,* November 5, 2018, https://www.forensicmag.com/news/2018/11 /bite-mark-evidence-skin-should-be-deceased-dentist-says.

7. Paul C. Giannelli, "Forensic Science: *Daubert's* Failure," *Case Western Reserve Law Review* 68 (2018): 869.

8. Schuppe, "We Are Going Backwards."

9. NAS Report, 53 (italics added).

10. Randy Balko, "Judges Are Terrible at Distinguishing Good Science from Bad: It's Time We Stopped Asking Them to Do It," *Washington Post,* September 28, 2017, https://www.washingtonpost.com/news/the-watch/wp/2017/09/28 /judges-are-terrible-at-distinguishing-good-science-from-bad-its-time-we-stopped- asking-them-to-do-it/?utm_term=.66ec9c061d87.

11. PCAST Report, 18, 65–66.

12. PCAST Report, 18.

13. PCAST Report, 19.

14. Findley et al., "Shaken Baby Syndrome, Abusive Head Trauma, and Actual Innocence," 212.

15. Alex Kozinski, "Criminal Law 2.0," *Georgetown Law Journal* 44 (2015): iii, v.

16. Balko, "Leigh Stubbs."

17. Brandon L. Garrett and Peter Neufeld, "Invalid Forensic Science Testimony and Wrongful Convictions," *Virginia Law Review* 95 (2009): 1, 14–15.

18. Tim Novak and Robert Herguth, "Freed Murder Defendant Says He Was Jailed 19 Months Because of Botched Autopsy," *Chicago Sun Times,* August 31, 2018, https://chicago.suntimes.com/news/freed-murder-defendant-jailed-because- botched-autopsy-cook-county-medical-examiner-adrienne-segovia/.

19. Novak and Herguth, "Freed Murder Defendant Says He Was Jailed 19 Months."

20. Scheck, Neufeld, and Dwyer, *Actual Innocence,* 122.

21. NAS Report, 23–24.

22. Mark Hansen, "Crime Labs under the Microscope after a String of Shoddy, Suspect, and Fraudulent Results," *A.B.A. Journal,* September 1, 2013, http://www .abajournal.com/magazine/article/crime_labs_under_the_microscope_after_a_ string_of_shoddy_suspect_and_fraudu/.

23. Spencer S. Hsu, "Sessions Orders Justice Dept. to End Forensic Science Commission, Suspend Review Policy," *Washington Post,* April 10, 2017, https:// www.washingtonpost.com/local/public-safety/sessions-orders-justice-dept-to-end- forensic-science-commission-suspend-review-policy/2017/04/10/2dadaoca-1c96– 11e7–9887–1a5314b56a08_story.html.

24. Liliana Segura and Jordan Smith, "Ten Years after a Landmark Study Blew the Whistle on Junk Science, the Fight over Forensics Rages On," *Intercept,* May 5, 2019, https://theintercept.com/2019/05/05/forensic-evidence-aafs-junk-science/; Meehan Crist and Tim Requarth, "Forensic Science Put Jimmy Genrich in Prison for 24 Years: What If It Wasn't Science?" *Nation,* February 1, 2018, https://www.thenation.com/article/the-crisis-of-american-forensics/.

25. Department of Forensic Science, Washington, DC, https://dfs.dc.gov/page/about-dfs.

26. James McNamara et al, "Characteristics of False Allegation Adult Crimes," *Journal of Forensic Science* 57 (2012): 3.

27. Anthony W. Batts, Maddy deLone, and Darrel W. Stephens, *Policing and Wrongful Convictions*, New Perspectives in Policing Bulletin (Washington, DC: U.S. Department of Justice, National Institute of Justice, 2004), https://www.ncjrs.gov/pdffiles1/nij/246328.pdf.

28. Batts, deLone, and Stephens, *Policing and Wrongful Convictions,* 535.

29. PEACE stands for Preparation and Planning, Engage and Explain, Account, Closure, and Evaluate. To read more about the PEACE model of interrogation, see Mary Schollum, "Bringing Peace to the United States: A Framework for Investigative Interviewing," *The Police Chief,* November 2017, available at *fis: Forensic Interview Solutions,* https://www.fis-international.com/assets/Uploads/resources/Schollum-PEACE.pdf.

30. Tom Jackman, "New Orleans Police Pioneer New Way to Stop Misconduct," *Washington Post,* January 24, 2019, https://www.washingtonpost.com/crime-law/2019/01/24/new-orleans-police-pioneer-new-way-stop-misconduct-remove-blue-wall-silence/?utm_term=.8e40144bc6d9.

31. Amy Novotney, "Prevent Police Misconduct," *Monitor on Psychology* (American Psychology Association) 48(9) (October 2017), https://www.apa.org/monitor/2017/10/police-misconduct.

32. Jackman, "New Orleans Police Pioneer New Way."

33. Cynthia Lum et al., "Research on Body-Worn Cameras: What We Know, What We Need to Know," *Criminology and Public Policy,* March 24, 2019, https://doi.org/10.1111/1745-9133.12412.

34. Alan Dershowitz, *The Best Defense* (New York: Random House, 1982).

35. D. Kim Rossmo and Joycelyn M. Pollack, "Confirmation Bias and Other Systemic Causes of Wrongful Convictions: A Sentinel Events Perspective," *Northeastern Law Review* 11 (2019), 791, 832, Cheryl Staats, *State of the Science: Implicit Bias Review 2014* (Columbus: Kirwan Institute for the Study of Race and Ethnicity, Ohio State University, 2014), 20, http://kirwaninstitute.osu.edu/wp-content/uploads/2014/03/2014-implicit-bias.pdf.

36. Rachlinski et al., "Does Unconscious Racial Bias Affect Trial Judges?" 1225.

37. Jerry Kang et al., "Implicit Bias in the Courtroom," *UCLA Law Review* 59(5) (2012): 1124, 1169–76.

38. Rachlinski, "Does Unconscious Racial Bias Affect Trial Judges?" 1195, 1218, 1221.

39. Stephanos Bibas, "Plea Bargaining Outside the Shadow of Trial," *Harvard Law Review* 117 (2004): 2543–47.

40. Rossmo and Pollack, "Confirmation Bias and Other Systemic Causes of Wrongful Convictions," 818–30.

41. Michelle Alexander, "Go to Trial and Crash the Courts," *New York Times,* March 11, 2012, https://www.nytimes.com/2012/03/11/opinion/sunday/go-to-trial-crash-the-justice-system.html.

42. *Brady v. United States,* 397 U.S. 742 (1970).

43. For a compendium of documents about New Jersey bail reform and its implementation, see Criminal Justice Reform Information Center, New Jersey Courts, https://www.njcourts.gov/courts/criminal/reform.html. On New York State, see Michael Rempel and Krystal Rodriguez, *Bail Reform in New York: Legislative Provisions and Implications for New York City* (Center for Court Innovation, April 2019), https://www.courtinnovation.org/sites/default/files/media/document /2019/Bail_Reform_NY_full_0.pdf. On California, see Jazmine, Ulloa "California's Historic Overhaul of Cash Bail Is Now on Hold, Pending a 2020 Referendum," *Los Angeles Times,* January 16, 2019.

44. See The Bail Project, https://bailproject.org/; and the Bronx Freedom Fund, http://www.thebronxfreedomfund.org/.

45. Dylan Walsh, "On Plea Bargaining, the Daily Bread of American Criminal Courts," *Atlantic,* May 2, 2017, https://www.theatlantic.com/politics/archive/2017 /05/plea-bargaining-courts-prosecutors/524112/.

46. Jenia Iontcheva Turner, "Judicial Participation in Plea Negotiations: A Comparative View," *American Journal of Comparative Law* 94 (2006).

47. Walsh, "On Plea Bargaining."

48. Jonathan Rapping, "Who's Guarding the Henhouse: How the American Prosecutor Came to Devour Those He Is Sworn to Protect," *Washburn Law Journal* 51 (2012): 513, 555.

49. National District Attorney Association, National Prosecution Standards, 3d ed. (2009), § 1-1.1, https://ndaa.org/wp-content/uploads/NDAA-NPS-3rd-Ed.-w-Revised-Commentary.pdf.

50. Justin Miller, "The New Reformer DAs," *American Prospect,* January 2, 2018, https://prospect.org/article/new-reformer-das.

51. Rapping, "Who's Guarding the Henhouse," 538–39.

52. Adam M. Gershowitz and Laura R. Killinger, "The State (Never) Rests: How Excessive Prosecutorial Caseloads Harm Criminal Defendants," *Northwestern University Law Review* 105 (2011): 261, 287.

53. *Missouri v. Lamar Johnson,* Brief of Amicus Curiae, "43 Prosecutors in Support of the State's Motion for a New Trial" (Circuit Court City of Missouri, No. 22941-03706A-01, August 15, 2019), 1, https://fairandjustprosecution.org/wp-content/uploads/2019/08/Missouri-v.-Johnson-Brief-of-Amici-Curiae.pdf?utm_source=The+Appeal&utm_campaign=098705f9c0-EMAIL_CAMPAIGN_2018_08_09_04_14_COPY_01&utm_medium=email&utm_term=0_72df992d84–098705f9c0-58403447.

54. Exonerations in 2018, *NRE*, (April 9, 2019), 2, 12.

55. *Missouri v. Lamar Johnson,* Brief of Amicus Curiae, 18.

56. Prosecutorial immunity depends on the prosecutor's function at the time of the misconduct. Prosecutors have absolute immunity for their misconduct performed in the advocacy function (*Imbler v. Pachtman,* 424 U.S. 409, 427 [1976]), but have qualified immunity when they act as investigators or administrators (*Buckley v. Fitzsimmons,* 509 U.S. 259, 268–70 [1993]).

57. Margaret Z. Johns, "Unsupportable and Unjustified: A Critique of Absolute Prosecutorial Immunity," *Fordham Law Review* 80 (2011): 509, 535.

INDEX

Names in bold typeface indicate exonerees.

Central Park 5, 103–4, 217n70
Chapman, Ron, 75
Chicago Police Special Operations Section (SOS), 71–72
child abuse (non-sexual), 25, 31, 48, 53, 57–58
child abuse (sexual): actual-crime exonerations in cases of, 12, 13*table2*; consequences of, 53; and divorce, 53–55; false accusations of, 53–60, 79, 119–20, 123–24; and false memories, 57–58; and hysteria, 56–59; and mass hysteria, 13, 53; in no-crime convictions, 53; no-crime exonerations in cases of, 13*table2*, 53
CIUs (Conviction Integrity Units), 13, 162, 192
Clark, Donald, 36–37
Clark, Stephon, 69
Clarke, William, 97–99
class bias, 18
Clean Halls policy (New York City), 164–65
cognitive bias: in child sexual abuse cases, 58; defined, 26–27; in forensic science, 42, 179; of judges, 42, 183; in lie detection, 47; and mechanical malfunctions as murder, 29–31; and medical examiners, 35, 42; and no-crime convictions, 31; other types of, 200n9; of police, 42; premature cognitive commitment in, 58–59; of prosecutors, 42, 183; and suicide ruled as murder, 27–29; training, 20, 183–84
cognitive dissonance, 102–3
Coleman, Tom, 74–75, 125
Color of Change (racial justice program), 87
Colvin, Richard, 5, 38
Community Resources Against Street Hoodlums (CRASH) (Los Angeles), 73–74
comparison line experiment (Asch), 104–5
confessions. *See* false confessions; guilty plea(s); recanted confessions
confirmation bias, 27, 85, 179, 183
Consiglio, Richard A., 174–75

Contee, Darian, 118
Conviction Integrity Units (CIUs), 13, 162, 192
Cooper, Anthony, 54
Cornell, Matthew, 77–78
Counts, Gregory, 17
courts of appeal. *See* appellate courts
Cox, Dale, 2–3
CRASH (Community Resources Against Street Hoodlums) (Loa Angeles), 73–74
Crawford, Rodricus, 1–5, 179, 197n2
crime fabrication/invention, 61–81; for arrest quotas, 64–66, 81; for career advancement, 81; and false confessions, 78–80; for financial gain, 70–74, 81; to justify unwarranted fatal shootings, 69; noble-cause corruption in, 76–78, 81; and no-crime convictions, 60; as police brutality cover, 66–70, 81; in poor/marginalized communities, 74–76, 81
crime labs, 162–63, 174, 177–79, 188
Crowell, Catherine (Catherine Crowell Webb), 43–44, 50–51
Culver, Cathy, 82–83

Daubert test, 138–39, 176
Davis, Dewey, 40–41, 101
Davis, Gerald, 40–41, 101, 176
death penalty/sentence: of the **Boorn brothers**, 5–6; of **Butler**, 34; Cox on, 2–3; of **Crawford**, 1, 4; error rate vs. non-death sentences, 9; forensic errors in, 122–23; innocence proven after, 8; and "legal" lynchings of African Americans, 109; for no-crime convictions, 39, 92, 109; and pressure on prosecutors, 8; of **Robins (Ha'im Al Matin Sharif)**, 102, 106; in the **Salem Witch Trials**, 4; in the **Scottsboro cases**, 109–10; of **Willingham**, 35–38, 122–23; wrongful conviction percentages, 8–9. *See also* exonerees
defense lawyers, 106–26; and assembly-line justice, 20, 112–13; author's proposals addressing, 176, 193–95; bad lawyers among, 108–10, 112–13, 122–23; case overloads of, 19, 110–14, 121–22, 124,

interrogation (continued)
33; in child sexual abuse cases, 59; in the Clean Halls program, 164; as exoneration factor, 213n75; false confessions induced by, 28–29, 33, 39, 78–80; of **Nicole Harris,** 79–80; of the **Kellers,** 59; of **Marie** (pseudonym), 49; of **Monroe,** 28–29; and no-crime convictions, 20–21; and no-crime exonerations, 78–80, 81; of **Doug Perry,** 59; in the TAP program, 164; of **Winfield,** 176–77

interrogation (PEACE model), 181

interrogation (recorded/unrecorded), 24, 181

jailhouse snitches, 99. *See also* informants

Jenkins, Wayne, 72–73

Jones, David (pseudonym), 169–70

judges (appellate), 19, 88, 128–29, 141, 146–47, 189–90. *See also* appellate courts

judges (trial), 127–51; as addicts, 134–36, 223n33; African Americans as, 131–32; and Alford pleas, 144–45; and assembly-line justice, 20; author's proposals addressing, 150–51, 187–88; as bad judges, 130–38, 222n12; bad lawyering tolerated by, 141; bail/bond determined by, 157; in bench trials, 127–30, 145, 188, 221n1; biases of, 19, 42, 130–34, 184; cognitive bias training for, 183; contempt of court powers abused by, 137–38; and courtroom backlogs, 158; vs. defense functions, 136–37; defense lawyers' incentives to please, vs. clients' interests, 121–22; electoral politics influencing, 136; evidence accessible to, 187; forensic training recommended for, 176; greed influencing, 136; and juries, 130; lawyers appointed by, 130; and mandated sentencing, 145; misjudging the law, 138; no-crime guilty pleas accepted by, 143–44; and plea bargaining, 143, 187; prosecutorial misconduct tolerated by, 141–42; and racial prejudice, 184; retaliating against defense lawyers, 142, 145–46; roles of, 129–30,

187; sentencing power abused by, 138; unreliable evidence admitted by, 101–2, 138–41

judicial misconduct, 19–20, 124–25, 137, 183

juries: African Americans excluded from, 2–3, 134; in the **Agnew** case, 148; all-white juries, 2–3, 69, 109; author's proposals addressing, 181; and bad lawyers, 115–16; and bench trials, 127, 130, 188; in the **Butler** case, 34; in the **Carter** case, 82–83, 100; in the **Cooper** case, 54; in the **Crawford** case, 2–3; and the death penalty, 91, 106; in the **Edmunds** case, 32; and false accusations, 17; and false confessions, 34, 78–80, 94; and forensic error, 3, 41, 176; good-faith deliberations of, 8; grand juries, 30, 102, 130, 152; in the **Clinton Harris** case, 94; in the **Nicole Harris** case, 79–80; in the **Horner** case, 55; and judicial misconduct, 137–38, 145, 148–49; and the **Kern County, California defendants,** 57; in the **Raynella Leath** case, 135; and lie detection, 60; and mass hysteria, 57; in the **Monroe** case, 24; in the **Mora** case, 36; in no-crime convictions, 60, 185; and perjury, 98–99; and police misconduct, 81; and propensity evidence, 116; and prosecutorial misconduct, 85, 98–100, 170, 189; in the **Stubbs** case, 100; and trial judges, 130; in the **Jessica Trump case,** 145; in the **Raymond Tucker** case, 128; in the **Tulia, Texas defendants** case, 10; in the **Clinton Turner** case, 98–100; in the **Vance** case, 100; in the **Villalobos** case, 36; in the **Edward Williams** case, 67–68; in the **Willingham** case, 38

Just Mercy (Stevenson book and film), 132

Kaczemarek, Anne, 89

Kahneman, Daniel, 147

Kang, Jerry, 184

Kassin, Saul, 79

Keller, Dan, 56–60

Keller, Francis, 56–60

Kelling, George L., 165

Kelly, Regina, 75–76
Kern County, California defendants, 57
Kids for Cash scandal, 136
Koury, Michael J., 145
Kozinski, Alex, 97, 99
Krasner, Larry, 191

Lackey, Dan, 52
Landry, Herbert, 117
Leath, David, 134–35
Leath, Raynella Dossett, 134–36
Lee, Kuao Fong, 201n30
LeFever, Virginia, 201n24
Lefstein, Norman, 137
Lentini, John J., 36
lethal force, 66, 69–70
Lewis, Andrea, 25
lie detection and detectors: advanced
   technologies' reliability in, 46–47;
   behavioral markers lacking/unreliable
   in, 45; biases in, 46–47; cognitive
   bias in, 47; and false accusations,
   44–48, 52–53; fMRI lie-detection,
   46–47; in the Nicole Harris case,
   80; National Research Council on,
   46; No Lie MRI lie-detection, 47;
   physiological behaviors unreliable in,
   45–46; and police, 47, 52–53; and
   polygraphs/polygraph examiners,
   45–46; reliability/unreliability of,
   44–48, 52–53, 60
Ligon, Jeanine G., 166
Ligon v. the City of New York, 166
loitering, 154–56, 158, 168–69, 171, 188
Louima, Abner, 63, 208–9n8
Love, Corey Anthony, 162
Love, William Cash, 146

"Making of a Murderer" (TV show), 6
Marcus, Paul, 115
marginalized communities. See poor and
   marginalized defendants
Marie (pseudonym), 49
Marion, William Jackson, 5–6
Marquez, Segundo, 142
Martin, David, 122–23
Mary (pseudonym), 113–14

mass arrests/incarcerations, 57, 162, 181–83,
   191
mass/group exonerations, 4, 9, 11, 13, 20,
   73–75, 89, 162
mass hysteria, 6, 55–60
Matthews, Craig, 64–65
McCaffrey, William, 51
McDonald, Laquan, 69–70
mechanical malfunctions mislabeled as
   homicide, 29–31
medical examiners: in the Butler case,
   33–34; and cognitive bias, 28; in the
   Crawford case, 4, 179; in the Nicole
   Harris case, 80; lacking criminal investigation training, 35; in the Monroe
   case, 23–25, 27–28; in the Robins case,
   106; in the Stallings case, 34–35; in the
   Winfield case, 177
Medwed, Daniel, 101–2
mental illness as sexual-assault false-accusa-
   tion motive, 51–52
Michelle "Kelly" Michaels, 57
Milan, Stephen, 133–34
Miranda v. Arizona (U.S. Supreme Court),
   215n27
mirror test for counsel competence, 19, 144,
   150, 226–27n85
misdemeanors, 152–71; appellate review
   lacking for, 159–60; author's proposals
   addressing, 188; bail/bond for, 156–58;
   case overloads of, 9, 111; consequences
   of, 19–20, 160–61, 166, 171; as convictions, 158; defined, 153–54; discovery
   lacking in, 159; exonerations rare in, 9,
   154, 156, 158–60; false confessions to,
   20; guilty pleas to, 157–61; innocence
   projects' inability to consider, 159,
   227n15; loitering, 154–56, 158, 168–69,
   171, 188, in the Louima case, 63; no-
   crime misdemeanors, 9–10, 20, 154–55,
   160–61, 188; and plea bargaining, 188;
   poor and marginalized defendants, 20;
   processing of, 154–63; prosecutors'
   unnecessary pursuit of, 169–70; public
   defenders' excessive caseloads of, 111–12;
   trespassing, 153, 158; vagrancy, 168–69;
   in the Edward Williams case, 67–68

mislabeling/misclassification of crimes, 23–42; arson, 7, 12, 35–38; cognitive biases in, 26–29; in the **Crawford** case, 1–5; as exoneration factor, 201n24; gender bias in, 25; mechanical malfunctions as homicide, 29–31; by medical personnel, 17, 58; in the **Monroe** case, 25, 27–29; by police, 16–17; police handbook's influence on, 28; of rape, 52; and sexual assault, 52; suicides misclassified as murders, 16, 24–25, 27–29, 82–83, 134–35, 201n24

Mohammed, Kallatt, 70

Mollen Commission police corruption study, 62

Mollen, Milton, 62

Monroe, Beverly, 23–24, 27–29, 31, 78

Monroe, Kate, 24–25

Mora, Raymond, 35–37

Morton, Michael, 105

Mowbray, Fredda Susie, 201n24

Mundy, Amber, 52

Munoz, Cesar, 201n24

murder/homicide: in the **Candice Anderson** case, 29–31; in the **Victoria and Medell Banks** case, 39; bite mark evidence in, 174–75; in the **Boorn Brothers** case, 5–6, 78; in the **Burroughs** case, 55–56; in the **Butler** case, 33–34, 173; in the **Carter** case, 82–83, 100; in the **Contee** case, 118; in the **Crawford** case, 1–5, 179; deaths assumed to be, 28; DNA exonerations in, 148; in the **Edmunds** case, 32; exoneration data in cases of, 12, 13*table2*; false confessions in crimes of, 79; in the **Fraser** case, 39; in the **Nicole Harris** case, 79–81; in the **Landry** case, 117, 173; in the **Raynella Leath** case, 134–36; in the **Marion case,** 5–6; mechanical malfunctions mislabeled as, 29–31; medical evidence standards in, 179; medical misdiagnoses in, 31–35; in the **Monroe** case, 24–25, 27–29, 31; in the **Mora** case, 35–37; in the **Robins** case, 106–7; in the **Ross** case, 174–75; in the **Stallings** case, 34–35; in the **Diane Tucker** case, 39; in the **Vasquez,** case,

35–37; victims found to be alive, 38–39; in the **Villalobos** case, 35–37; in the **Willingham** case, 35–38, 99, 122–23; in the **Winfield** case, 177, 184; women's vulnerability to convictions of, 25–26; and worst conviction cases, 199n39; in the **Zuohai** case, 38. *See also* forensic error; mislabeling/misclassification of crimes

NAACP (National Association for the Advancement of Colored People), 75, 155

National Academy of Sciences (NAS), 138, 174–75, 178

National Commission on Forensic Science (Washington, D.C.), 178

National District Attorneys Association, 174

National Registry of Exonerations (NRE) (Washington D.C.): actual-crime exonerations in, 11–12, 12*table1,* 13*table2;* CIU exonerations of drug crimes, 162; by crime type, 12–13, 13*table2;* exoneration data in, 9; on forensic science, 12, 141; function of, 11–12; mass/group exoneration data excluded from, 13; on murder vs. suicide exonerations, 29, 201n24; no-crime exonerations in, 12*table1,* 13*table2,* 25; on women exoneree percentages, 25

National Research Council, 37, 46

Nelson, Rashon, 167

Neufeld, Peter, 177–78

New York Civil Liberties Union, 166

New York State Commission on Judicial Misconduct, 142

Nifong, Mike, 87–88

no-crime convictions: and actual-crime wrongful convictions, 7, 11–15, 12*table1;* author's proposals addressing, 20, 173–95; consequences of, 14–16; exoneration data on, 12*table1;* gender stereotyping in, 25; introduction, 1–21; mass exonerations in, 73–75; prevalence of, 4–5, 8–14, 63; women's exoneration percentages, 25. *See also* actual-crime wrongful convictions; biases; child abuse (physical); child abuse (sexual); CIUs; crime fabrication/invention; death penalty/sentence; defense lawyers; drug crimes; false accusations; false confessions; *headings under exonerees; headings under forensic;* judges (trial); judicial misconduct; juries; mass hysteria; misdemeanors; mislabeling/misclassification of crimes; National Registry of Exonerations; perjury; police corruption and misconduct; poor and marginalized defendants; prosecutorial corruption and misconduct; rape (adult); SBS; sexual assault (adult)

No Lie MRI lie-detection, 47

North Carolina Innocence Inquiry Commission, 117

Northwestern University Center on Wrongful Convictions, 25

NRE. *See* National Registry of Exonerations

NYPD 12 (minority police officers challenging arrest quotas), 65, 209n18

Obama, Barack, 178

official misconduct, 11, 12*tabler*, 93, 124–25, 183

Ogg, Kim, 190–91

Operation Clean Halls (Bronx, New York), 164–65

Oscar (fire accelerant detection dog), 117, 176

Ozzborn, Thomas, 78

Papachristou v. City of Jacksonville (U.S. Supreme Court), 168–69

Patterson, Betty "Mizzie," 77

PCAST (President's Council of Advisors on Science and Technology), 174–75

PEACE model of questioning (United Kingdom), 181, 231n29

Peak, Carolyn June, 201n24

Perez, Raphael, 94

perjury: by Beale, 51; in the **Carter** case, 83; in the **Cassim** case, 52; by Coleman, 74–75; in no-crime convictions, 11, 12*tabler;* by police officers, 68, 74–75, 96; and prosecutors, 85, 88; in the

Clinton Turner case, 98–99; by Vandergrift, 83

Perry, Doug, 59–60

Perry, Rick, 75

Perry, VanDyke, 17

phantom crimes. *See* no-crime convictions

Pinocchio (fairy tale), 45

plea bargaining: Alford pleas, 144; author's proposals addressing, 185, 188; elimination of, 186; and exoneration data, 10; fact-finding circumvented by, 185; as false confession, 157; judges' roles in, 143, 187; judges' threats of penalties to induce, 145–46; as loss of appellate rights, 94; and misdemeanors, 188; and police misconduct, 81; prosecutors' roles in, 143; reasons for accepting, 143–45; role of, vs. no-crime prosecutions, 185; Supreme Court ruling on, 186; of the **Tulia, Texas defendants,** 146. *See also* guilty plea(s)

Plendl, Adam, 118–19

police: arrest powers of, 155–58, 170–71; author's proposals addressing, 165, 179–83, 191, 194; cognitive bias training for, 183; community relations with, 62; difficulties faced by, 62; lethal force used by, 66, 69–70; and lie detection, 45, 47, 52–53; reform, 20, 179–83

police corruption and misconduct, 61–81; author's proposals addressing, 179–83; and the blue wall of silence, 62–63, 208–9n8; and cognitive bias, 27, 35; convictions called into question by, 77–78; as crime, 18; crime fabrication/invention, 64–78; defense lawyers' effectiveness compromised by, 124–25; of Dowd, 62; evidence-planting, 7, 9, 13, 17–18; as exoneration factor, 13, 20; framing the innocent, 18; Mollen Commission investigation of, 62; motivations for, 18, 64–78; noble-cause corruption, 18; as no-crime conviction factor, 9, 125; organizational norms in, 62–64; and police brutality, 61–63, 66–68; police officers prosecuted for, 62, 70–71, 73, 75, 77–78; police perjury as, 68, 74–75; police shooting unarmed people,

police corruption *(continued)*
69–70; and prosecutors' guilty plea
offers, 93–94; protection money
demanded by police as, 70; and restrictions imposed on police, 62; tunnel
vision, 27. *See also* crime fabrication/
invention
poor and marginalized defendants: as arrest
quota targets, 64–65; bad lawyers
assigned to, 194; bail for, 156; with
criminal records, 70–71; in detention
prior to trial, 10; funding models for
representation of, 110–12; judges' biases
against, 131–34; and malign neglect, 171;
no-crime convictions of, 6, 18; no-crime
wrongful convictions of, 39, 61; people
of color as, 18; plea offers accepted by,
125, 153–54, 157–58; police crime-inven-
tion against, 74–75; police declaration
of, as the enemy, 182; and the right to
counsel, 110–11, 156; trespass charges
against, 165, 167; vagrancy charges
against, 169; vulnerable to misdemeanors, 20, 171. *See also* **Tulia, Texas
defendants**
Poppa, Douglas, 83
Powell v. Alabama (U.S. Supreme Court),
109–10
Pozonsky, Paul Michael, 223n27
Practical Homicide Investigation (Geberth),
28
President's Council of Advisors on Science
and Technology (PCAST), 174
presumptive bias, 183
professional snitches, 29
propensity evidence, 116
prophylactic rules, 88, 215n27
prosecution complex, 101–4
Prosecution Standards of the National
District Attorneys Association, 190
prosecutorial corruption and misconduct,
82–105; accountability lacking in, 88;
and the adversarial system, 85; of Ken
Anderson, 105; and assembly-line justice, 20; author's proposals addressing,
185, 190–96; in *Berger v. United States,*
84–85; bureaucratic legitimization of,
104; and coercion of witnesses, 85;

cognitive bias in, 42, 85; confirmation
bias in, 85; and deals with prosecution
witnesses, 85; in the Duke University
lacrosse case, 87; electoral politics in, 85,
87; exculpatory evidence withheld by,
187–89; as exoneration factor, 20–21;
false confession inducement as, 18; and
falsified evidence, 16, 85; and faulty
forensic science, 85; of John Foster, 89;
of Ken Foster, 89; harmless errors
overriding, 88; institutional disincentives promoting, 86–89; internal oversight lacking in, 85–86; judges ignoring,
138; of Kaczemarek, 89; and misstate-
ments of fact, 85; in the **Monroe** case,
24; as no-crime conviction factor, 18;
and perjured testimony, 85; preventative
measures against, 88; and prosecutorial
culture, 150, 190; prosecutors cleared of,
84; prosecutors' improper arguments as,
100–101; prosecutors penalized for,
87–88, 105; prosecutors taking advantage of, 94–97; in the **Robins** case, 107;
sanctions rarely imposed against prosecutors for, 87–88; and state bar associations, 88–89; trust in justice system
eroded by, 192; withholding exculpatory
evidence as, 97–99; witness threaten-
ing/intimidation as, 85, 95–96, 107. *See
also* prosecutorial immunity
prosecutorial immunity, 85, 88, 104–5, 193,
233n56
prosecutors, 105–26; and assembly-line
justice, 20; author's proposals addressing, 187–89; bail/bond determined by,
157; case overloads of, 10, 191–92; in
child abuse cases, 31; cleared of miscon-
duct/corruption, 84; cognitive bias
training for, 183; cognitive dissonance
among, 102–3; conviction scorekeeping
by, 85; and CUIs, 192; defendants
dehumanized by, 103; evidence assessed
by, 181, 191–92; evidence retesting
ordered by, 35; evidence screening by,
191–92; exculpatory evidence withheld
by, 19, 83, 85, 87; false evidence introduced by, 16; false testimony coached by,
83; improper arguments by, 100–101;

Founded in 1893,
UNIVERSITY OF CALIFORNIA PRESS
publishes bold, progressive books and journals
on topics in the arts, humanities, social sciences,
and natural sciences—with a focus on social
justice issues—that inspire thought and action
among readers worldwide.

The UC PRESS FOUNDATION
raises funds to uphold the press's vital role
as an independent, nonprofit publisher, and
receives philanthropic support from a wide
range of individuals and institutions—and from
committed readers like you. To learn more, visit
ucpress.edu/supportus.